D0886214

THE FIRST ANTHOLOGY

OF MISSOURI WOMEN WRITERS

SHARON KINNEY-HANSON, SENIOR EDITOR

SHEBA REVIEW, INC. ● JEFFERSON CITY, MISSOURI ● USA

Hanson photo

The Editorial Board with hosts during one of several selections meetings, ACTS Institute, Lake Ozark, Missouri. L to R (standing) Jo Schaper, Char Plotsky (ACTS Director), Edith McCall, Evadine Judge (Ragdale Foundation), Pam Goldstein, Mary Beth Llorens; (seated) Mariane Fleischmann, Helen Patmon, Alice Brand. Sharon Hibdon and Sharon Kinney-Hanson not shown.

MISSOURI WOMEN WRITERS

Dedicated to:

Marianne Moore, Poet

[1887 — 1972]

Marianne Moore graduated from Bryn Mawr in 1909 and first published in *Poetry* in 1915. She wrote poetry, plays, essays, and translations; edited *The Dial* 1925– 29. Among her many honors are a Pulitzer Prize, the National Book Award for Poetry, the Bollingen Prize. She was born near St. Louis on November 15, 1887.

CONTENTS

PREFACE

by Lieutenant Governor Harriett Woods

How do we get a sense of who we are—a feeling of self or identity? People often ask me how I've been able to achieve so much as a woman, and I sense in the question the assumptions that being a woman is different, and that is probably a handicap. Well, I certainly accept that it's different, but *never* that it's a handicap!

I didn't really understand the feminine differences as I grew up, in the years before "women's liberation." There were very few real-life role models, and the ones in literature seemed far removed from my reality. Women in books always were devoting themselves to some romantic hero, and even those with spunk and wit seemed relegated to second place.

That wouldn't happen to me! I turned my back on any exploration of myself as a woman and went after a journalism career desired by men. There were few clues in school as to what made me special: not very much in the required reading in literature, and my college philosophy major just immersed me in the metaphysics of men.

So I became a barrier breaker, like many women of my generation, working harder and reaching farther, just so we could be equal. Gradually I invented my own identity, as journalist, wife, mother, and then as elected official. Only in the last decade have I really become aware of a host of voices around me that talk about experiences very much like my own. They aren't talking just about political experiences, but about sharing and caring, and the strength and power within women. Some of those voices belong to women poets and novelists, and they are the most insightful of all.

So it is important to me personally, as well as for all those who will read this book, that we have a first anthology of Missouri women writers.

It's also important for the writers, who too often are dismissed as lightweight by male editors who fail to understand the female agenda.

Anne Bradstreet, our first American poet, captured in "The Prologue" some of the frustration of the women writer seeking recognition:

> I am obnoxious to each carping tongue
> Who says my hand a needle better fits,
> A Poet's pen all scorn I should thus wrong,
> For such despite they cast on female wits:
> If what I do prove well, it won't advance,
> They'll say it's stol'n, or else it was by chance.

Well, we know better today. We have enjoyed the power and imagery of a great variety of women writers, including a suprising number from Missouri. We have come a long way in the view we have. Now we need to reflect again on who we are and what of ourselves makes us special.

In the political world, the pundits talk about something called the gender gap. It seems that women cast their votes differently than men, reflecting different positions on issues like war and peace and social welfare concerns. This came as a terrific surprise to politicians who were accustomed to women voting the way their husbands told them. Politicians began appearing before women's groups asking them what they wanted!

Very few of these analysts and vote-seekers look beyond the current issues to ask about differences in underlying values. But that's what interests me the most. For surely that gender gap in voting reflects a difference in perceptions and life experiences that also is expressed in women's writing.

It's time for us to pause to hear those words, the spirit of the emerging voice of women. For wouldn't it be a waste to win some kind of numerical battle for political and economic representation without also winning respect for women's messages? Indeed, women have been largely missing from history, and the world is the worse for it. Our concern for nurturing, empowering, sharing, enlarging, and caring is a strength, not a weakness. We find beauty in many little things, and we can turn the ordinary into the extraordinary.

Missouri, too, has suffered from its share of snubs and misconceptions—its rich literary diversity too often summed up in a collection from Mark Twain. Well, we will show them a contemporary collection of literature written by talented women in Missouri.

Women will speak for Missouri in 1987, as leading women authors tour into many communities of the state. The impact of their voices will raise the consciousness of all of us. It's time to be proud of their abilities and their songs.

In a world of violence and abuse, it is time for women to make their private values, the public values. It is time for us to frame the public debate and to offer our visions for the future. The selections in this anthology are part of that process. They give us pleasure. Whatever we are, as Missourians and as women, is here. I am confident this is just the beginning for women writers in our state.

MAYA ANGELOU

STILL I RISE

You may write me down in history
With your bitter, twisted lies,
You may trod me in the very dirt
But still, like dust, I'll rise.

Does my sassiness upset you?
Why are you beset with gloom?
'Cause I walk like I've got oil wells
Pumping in my living room.

Just like moons and like suns,
With the certainty of tides,
Just like hopes springing high,
Still I'll rise.

Did you want to see me broken?
Bowed head and lowered eyes?
Shoulders falling down like teardrops,
Weakened by my soulful cries.

Does my haughtiness offend you?
Don't you take it awful hard
'Cause I laugh like I've got gold mines
Diggin' in my own back yard.

You may shoot me with your words,
You may cut me with your eyes,
You may kill me with your hatefulness,
But still, like air, I'll rise.

Does my sexiness upset you?
Does it come as a surprise
That I dance like I've got diamonds
At the meeting of my thighs?

Out of the huts of history's shame
I rise
Up from a past that's rooted in pain
I rise
I'm a black ocean, leaping and wide,
Welling and swelling I bear in the tide.

Leaving behind nights of terror and fear
I rise
Into a daybreak that's wondrously clear
I rise
Bringing the gifts that my ancestors gave,
I am the dream and the hope of the slave.
I rise
I rise
I rise.

MAYA ANGELOU

CAGED BIRD

A free bird leaps
on the back of the wind
and floats downstream
till the current ends
and dips his wing
in the orange sun rays
and dares to claim the sky.

But a bird that stalks
down his narrow cage
can seldom see through
his bars of rage
his wings are clipped and
his feet are tied
so he opens his throat to sing.

The caged bird sings
with a fearful trill
of things unknown
but longed for still
and his tune is heard
on the distant hill
for the caged bird
sings of freedom.

The free bird thinks

reprint permission for "Still I Rise" from *And Still I Rise* (1978), and "Caged Bird" from *Shaker, Why Don't You Sing?* (1983) by Maya Angelou granted from Random House, Inc.

of another breeze
and the trade winds soft
through the sighing trees
and the fat worms waiting
on a dawn-bright lawn
and he names the sky his own.

But a caged bird stands
on the grave of dreams
his shadow shouts
on a nightmare scream
his wings are clipped
and his feet are tied
so he opens his throat to sing.

The caged bird sings
with a fearful trill
of things unknown
but longed for still
and his tune is heard
on the distant hill
for the caged bird
sings of freedom.

Maya Angelou

JEAN MORRISON BAKER

I LEARNED TO BE QUIET

I learned to be quiet
shelling corn for speckled Plymouth Rocks
when I was ten. On October days
I sat in golden gloom on corn-ear hills
in the farm granary. Broke kernels loose from cobs
with strong thumb pushes,
filled my bucket, then sat waiting,
barely breathing, eyelids nearly closed
so even blinking would be slight,
listened to wind sing through rafters,
watched dust dance in sunlight columns,
until corn husks rustled, and fat gray satin mice
came from secret passageways to play games of tag.
I watched their wide eyes scan like radar screens,
their needle teeth crack kernels held in tiny hand-like feet.
Then jealous of their freedom, I would move
and make them disappear.

ALICE G. BRAND

VITAL STATISTICS

His cover letter read
dear personnel director
I have been promoted on every job
hiring me is as right as rain
now that's a man for you
because no woman would be promoted
with a swagger in her mouth
rings in the side of her nose
you couldn't promote a woman unless she wore
a blazer and a string tie
now that's a woman for you
feminine but not quite
jewish but not Joan Rivers
black but not Shange
and you don't talk
and you don't ask for raises
and you mind your own business, girl
cause you're here
to work for the rest of us
the best of us.

So I said
dear father superior
I would like returned to my office
the phone that was removed without
permission or warning the day I was sick.
I would like returned my bulletin board
that was taken when you moved my room
to the back and scribbled all over my pride
and we ran out of good feelings
and it disappeared along with my stamp pad
and my self-respect. and while I'm thinking of it,
I want back my typewriter that you so cannily borrow
every few days to remind me that
I still work for you and everything here is yours
and the civil rights that were purchased
for me four years ago when you liked me better
because I was tentative and nondescript.
I'll have back my secretary whom you confiscated
when you prayed I wouldn't last
and my achievements which you annexed for yourself.
I'll keep my own achievements, thank you.
I'll take back my dignity, whole and unharmed,

5

and my bonus that you appropriated for
your secretaries to break and enter my office,
rifle through my desk and my morals,
my tried and my true to see if I'd left any of it
lying around along with my checkbook and my accounts
receivable.

And you ain't heard nothing yet
I'm going to march you into the VPs and tell them
that you lie, you thieve
not only have you stolen my name,
repossessed my title and shanghaied my space,
you have picked my pockets, rigged the deck,
and walked off with my words.

When I'm through with you,
we're going to trade places.   and
I'll have the 4 phones, 3 secretaries, 2 office boys,
kitchen privileges, conference calling,
windows, drapes, and your more-bang-for-the-buck.
and don't make fists at me in your pockets
'cause if you keep messing with me
you're gonna find yourself in a poem.

Alice G. Brand

6

ALICE G. BRAND

FLORIDA

DECEMBER

On Siesta Key I roll in the sand
And take on its talcum
But it's like making love on dry ice
So I bring a sweater to warm me
Take amaretto in my coffee
The gulls are on nodding terms
With the sandpipers who overhear
That Jennie has taken a black lover
It will kill her family
In a cold heat
That makes us all brown.

I wish there were a way to build
A greenhouse over Punta Gorda
Powder could perfume this sand
And send sweet whiteness all around
The banyan, bougainvillea
I will tell you how expensive are
The colors of the orchid trees
Magenta and pink are ladies'
down here, everywhere

On this beach
Abalone, venus clams, spindle shells,
Cochina, the grieving waters and amaretto
So smooth, the gulls, observers
Of this meeting, of my browness,
Of the sandpipers, stilt-leg scurring

ALICE G. BRAND

WARNING:

aerosol cans
or any container using
air pressure must be punctured
before depositing in this incinerator.
Throwing carpet sweepings containing napthalene,
camphor, or any other flammable or highly combustible
substance into this incinerator is unlawful. Depositing
paint cans, floor scrapings, oily rags, or her gold compact,
cigarette holder, or her rhumba, Roseland, or Xavier Cugat maracas
into the incinerator, or her upsweep, mouton hat and wigs or her sweater
from Hong Hong sequined with palm trees, or her Lewyt, Victrola, Brownie
Hawkeye, photos and love letters into the incinerator, or her headaches
or chills or blackouts, or her x-rays, cat scans, intravenous, or her
flexible straws, walker, bedpad, bone and bandage, or her pills,
her pain, surgery and sutures into the incinerator, or her
hollowed eyes, her chalky skin and hair, or her morphine,
delirium, barest breath, headstone, footstone, dwarf
yews set between, or the ground cover, prayer
pebbles and unveiling, or ashes from
traffic and tears, dung and dust,
into this incinerator is unlawful.
Failure to comply with federal
air standards subjects the
patient to penalties
or death.

MARILYN CANNADAY

A BOLD PROPOSAL

What is all the fuss about right-to-life and the question of when life begins? It seems fairly simple to me. If it wiggles, it's alive, and if it's alive, it has certain rights. What naturally follows is that the government has the responsibility of protecting those rights. I think not ony fetuses and embryos should be protected by law, but spermatozoa as well. Have you ever seen those cute little squiggly sperm under a microscope or in living color on film? Without a doubt they are alive, and each one has the potential to fertilize an ovum and become a living, breathing human being. I think we should launch a whole new campaign to protect the sperm's right to life. And to carry the idea a bit further, why should only an *occasional* sperm hit the mark and realize its potential? We should make whatever arrangements necessary to save and freeze all leftover sperm. Since they so outnumber ova produced by women, we should put our best scientists to work to artifically create life from those wonderful little bits of protoplasm.

Why not legislate that *every* ovum be fertilized whether in the womb or in the test tube? Perhaps science could discover a way for spermatozoa to be developed *independently* into half-persons. These fractional persons would eat less than whole persons, would cost less to support, and perhaps could be given a half vote. They could be taught to hop around on one leg, and being smaller and slimmer than whole regular persons, think how many you could get in a bus or grocery store.

Some people get hung up on the rights of adult women as opposed to rights of the unborn. Irrelevant. The women have had their chance at life. The government's more pressing concern is the generation of new lives. The more people you have, the more taxes you can collect. Greater numbers mean potential progress and a better economy. Child abuse, crime and poverty are the concern of pessimists. These things will take care of themselves if we can legislate a great humanitarian society. If we can force the issue on sperm right-to-life, other things will fall into place. If we protect *every* life, regardless of its inception, who knows—maybe our next president will be a half-person generated in a test tube or even the product of incest or rape. The mother-incubator is not important when you keep your sights on the end result—more babies. And if we have more girls than boys, think of their potential for giving birth to even more children.

Women should spend more years in pregnancy and child care. They should feel honored to be receptacles for the generation of human life in any number and condition. Their God-given right is to bear and nurture, and free choice doesn't have anything to do with that. Quantity is more important than quality. And, incidently, more pregnancies would definitely keep women down and out of politics, and would free up jobs for half-men.

If this campaign catches on—and I think it will under the present administration—we will not rest until we have given every sperm its inalienable right to life. First we will legislate against abortion for *any* reason, and then we will legislate against all birth control. If, after their birth, any human beings or semi-human beings die, that's not the government's problem. The government has protected the right to be *born*, and if they die from natural causes, so be it. Even a gradual starvation could be considered a natural cause. The key word is "natural." The United States of America has the potential to be a great humanitarian society—with the passage of the right legislation. All it takes is the balls to vote for it.

Marilyn Cannaday

LENORE CARROLL

COLLAGE

Since I have fibrocystic disease, I must check my breasts every month and every month I must remind myself to do it. It scares me, but I do it anyway and try not to get depressed. I see a doctor every six months. The last time I went, she found a lump she didn't like and she referred me to a radiologist. I had to go, even though I was afraid. My breasts are lumpy and all lumps feel the same to me.

So it wasn't the first time I had had to wait days while fear settled through me like fog, not the first time I had had to think about what would happen if there was something there.

The radiologist's office—on the top floor of a doctor's building—has a skylight which illuminates a huge planter. It distracted me from my brooding. I was shown to a cubicle to change into a smock, then taken to an alcove where I watched a slide presentation. I've no memory of what I watched. It must have had something to do with breasts and lumps.

The fear is familiar, but the procedures were new. Anxiety made me giggly. First, the sonogram. I had to lie on a table with one breast dangling in a tank of water. Turned away from the equipment for the left breast, I could see my right one on the monitor. Subsequent cross-sections were shadows on a screen, as imponderable as Greek. I felt I'd been invited to a strange rite where secrets were revealed. But, what the secrets meant was not to be explained.

I dried off. Then Xeromammographic shots captured each breast. I made feeble jokes. No one laughed. Back in the dressing cubicle, I took off the damp smock and put on my own clothes—a plaid shirt faded and familiar, a wrap skirt with an applique like one of my son's childhood paintings. I tried to study the Picasso print, but only registered the wall paneling. I cracked the door, indicating I was dressed and waiting for the doctor to read the results.

My mind wouldn't stay on one thought.

. . .I was taught not to touch myself. Especially not breasts. I get around the old prohibition by checking in the shower. I must touch them then. . . I don't want to because I'm afraid I'll find something. I always feel lumps. . .those monthly reminders. . . my breasts could be cut off. . .and what a shame because they're so sensitive I scarcely can bear to have my husband touch them as we begin to make love. . I wonder if I could orgasm by breasts alone. But. . .I'm getting older. Making love gets better. . .that's hardly fair. My sagging body can still do it in spite of belly crisscrossed with scars, breasts and hips maintained only by swimming, granulations of cellulite on thighs, vericosities in my legs like new blue streams on a watershed. Hair thins. . .membranes dry. . . in the YMCA shower room, I always avoid looking at that old

11

woman who has had a mastectomy. . .Virginia Woolf has a character in *Mrs. Dalloway* who thinks the compensation of growing old is simply: "passions remain as strong as ever, but one has gained—at last! the power which adds the supreme flavour to existence—the power of taking hold of experience, of turning it around, slowly, in light.". . .forty's too soon to be old. But that's what I'm doing, turning it around, looking at my fears.

I remove some old woman's grey hair from my plaid shirt.

Flo: I saw something the other day that scared me to death.
Alice: What was it?
Flo: My mother's hand coming out of the sleeve of my coat.

My skin's freckled. . .I used to joke about "liver" spots. They always faded. Used to. . .now there's one on the back of my left hand, just over the thick vein that rides the ligaments. . . it's been there. . .ten years. . . Teenager boys like movies like *Star Wars, The Terminator, First Blood*, full of ejaculatory explosions and. . .and violence. The physical, exterior violence of blows, cuts, bruises, wounds. Flashfights. Kung Fu dance. Masculine display to establish dominance. Women's violence is different. . . it's interior. Each month her body verifies in blood she is female. The growing fetus performs a slower violence, persistently changing physiology forever tearing apart what then must heal. . .and shrink. A woman pays with her body in exchange for that gift. . .accustomed to disfigurement and violence. . .mastectomy is just one more mutilation. . .everything sexual, from the first tearing of the hymen, is eventually connected with pain and loss. . .all internal. . .

The X-ray technician leads me to the physician who, standing, reads the print. Rather than shadows on film stock, Xeromammography produces an opaque sheet looking like a blueprint of my breast's interior.
"Everything's fine," he says, and breezes to his next patient.
It is perfectly symmetrical, this arcane view. It's a map of a mountain whose streams run to the peak, gradually growing wider and more crowded. I see the topography of hidden flesh where lymph nodes and milk ducts tangle, twine as they rise to the nipple.
Too soon the assistant removes the picture. I gather my purse and coat and leave with a light step.
Home free, this time. But each month, I remind myself, someday some doctor may want to cut off my breasts.

Sometime after the sonogram I'm in the locker room at the Y where I swim, and I notice a woman stuffing foam falsies inside her bra. I feel the fog settle in my gut. Does she have a double mastectomy? We've showered together in the communal room several times, but we try hard not to see each other. Staring's an invitation, or voyeurism. When a mother brings a small child into the locker room, the child looks directly at those places adults pretend not to see. Staring violates the privacy each of us tries to hold around herself as we undress and shower and walk naked though towelled through the moist warm room.

I've seen breasts of every shape, size, age, responding to gravity in these locker rooms and dressing rooms. But I've not been able to bring myself to look at that old woman's chest as she gently scrubs her body, her cloth foamy with soap.

We've chatted as we dress. She's told me of sewing her own swimsuits—where she buys fabric and how she manages the bosom. She's friendly, asks what I do while pulling on her stockings and buttoning her blouse. She tells me she and her husband are retired and describes some of the things they do together now. Her hair, dry and fine as white mirabou, floats around her head until she goes to the mirror, brush in hand.

Another week and we're leaving the pool after an Open Swim. The smell of chlorine follows us into the locker room. We go the shower stalls together. I close the frosted glass door, put my bag on a plastic stool. There're four shower heads, two drains, the entire 10 by 12 foot room is tiled, floor to ceiling. We lather and scrub; sweet shampoo and soap smells rise in the heat. I finish first and bend over so the water from my hair drips on the floor while I dry my body, then I wrap the towel around my head, prepared to leave. She's still slowly stroking her washcloth down her legs.

I look and there are the scars on her chest. They're ropy half-circles, like crooked grins, the scar tissue fine and white. They're old scars and this woman is alive.

JAN CASTRO

MONGOOSE AND COBRA

On a rock beside the rushing waters, Mongoose was watching the reflection of her delicate ribcage covered with sleek brown fur as it multiplied in the eddies and currents. Her brown saucer eyes spied a cobra in the dry red dirt and grasses along the shore. She admired the diamond-shaped, bulbous yellow-and-black head, the wily forked tongue, the supple, iron-hard neck and body.

"Come closer, friend," she said. "Look at your beautiful eyes in my mirrors."

He stared boldly at her, and she noticed that his eyes, instead of reflecting the yellow-green of the land, contained the blue of the sky. This must be a juicy cobra, she figured to herself.

"Let us lie on our backs and watch the tiny clouds and tell stories," she offered.

Cobra smelled something about her. He smelled something juicy. He could eat her in one bite. He slithered over and lay in the sun, letting the light warm his scaly diamond back.

"What's your story, Mongoose? How did you come to the riverbed? This is my territory."

"I followed the northern route from the east. I run fast. The woods back there are drying up. There aren't many fine cobras left back there. Here the winds smell fresh. They send sweet invitations. The climate is good and there are plenty of contests to keep me amused."

"Contests?"

"Yes. Races, endurance, hide-and-seek."

"Do you want to race?"

"I can run much faster than you, so there's no contest. How did you get your blue eyes?"

"I came here from the north. My mother says I have double vision. I can see inside things."

"Me?"

"You."

"So you see what I'm thinking."

"Yes."

The clouds were dissolving in twilight. A pale rainbow of red, yellow, and blue cast its colors across the waters. The wind sighed along the edges of the racing, prism-colored currents. A few birds, black-banded and grey and blue-white, yellow-headed birds, cried out from the branches.

For one second, there was a contest of wills, the brown and blue eyes staring into each other's, clouds dissolving in the tiny mirrors of their pupils glinting in the last rays of sunlight.

In an instant, the fleet mongoose sank its razor teeth into the fine neck of the cobra, whose tongue released green juice onto the smooth grey stone as its raised jaws fell short of sucking in the tiny brown mirrors and body. The contest was over. Mongoose salivated along the edges of the thick head, carving a meal of flesh, swallowing, swallowing with the undulating motions that once belonged to the elongated body, licking the edges of the wound, sucking meat, fresh and juicy, taking and losing the companion of a sunny afternoon as they lay side by side on the grey rock by the reflecting pools.

"You got me," said the ghost of Cobra.

"You knew I would," said Mongoose, licking the ribbon of rough skin absorbing the rosy light of dusk.

"You are a fine one," said Mongoose. "I wish you would come back to life so we could play this game again, so I could taste you again, whole."

"I am inside you, and you can let me out," said Cobra.

"That is a new game," said Mongoose, and she yawned, satisfied and full, and Cobra sprang out. Cobra knew that he could not win, but he won anyway. And both creatures sank into the night as they had sunk into each other, leaving a bright stain on the grey rock.

T. D. CIACCHI

ROSES: AMI, AMO

We wave bon voyage to friends,
their breath turns to steam on the windows.
Slowly, droplets condense and fall away.
When you start the engine
I pull our intimacy over me
as a winter coat on the first frost-filled morning.
Hearing the gallop of your foot
relentless on the gas pedal,
I smile at my reflection in the rearview mirror.

Others whiz by
intent on journeys of their own making
trailing ribbons of smoke
that never quite disappear.
Your hands swing with the steering wheel
and mine are busy too
(one holding my knees to my chest
the other gripping the door handle
with a sweat moistened palm).
As we rocket down this tunnel
We shake We rattle We chatter.

Here we are, dancing on this pinhead.
A magnet whose predetermined forces
pull us forward and back,
straining to define these rhythms.
We sway on the outer edge
bumping elbows, bumping knees, touching foreheads
with a gentle rumble that reminds me of my grandmother
speaking in her native tongue.
The lyrical vowels of Italian
forming small blossoms in her mouth.

S. R. CLEMENT

THE SUMMER BOX

The grandmother rocked gently in the porch swing, fanning away mosquitoes in the warm air of the summer evening. In the distance she could hear the piping voices of her three grandchildren as they were drawn home to dinner, television, and her. The grandmother often imagined that she, alone, drew them home—reeled them in like so many minnows flashing at the end of a bamboo pole. She had loved to fish; had fished, in fact, every summer for sixty years until a badly broken hip ended her fishing days and sent her to live with her daughter's family. It was not a bad life, but not an active one.

Except that she still fished—only now she used the children instead of hooks.

Each morning she'd stand at the front door with her walker and send the children out on invisible lines, letting them drift to the front gate, playing them down the street, then letting them go bobbing over fences and under tree branches, whirling in the dust until they were caught up in a current with a dozen other little bobbers let loose in the morning tide.

The children drifted back at various times during the day, usually to eat. "What, baiting your hooks again?" she'd ask, and "Aw, Grandma!" they'd laugh before being swept back into the dry grass current. They were ages twelve, eleven, and nine. Just right to fish with, the old woman thought. Too young to think you're batty, and old enough to be too polite to tell you if they did.

Each evening, she'd sit out on the porch swing and, as the sun began to set, slowly draw them home again on invisible lines. They always had a catch for her; treble hooks, everyone of them, she thought. There might be a blue jay's feather, a green jewel found in the ruins of an old Coke bottle, pebbles, fossils, milkweed fuzz, or old clay marbles found in the wake of a garden tiller.

She'd put each find that a child considered extra special in her "summer box"—an old tin tackle box she'd had for years, and which still held a few of her favorite flies.

Each summer they filled the box with memorabilia: shells from vacation, a lock of hair from a girl friend's ponytail, the first cicada skeleton, the last robin's egg.

Each winter when the snow fell too deeply to play in, and ice pushed across the walks and edged the windows, she got out the summer box and they relived their summer. When spring came, they'd throw it all out—except for her flies—and a few things went into the children's drawers or scrapbooks, to make ready for the coming summer.

The other night the children brought her an old tooth they'd found in a vacant lot. "Maybe it's an injun's, Grandma!" nine year old Brian exclaimed. "It looks old," he added. Looks like a dog's, the old woman thought to herself, but it went into the summer box as a possible Indian relic. Brian had hugged her, eyes shining with stolen sun, the dust of summer hidden away in creases in his neck and arms. A regular little summer box himself, she had thought.

This night, however, as the two older ones placed a bouquet of goldenrod in her arms, Brian moved past in a quiet, dark eddy, barely smiling, letting the screen door slip quietly from his fingers as he went inside and up the stairs to his room. The grandmother heard a quiet "snick" of the lock on his door and, somewhere inside her, felt an invisible line tugging at her.

A hour later, "Mother, I can't get Brian out of his room to come to dinner." Her daughter stuck her head out the porch door, trying to peer into the darkness where the porch swing creaked. "Kevin and Julie say he's upset about something, but they don't know what." The porch swing creaked. "Talk to him, will you? Mother, are you listening?"

"He won't starve in the next couple hours, Lydia," the old woman finally said. "Let him have a little privacy—Brian'll tell us what's wrong when he's a'mind."

Lydia sighed, closed the door. The porch swing creaked, and continued creaking long past the time when the grandmother usually went to bed. Finally, the screen door opened and Brian wandered out onto the porch. He stood for a moment, hands in his pockets, and then, "Grandma, can I talk with you for a minute?"

"Surely, boy. Come over here and sit by me so's I can see you better. I won't have the porch light on drawin' mosquitoes." Brian sat down on the swing carefully so he wouldn't jar his grandmother, and swung his legs, thinking.

"Grandma, would you go some place with me tomorrow?"

"What? Wade out there with the rest of the fish?"

Brian gazed up at her in the dim moonlight, his head cocked. "It's important. I want to show you something."

"I'm too stove up to walk any far place, 'less you'd like to ask your mother to drive us?" She couldn't see his face clearly, but felt the boy tense up.

"Oh, no, I don't think Mom'd understand. It's at the cemetary," Brian told her.

"Your mother's a wonderful person, Brian," the grandmother started. "I ought to know—I raised her. But she hasn't got an imaginative bone in her body, for all her college education. I think you're right," she sighed. "She probably wouldn't understand about us going to a cemetary. I'm not sure *I* understand your reasons, so maybe you best just tell me all about it."

"Well," Brian started, "I was out at the cemetary today with some other kids. . ."

"You know, the cemetary's no good place to play in," she admonished.

"I wasn't playin', just lookin' at the headstones and statues and stuff. Not playin'," he said again, firmly. "Anyway," he continued, "I was out where Grandpa's buried, and I saw some other old graves with our names on them, and I started lookin' for other names I know, and pretty soon I was off in this real weedy patch under this big ol' tree and that's when I found them." He stopped a moment to catch his breath.

"Found what?" she asked, not sure where he was leading.

"These two little headstones, kinda fallen over and hidden in the grass," Brian told her. "They're real old. I could hardly read the writing on them, and Grandma," he went on, turning wide eyes up at her, "They were kids' graves."

The grandmother was puzzled. "You've seen childrens' graves before, Brian. You know where cousin Donna's baby is. . .there's a whole section for little babies on the east side."

"Yeah, well, sure, but they're *new*—they're taken care of." He struggled to find the right words. "The ones I found are lost—nobody takes care of them." He was silent for awhile, obviously frustrated at not being able to say what he wanted.

"You said there's writing on the stones?" she prompted.

"Yeah, I wrote it down," Brian brightened a little. He pulled a crumpled piece of scrap paper from his back pocket and struggled to read the scrawled words in the dim light.

"*Richard DeHar*-something. *1847*," he read, squinting. "I wonder if that was when he's born or when he died."

"Could be both," his grandmother said, putting an arm around him. "There was lots of sickness back then, and not many fancy doctors, either. What else did it say?"

"*I wonder what I was begun for, when so soon it is that I am done for.* That's kinda sad, Grandma," Brian said, snuggling under her arm.

"Yes, 'tis, Brian. But I still don't understand why you. . ."

"Wait, Grandma. There's something written on the other one, too." Brian bent his head over the paper again. "*In sol-i-tude I often sit, my child and think of thee. The little word thy tongue hath lisped will not forgotten be.* Don't you wonder what that word was? Don't you see why it's so sad?" Brian's voice rose in agitation, and he continued before his grandma could answer.

"It's *all* forgotten now, not just the word, but everything. No one 'members they're there! No one takes care of 'em. The other graves are taken care of, people put flowers and flags and statues and all kinds of stuff on 'em, and mow the grass, too. But maybe, someday, they'll all be forgotten, too. Maybe someday, someday. . ." He paused, uncertain again, and panting a little.

"Maybe someday you'll be gone and forgotten, too," the old woman finished. "Is that why you're so upset? Lord, child, that happens to everybody and everything, someday. Just make sure it don't happen to you while you're still alive, that's the trick!" She laughed at herself. Brian stared down at the top of his dirty tennis shoes.

"Well," he said, "it's the first time I've ever thought about me . . .dyin'." He whispered the last word, and the grandmother was immediately contrite.

"So it is, I guess," her voice softened. She hugged him to her. "You're such a sensible boy, I forget sometimes that you *are* a boy. But a big boy, and gettin' bigger everyday." She held him away from her, as though looking to see how much he'd grown in the last few minutes, and Brian smiled.

"Grandma," he asked, snuggling under her arm again, "What will really happen when I die? I mean, after I die? I mean. . .?"

"I know what you mean. Nobody knows for sure, and I hope I won't find out for myself for a little while longer. But what *I think* happens is that your soul goes up to Heaven to live with God. Your soul," she added, "is kind of like God's summer box. When you get to Heaven He takes hold of your soul, which is full of all the good things and all the bad things you've ever done, and he gives it a good shake."

Brian giggled, "Why's He do that, Grandma?"

"Well, He shakes out all the bad things, so's there's nothing left but all the good things that make you so special. That way, He can enjoy you just like we enjoy all the special things we save in our summer box every year." They sat together silently in the swing for awhile, listening to the crickets.

"It's still not fair," Brian mumbled more to himself than to his grandmother.

"That there's no one to take care of those little graves?" she asked. "Well, now, I wouldn't say that, exactly." When Brian looked up at her, she stretched herself and reached for her walker. "Seems to me, when someone thinks something's unfair, he ought to do something about it. Help me up, boy. It's way past our bedtime."

The next morning the grandmother slept late, and missed sending the children out for the day. But, she was there on the swing that evening to draw them home.

"Look, Grandma!" Kevin and Julie sat on either side of her, and Julie held out her hand. "We found the first cicada shell on the sugar maple this year. Can we put it in the summer box?"

"Of course! Run along inside and get it," she replied. She watched them go in and then turned to Brian, who was leaning over the arm of the swing.

"And what did you bring me tonight?" she asked.

Brian held out his hands. They were covered with dirt and grass stains, as was the rest of him. "Nothing you can put in the summer box, Grandma," he said, giving her a wink.

She reached out and gave his dirt-smudged cheek a pat, saying, "Run along inside and get cleaned up before your mother sees you, dear. And don't be too sure about what I can and can't put in my summer box," she gave a wink back at him.

She watched the boy scamper inside, and looked down at the dirt on her hand. Taking her handkerchief out of the front pocket of her blouse, where grandmothers are apt to keep such things, she wiped off the dirt and then, carefully, folded the lace square and tucked it inside her blouse again, over her heart. Treble hooks, she thought, everyone of them.

THE JOYFUL GARDENER

Have fun while you garden. Once in a while plant something where you want it to be regardless of what the catalog says. Flowers and shrubs must find it quite dull with spittlebugs weaving webs on leaves, sowbugs nibbling at root stems, and bees poking inquisitive tongues overall.

When I heard that Oriental poppies resented being transplanted, I got a spade and moved one just to see how a resentful poppy reacted. Know something? It was tickled pink.

One day I decided that my Japonica bush was too squat. To make it tall and tree-like I clipped the overgrown shrub down to one sturdy sprout. It was furious and said so in strong Japanese Quince language, but I whacked and slashed on it for two years. Now I am asked, "What kind of tree is that?"

From the red soil of Georgia I brought a Texas Star to our Missouri garden. Now the beauty stands 15 feet tall, but it has not yet caught on that it's in Yankeeland. My little secret gives me pleasure.

Someday I plan to have a spindle tree. I know nothing about spindle trees—what they do or look like—but I imagine myself remarking casually to a visitor, "By the way, have you seen my new spindle tree?"

Thus, I take pleasure in a spindle tree I do not possess.

DROP THAT HOE

I got carried away with emotion considerably in excess of the situation. There are some things that the human spine simply will not do simultaneously. Before the back will turn, twist, and bend backwards, it will crack.

Mine cracked.

I now sing a new song. Better than physical exercise is to just keep breathing. Skill in lung-filling is not necessary. Do it. Daily. No need for duck-hunting underpants. Only a rocking chair where you can rock back and forth, back and forth. I said rock—not rock-and-roll—and wait for Spring, all the while breathing quietly.

What has this to do with gardening? Well, should you suddenly stop breathing you'll probably receive floral arrangements. But that isn't what you want, is it?

NADINE MILLS COLEMAN

THE EXCEEDINGLY GOOD EARTH

My mister, the agronomy professor, kept at me to save vegetable and fruit parings instead of swishing them down the garbage disposal. He handed me a bulletin on soil science (one that he himself had written), but when I read "organic residue. . . collodial soil. . .per ton of dry organic material to 60 pounds," I shook my head and handed it back.

What I wanted, I told him, was a cute little compost place with a brick walk down the middle. "On the North I put kitchen gleanings— and leaves and grass clippings on the South. It will be neat. No flies. No odor."

"I suppose you'll hang curtains, too," said the professor.

The pay off came two years later when with a lavish hand I banked the precious nutrients around flowers and shrubbery. Soon the humus seeped down where raindrops would work their chemistry.

"Hon, just look at all of this black dirt."

"*Soil*! Don't call it dirt. S—O—I—L!"

"Whatever—it's a real treasure. See, I banked the althea bush knee-high in the stuff."

"Altheas don't have knees," he reminded me. "Now you'll see a big difference in the garden. It's like this: when you decompose organic matter into humus, certain gums are produced which bind soil particles into clumps and create a porous soil." He took a bulletin from his pocket. "It says here. . ."

from *The Joyful Gardener*, Published 1985, *Columbia Daily Tribune*

ELLEN COONEY

ALICE AND THE DONUTS

Alice was terribly organic
Alice was terribly politically correct
one day however Alice raided a couple
of Hostess raspberry donuts from work
well she rationalized the donuts were
paid for the bombs already subsidized
and the donut pleasure was so pure
that the next time Alice bought groceries
she bought a box of those raspberry donuts
and as soon as she got home
she greedily ate three of them
but this time the pleasure was not so pure
Alice was always reading something
and she read the list of ingredients
it was the beef fat that seized her with horror
beef fat as well as bombs and sugar
Guilt climbed on Alice's back like a hump
the afternoon movie she saw
was unmemorable and unmoving
serves me right thought Alice
she went home and drank shooting sherry
and stared at the rest of the donuts
she would throw them away
no she would take them to work on Monday
Alice went to bed to forget about the donuts
but Sunday morning came soon enough
Alice would go on a three day fast
but the beef fat sugar bomb donuts
haunted her as she read
as she listened to baroque music
as she did her laundry
the only way to forget about those donuts
Alice thought was to eat them
so she did
then she brushed her teeth
but it was too soon
the hideous neon raspberry color
poured into the sink
the sight of it made her throw up
the baroque music was still on
how pure a pleasure this music
usually was but she thought of the fat
selfish dissipated kings these musicians

entertained and how disgusted
they must have been at their
beef fat and their sugar
and their terrible weapons

ELLEN COONEY

THE DAY AFTER MARTINMAS

the day after Martinmas
the two sisters in pea coats
arm in arm circled the
pond in the park
do you remember said one
we were here once before
swinging by a rope
in the sign of the cross
for what heresy or witchery
I know not
for misdeeds perhaps of
earlier lives left in
peace within cloistered walls
or silent anonymous cities
we were young maids then
sisters together
or lovers living like sisters
but I remember no more
of that day after Martinmas
but the swinging
north to south to center
east to west to center
beyond the pain the center
that finally opened and held
then severed us

MARY K. DAINS

THOMAS JEFFERSON'S TOMBSTONE

Thomas Jefferson's original tombstone, over 150 years old, still stands, albeit some 900 miles from its intended site. The third president of the United States left specific instructions for his gravemarker: it should be "a plain die or cube surmounted by an obelisk." Inscription would be: "Here was buried Thomas Jefferson, Author of the Declaration of American Independence, of the Statute of Virginia for Religious Freedom & Father of the University of Virginia." The base would record birth and death dates. Jefferson stated he wanted the memorial to be made of coarse stone so that no one would destroy it for the value of the materials.

Jefferson died July 4, 1826. He was buried in the graveyard at Monticello, his home near Charlottesville, Virginia. His family endeavored to carry out his wishes regarding his tombstone. Because Jefferson's estate was encumbered with debts, the family decided to sell Monticello, but retained the gravesite. In 1833 they erected a monument according to Jefferson's instructions. Instead of carving onto hard granite stone, the inscription was inset on a marble plaque and placed onto the face of the obelisk.

As years passed, the graveyard suffered neglect, and vandals and souvenir hunters chipped away at Jefferson's monument. Finally, in 1882, congressmen felt ashamed that no suitable memorial honored the man who held the offices of: President of the United States, Vice-president of the United States, Secretary of State, American Minister to France, and Governor of Virginia. Congress appropriated funds to repair the cemetary and to erect a new monument to Jefferson. What then, would become of the old monument? Jefferson's decendents received numerous requests for the relic.

Professor of Greek and Comparative Philology at the University of Missouri, A. F. Fleet brought the matter to the attention of Samuel S. Laws, university president. Fleet was aware of Laws's fondness for museum pieces; he knew that Laws purchased large scientific collections including the skeletons of animals for the university's museum; he knew that when a circus elephant died at Liberty, Missouri, Laws had acquired the carcass and sent it to New York for mounting; that Laws personally had bought from a private dealer, a life-size bronze equestrian statue of George Washington which he'd placed in front of his home on the university campus in Columbia, Missouri.

Jefferson's "old" monument appealed to Laws. He made official request for it, and pointed out that Missouri had established the first state university in the Louisiana Territory which Jefferson was so instrumental in acquiring during his presidential administration. Jefferson had labored during much of his life on behalf of state-supported education; furthermore, many settlers of Boone County (home of Missouri's state university) originally came from Virginia. Laws himself, was a native Virginian. Also, Missouri's capitol city was named in Jefferson's honor.

After Jefferson's descendants agreed that the University of Missouri should receive the relic, Fleet went to Monticello in 1883 to supervise packing and shipping of the stone to Missouri.

Once in Columbia, it was placed near the entrance of the campus administration building. For safekeeping, the inscribed marble plaque was stored in Academic Hall. When that building burned in 1892, the plaque (unfortunately burned and cracked) was found in the rubble. Later it was restored, and it remains today in a safe in the present administration building.

When Laws left the employ of the university, he took his Washington statue with him, because the board of curators had never reimbursed him for it. But, the Jefferson monument, of course, remained on the campus grounds.

In 1904, the board of curators loaned the Jefferson monument to the St. Louis World's Fair. They sighed with relief when it returned to Columbia in good condition. A short time later, a loan request for the monument for the Jamestown (Virginia) Exposition was denied for fear that the marker would not be returned.

Largely ignored for many years, by students, by faculty and residents, the Jefferson monument was moved to various locations on campus. During the American Bicentennial, it moved to an historical site known as "Red Campus." It now occupies a prominent place adjacent to the Chancellor's residence on Francis Quadrangle, a site listed on the National Register of Historic Places. Benches near the monument make the area a favorite resting area for visitors and students. Today, it receives the attention it deserves. Thomas Jefferson, without doubt, would be pleased to see what has become of his original marker, a historic landmark on the campus of the University of Missouri.

CAROLYN DELOZIER

ROOM 341

She lay, all curled up into that final question mark
That no longer asks "How?" or even "Why?"
Just "When?"

I saw her in her room each day,
As I hunted the hall for other rooms,
Other patients,
Checking their Medicare and Tie-In plans,
Answering insurance questions,
And getting shaky signatures on endless forms.

Although her file was all in order,
And I had no need to interrupt,
I slowed one day,
And paused to look inside.

The foot of her bed held a hat thrown down,
And there he sat—in his overalls,
over by the window light,

And on his lap,
And on the floor around his feet,
A large white cloth
Spread to the other wall.

He held the nearest corner close to his glasses,
And patiently his needle slipped into the cloth,
Then burst forth a thread
Of brilliant blue!
Then turned and plunged, now down and through.
His slow, work-worn hand swept below
To catch the end,
And start its silver tip on its trip up again.

I stood and watched and saw
A pattern grow,
Of birds and flowers in a world of sunshine
That sprinkled empty areas of white,
And chased the gloom
From that gray, quiet room.
And I wanted to ask him,
And didn't, but walked away,
Back to my office, my desk,

My papers, and phones.

Perhaps he cross-stitched for a hobby,
Had done it all his life.
A craft to settle body and soul
enough to sleep at night.

I rather like to think
She started the cover,
Back in years when dreams
Still came true sometimes.

I can see her standing in her room,
Planning the cheerful colors,
Smiling as she chooses
Waves of scalloped quilting,
Soft and dancing gaily across the bed
To the floor,
And meeting
The bright ruffle that will match
Her curtains.

I'm inclined to think he never held a needle
Until now.

And I like to think
He tried to finish it
For her.

But it's none of my business.
I'm just an insurance clerk.

CAROLYN DELOZIER

A STATUE IN THE DESERT

It was summertime when the Germans came, just after World War II ended. All the kids were out of school, seeking diversions from boredom and the desert heat by gathering in the empty lot behind our house every morning to plan their day.

Boys, mostly, made up our group. A few girls would straggle in from time to time, but most of them complained that the boys were rough and insensitive as they went about their important business. The group's daily game that summer was to create great imaginary stages on which to act out interpretations of what our world really was like.

I was the only girl who stuck around. At the incredibly mature age of seven, I imagined myself, a tomboy, a fast runner, and very strong. With pigtails flying, bruised knees, skinny arms and legs, dirty shorts and t-shirt, I hung in there like glue as the boys planned their magnificent events.

Our small town, Alamogordo, New Mexico, was home for the families of many scientists and technicians working on the early American space efforts at White Sands Proving Ground. My father was one of many scientists.

One evening, Father mentioned over the dinner table that some German scientists and their families would arrive in New York by boat in a few days. They'd make a long journey across the United States on the Santa Fe, to help in our country's space research at White Sands. Father said many would come to Alamogordo to make their new homes. He looked at us, particularly my brother and me, and hinted with his eyes that we'd better be nice to these new people and help them get settled. German families would be moving into the new houses across from the lot behind our house.

But Father couldn't fool us kids! We'd seen the "News for the Day" at the local moviehouse; we knew what the Germans really were, or so we thought. Our town was being invaded, and we would stand against them, just as we'd seen our soldiers do in the newsreels.

The morning before our new neighbors were to arrive, a dozen or so of us milled around in the lot. As usual, I was the only girl. My brother, an organizer, split us into separate troops, and we began to plan and work. "Get more tumbleweeds over here!" he shouted. "Rock detail—we'll need twice that many! Now, man the fort! Every man to his post!" The practicing and drilling reached a fever pitch.

As a girl, I wasn't allowed in the front lines. I was given the job of message carrier to different sections of the tumbleweed wall, that, by noon, wove like a long bristly worm across the empty lot.

Finally the fort and our "soldiers" were ready. We all trudged to our homes to await the next day with much anticipation —and just a little fear.

Next morning, trucks arrived at the houses across the lot and men unloaded furniture like I'd never seen before. Large glass-fronted bookcases, beautiful gleaming wood chairs, sofas, bedsteads, stacks and stacks of linens, and what looked like enormous pillows, which I later learned were featherbeds.

Every so often, we'd see a child venturing out into the yard to survey the new surroundings. We'd shout *Comen sie hier*! but not one of the new kids advanced toward our tumbleweed wall.

We heard them calling each other by name—strange names, like Wolfgang, Helmut, Elke, Dieter.

Our platoon of soldiers watched all morning. As the day went on, more children gathered in their yards, looking our way, conferring. We knew they wanted to come across the empty lot to investigate us. We sensed they harbored fear for us, and this made us feel stronger and braver. We shouted all the German we knew: *Ja, ja, ja, nein, nein, nein*—and what we were sure was the ultimate insult: *Dumbkoff, dumbkoff, dumbkoff.*

Finally, several of the bigger boys came to look us over. Then they retreated, gathering the others, and all the German children disappeared behind a house.

We waited smugly, feeling proud that we'd scared them off. Secretly, each of us hoped they'd be back. And back they came, hands and pockets loaded with rocks and sticks. Slowly the group advanced toward our fort. My brother called me over to relay the message: Don't fire til you see the whites of their eyes. (He always got history mixed up.) I ran to the stations to report.

"Fire!" my brother shouted a message I didn't have to carry. The German kids returned our assault as fast as it came their way. Crude missiles flew from both sides, and for the first time I feared someone might get hurt. Insults filled the air: krauts, dumbkoffs, from our side; indecipherable gibes from theirs.

Suddenly a door slammed like thunder from a house across the empty lot. A giant of a woman came stomping through the desert sand. Tall and broad, but not fat, she wore a plain housedress, a spotless white apron, and Oxford shoes. As she barrelled down on us, she screamed, "Nein, nein, bitte, bitte!" One tall German boy grabbed her arm, but she didn't stop.

Up through the flying stones and sticks the woman marched, and I winced when something bounced off her cheek. But she just came on, hands on hips, her cheek reddening as she took a stance before us.

For a moment, she simply stared intensely at our dumbfounded collection—German and America kids alike. Obviously, a language barrier was keeping her from giving us all a royal "cussing out." She stomped over those tumbleweeds we'd worked so hard to build up, and turned to our side of the wall. It broken English, she said, "Ich bin—I—am— Frau Lau. We are told—come to America— help make the rockets go up. Be free—have wonderful life. See no more war!"

Sweeping her arms out to include everyone, she cried, "We come, and I see more war. In Germany is too much war, and here is too much war. No more, bitte, bitte!"

She paused, and the only sound I could hear was the dry desert wind whistling through the tumbleweed wall. She looked each of us in the eye, and I though I saw a twinkle of surprise when she realized I was a "girl soldier."

With her voice shaky and a tear rolling down the red mark on her cheek, she at last said, "When the boat comes to New York, we feel happy. We see your great country. We see—we see—in the harbor . . ." Her voice faltered, lacking the English to describe her feelings.

Her eyes searched among the lines of soldiers again and rested on me, with my pigtails full of tumbleweed burrs, my face grimy with sweat and dirt. She walked over and stood before me, whipped her apron off, and swung that crisp, clean whiteness around my shoulders so it draped to the ground. She picked up a short, fat stick, pulled my right arm into the air, and placed the stick into my hand.

Then turning to the kids, she pointed back at me, standing there with her white apron around my shoulders and my arm raised high, my hand holding the small stick. She smiled and walked past us and her own children, back through the dusty lot to her new home.

We were shocked. We merely stood there, and I realized that the other German and American kids were looking at me, with my long gown and my short stick held high.

I suddenly knew who I was. I raised my torch higher, and opened my arms and myself—to welcome these new people to America.

ANGELA DOUGHERTY

SO, YOU TOO

You go out freely,
& on the street
you see a woman,
whose arm falls off.
There is no blood,
no cry, nothing
other than separation
brings attention
to this catastrophe.
She picks it up,
lays it in a flower bed
in someone's yard,
& continues on.
You look around
for turning heads.
None but yours
seems to notice
(this is more frightening
than the lost arm);
she in turn
has no more reaction
than as if a barrette
had fallen from her hair,
& that she might
have put back.
So, you too
continue past her,
veering from her eyes,
a hint
of some extraordinary truth
that even she,
in her own severance
has denied.

DOROTHY DUNARD

HAIKU

Like a hermit crab
Shunning rooted heritage,
She pirates strange shells.

THE NOTE

Josh was nudging her awake, not so gently this time. "You were moaning in your sleep, Susan. You've been dreaming about it again, haven't you?" He stroked her hair, his fingers catching in its damp tangles. She nodded sleepily.

"Look. It's been over a month now. You've got to forget about it, huh? Get past it, you know? You did everything you could. Now quit beating on yourself so much. Ok?"

She rolled over to look at him.

"Ok, Susan?"

"Yes, ok," she replied, almost in a whisper.

He patted her shoulder and rolled over. She listened to his breathing slowing. She knew she wouldn't get back to sleep until it was early morning. She decided she would go down to the river tomorrow. She hadn't been back there since it happened.

It was mid-afternoon before she was able to get down to the bikepath along the riverfront. She rode past the phone booth at the gas station on 6th, squat aluminum box wavering in the heat of asphalt. She could feel the sun prickling on the last of those black scabs that ran like wavering graffiti down her shins. Her feet had kept slipping off the pedals as she had raced for the phone that morning. Their metal teeth had bitten long raw gouges, but she hadn't noticed them until much later. Her breath had come in great sucking sobs when she flew into the booth and fumbled with the cold circle of the O.

"I'm sorry, ma'ma," the operator said, speaking in the soothing tones of someone talking to a distraught child. "You're going to have to talk a little slower. I can't understand what you're saying."

So she'd pounded her fist on the smudged glass and tried again. Her tongue was swollen around this new language she was speaking for the first time, an important and fiendishly difficult language that allowed for no mistakes.

Everyone had said that the rescue team performed admirably; had been on the scene almost immediately, although they ran into problems retrieving the "rafter," reported as one George Fallon, age 24. They'd finally pulled him ashore two miles downstream. In the *Times* there'd been a photo of him lying stretched on the trampled weeds of the embankment, with rescuers leaning over him.

Susan had studied it for a long time. His eyes were closed. He looked like a young knight on a catafalque, his wetsuit gleaming like dark chainmail in the May sun. He was the only peaceful element in a study of frenzied movement. The paper said they had slashed open the wetsuit and prodded his faltering heart right there on the muddy bank.

The June afternoon sun was hot. Ellen wiped sweat from her eyes and coasted to a stop. Here. The thicket of chokeberries. She'd stopped to check their progress that morning. The year before she'd made jelly from their astringent fruit. She'd turned when she heard shouting, not sure at first what it was over the floodtide noise of the river, surprised anyone else was around so early on a Sunday. Then she'd seen him, crouched down in the black rubber raft.

Why hadn't she realized right away he was in trouble? She'd asked herself that every day since it happened. Now, down here on the bank again, she realized why. On first sight, she'd been momentarily entranced with him, an unexpected dawn gift from the river: beautiful blond god wrapped tight in the skin of a seal, coiled in the hollow of his shining black boat, calling out to her, the only person around, beckoning her maybe to come on the wild side.

She'd felt a kneejerk pulse of—what? Elation. Admit it, she told herself. That's how it had been. A split second, given over to the euphoria of possibility. When she finally had seen the fear in his face, she knew what she'd taken for a grin had been a grimace all along. And, his up-flung arms: no greeting, but a puppet reflex to the violence of water. His shouts: not *joie de vive*, but strangled desperation pure and simple. She'd been too slow in deciphering his terrible messages, she knew. Too slow.

His eyes had met hers then. She read resignation in them. Then the river surged, surged and pulled him into its cold brown rush. He never regained consciousness, they said, though he "lived" almost until evening.

She leaned against her bike for a long time, watching the river. The water had retreated far down the bank now. The dried mud of the bank was cracked and cardboard-looking as a jigsaw puzzle turned upside down. Bluebottles buzzed on the scattered piles of tangled debris left behind by the runoff. She saw chunks of styrofoam. Somebody's picnic cooler once full of beer for the long weekend.

Bicycling home, she swirved when an avocet shrieked and dive bombed her. His black beak curved toward her, sharp little scythe. She glimpsed a blur of the feathers around his head, bright pink as a fresh scar. Her bike wobbled and almost threw her.

That night she had the dream again. She was standing on the bank with her arms plunged to the elbows in the new green of a chokeberry bush. She was searching for something hidden there, something important to find. The leaves rustled so loudly she could hear nothing else. Then she realized the sound wasn't leaves, but feathers slithering. And the black glitter not ripe chokeberries at all, but a hawk's eyes, level with her own. She was staring into the tawny beaked face of a redtail as big as a man. Branches whipped against her face. She felt the push of a sudden cold wind. She rubbed her stinging eyes, turned to follow the hawk's flight. But he was gone. Then she saw the river runner on his raft. He stood upright now, balancing with an athlete's easy grace. His hair wasn't blond anymore, but pure white, stiff with frost, though it was late spring. Broken twigs were tangled in his hair, spiky as a laurel wreath. He still wore the wetsuit, but it was ripped now. His skin glimmered white through the slashes. She could see he was glazed with ice, sheathed in it as though he'd ridden the snowmelt river all the way down from the peaks of the Divide, from the very breaks where it rose, so high in the snowfields. He flung up his arm in a languid slow-motion gesture. The ice splintered, snared sunlight as it scattered. Glass arrows showered toward her, but melted as they reached her. She could feel their wetness cool her face. He waved again. She stood rooted on the bank. What did he mean? She had to know, before she could move, before her muscles would thaw. Tell me what you mean, she wanted to implore as the raft floated by her. But no words came. Not from her constricted throat. And not from him. His mouth was closed, not open or contorted with shouting as it had been once. The river began to take him now in dream-slow circles: circles nothing like the muddy deafening tumble the river had been earlier. Still he said nothing. His eyes fixed on hers. She couldn't read them. They were as dark as the redtail's, but without that eyeblink ferocity. And that last wintery second of animal bleakness she had seen once before was gone now. I'm sorry, she started to cry out, knowing it was hopeless, that she wasn't making a sound. Then she realized that he had closed his eyes. He couldn't even see her making an attempt. Her throat tightened further. An ache spread across her tongue and seeped back down, through her chest, her arms, her legs.

That was when she awoke. . .sprawled on her back, feeling as though she'd been dropped from some great height, saturated with the weight of enormous sadness. Josh was snoring with his usual soft pattern of hiccups. So she hadn't moaned in her sleep this time. That was something, anyway. The trip back down to the river hadn't exorcised the recurring dream, but at least she wasn't muttering unintelligible noises.

She lay gazing at the slant yellow bar from the streetlight. Words were just unintelligible noises most of the time, she thought. People opening their mouths so hopefully, and somebody else looking at them, intent, but not understanding anything that comes out. So what good are words?

She thought of George Fallon's mouth again: its distorted futility. And of her own frantic incoherence in the phone booth. And of Josh's lame attempts at comfort these days. Words should light up our dark spaces, our dark places, for us. But they don't. She turned her head away from the streetlight and closed her eyes, as though sleep would come faster if she mimicked it.

In the middle of the summer, the postman brought an envelope with handwriting Susan didn't recognize. There was no return address. She tore it open, pulled out a card whose front looked like the papercuts you find in Chinese import stores. Inside, the writing close to the top of the page was carefully done in ballpoint, the lines marching rigidly straight, as though the the writer had used one of those ruling devices that sometimes comes with stationery. The note began:

36

Dear Miss Gorman,

    I knew your name from when it was in the *Times*. I called them up down there and they gave me your address also, so I guess I should thank them too. That's what this is, a thank you note and I am sorry I took so long long to get around to writing you but this has been a pretty mixed-up summer as you can imagine. My nephew George Fallon was the man who fell off the raft that you phoned those rescue people about. We all just want you to know that we thank you for how you tried to help George.

                    Sincerely,
                    Mrs. Arnold Thatcher

There was a postscript that looked as though it had been written in a burst of scribbling, the lines slanting askew.

    PS I see now I was wrong to put off writing you the way I did. At first I just did not know why I was but then it came to me. He wasn't saved. I did not feel like thanking anybody right then. But I was wrong. I just wanted you to know. You tried and that is what counts. George would have wanted me to thank you, so once more I do. I know at least you tried.

Involuntarily, Susan turned the note to the back. At the bottom was a printed message.

Laserworks, Inc.
The traceries of this design were created
for your pleasure
by light itself.

Lighted words. Absolution from strangers. She put the note back in its torn envelope and laid it on the table.

CRYSTAL FIELD

12 MILES NORTH OF DULUTH

I.

The seagulls sound like kids
riding creaking swings
as a bald man in black and white swimsuit
throws them popcorn.
One or two trumpet
when his blond wife in yellow t-shirt
throws them popcorn too.
Last night in our cabin we heard thunder
along with soft rain. Today the water is so calm
the waves sound like someone in a bathtub.
Greg is painting his second north shore scene.
Yesterday two of the canvas rocks
made a gigantic black brassiere.
Today they're blended into gray rock.
I sit behind him watching the shore
transferred to canvas. We are free
12 miles north of Duluth.
Even in our worst times
we've been free here.

II.

On my gray rock
the water has worn a soft pouch
big enough for my bottom.
I'm filling up on reading.
The first day a novel:
In the Days of the Queen of Persia.
That's what my father called me—
due to my cantankerous ways.
The next day a guide for women in mid-life
that says the way to age sensually
is to love an idea—I could win a prize.
Yesterday *The New Male-Female Relationship.*
I smell the wet oils on Greg's canvas.
One leg cocked on a rock, his jeans stretch tight
across his ass.

III.

The water is so clear
I see the patterns of algae on the rocks beneath.
They look like evergreens on cliffs
seen from an airplane. Then the waves change.
The water crashes over a rock
and makes a waterfall for my feet.
Greg leaves his painting to slip a toe
in the icy water. "You could have a heart attack
falling in this water," he says. I smile and turn
to watch a freighter on the horizon.
When I turn back he's knee deep,
then waist deep, oohing and ahhing.
"Family jewels frozen?"
"I can say I've been swimming in Lake Superior," he says.
"I washed my hair in it years ago," I brag.
Several rocks away, the man throwing popcorn
now dangles his legs in the icy water.
"You could have a heart attack falling in this water,"
he says to his wife who smiles.

IV.

I move my feet like egg beaters in the water.
The waves move out from me
in ever larger circles,
no matter how the wind blows.

CRYSTAL FIELD

IN THE GARDEN

You have an apple butt, my sister says,
and bends her pear over
to weed green beans.
I get my fingernails dirty
when I weed, she says, but plants
love attention. I hover around
even if they don't need weeding.
Often Daddy's ghost visits,
gives me advice on asparagus.
I keep his roses large
and hum to the Swiss chard.
Plants grow better with attention.
And if this man doesn't work out,
I'm turning to a woman,
not a feminine woman
like my friend Mary,
but someone masculine enough
to haul manure and fix cars—
a woman, you know, like a man
I can trust.

PRUFROCK WAS WRONG

Cecilia is resigned
that another man will leave her
to be "free to love all women."
I know she thinks if she's beautiful
how come she's alone.
I have Greg who loves me
even though he knows me.
I take it in, feel very solid—very lucky.
And then fall in love with a Persian
whose dark eyes light up
when I enter a room.
And Cecilia leaves Carl for another potter
whose blue eyes light up
when she enters a room.
What we have here is a series of eyes
lighting up in a room.
Prufrock was wrong.
This is the way the women come and go.
They never mention Michelangelo.

MARIAN FLEISCHMANN

THE BLUETICK

The wailing scream of a Bluetick hound hot on the trail of a coon broke the stillness of the night. Hitching his blue jeans up over his rounded belly, Tom Swartz heaved his right leg over a barbwire fence and stepped down on the second wire. Holding a 12-gauge shotgun in his right hand, he grabbed the top of the fencepost with his left, putting his weight on his right foot. The wire sagged, straining against the steeple, as he struggled to get his left leg over. The hound bawled again, and swaying on the wire, he yanked his leg across, catching his pants on a barb and tearing himself free with a loud ripping noise. Ignoring the stinging scratch, he jumped to the ground. Staggering a little, he regained his balance and took off across the stubbled corn field. Ahead of him, he could see Joe Turner and Joe's cousin Steve running into the woods at the edge of the field. Panting, he ran after them. Joe's six-foot, four-inch frame towered over Steve, but they shared the blond hair and thin bodies of the Turners.

Other voices began to join the Bluetick's and he ran faster. Suddenly, the noisy chorus changed directions as the coon doubled back. Tom veered toward the sound, running full tilt along the edge of the field. He ran down the edge of a ravine toward the dogs who had treed the coon in a large walnut tree in the center of a grove on the banks of the Jim Henry Creek.

The Bluetick, his front feet resting high on the trunk of the tree, had his head back and was barking directly at the densest part of the tree. The other dogs ran in a crouch around the tree, jumping into the air, the click of their teeth as they snapped at the empty air adding to Tom's excitement.

Straining his eyes, his chest heaving, Tom looked for the coon among the tangled branches. Gradually he isolated a darker shape in a fork of the tree. Loading the shotgun, he aimed at the center and squeezed off a shot as Joe came running into the grove. Steve was a few steps behind, slowed by the three coons slung across his back.

The wounded coon held to the branches above their heads for a few minutes. He slowly let go and fell to the frenzied dogs below. The Bluetick jumped into the air and grabbed the coon as it fell. Shaking it viciously while the other dogs circled him, taking eager snaps at the dying coon, the Bluetick held his prize against the others.

"By God, you're lucky," Steve yelled over the noise of the dogs.

"Luck nothin'," Tom yelled back. "I knew that coon was headed for this side of the creek."

"Bullshit," shouted Joe as he began grabbing dogs by their collars and dragging them away. Steve began to pull dogs away too while Tom carefully took the coon from the Bluetick. He'd grabbed one from the big dog last year over by the Moreau River and got bit. He never rushed the Bluetick now. Taking a leather strap from his coat pocket, he tied the coon's hindlegs together and then got out his pocket knife and slit the animal's ruined throat to increase the release of blood. He noted with satisfaction the animal's healthy pelt and filled-out form. He'd freeze this one and barbecue it later when he had accumulated enough for a big meal. When the blood had slowed sufficiently to suit him, he slung the animal onto his shoulder so that it hung beneath his armpit.

"Well, it's goin' on four," said Steve. "Think we'd better be gettin' home?"

"Yeah," Joe answered. "I got some plowing to do down by the hog pens so I can put in the last of the winter wheat."

"I'm ready," Tom said. "Beth's at her folks so I'm gonna fix some bacon and eggs after I clean this coon, do chores, and then go over to Stegeman's sale. I could sure use old Ben's brush hog if it goes cheap."

"What the hell happened to Ben, anyway?" asked Steve as they started back to their trucks. He shifted the dead animals hanging on his back. Walking ahead of him, Joe carried two lifeless coons tied to his belt. Even as he waited for an answer, Steve was busy calculating the price of the pelts. That was his money to spend on tobacco and new shells and even an occasional cold beer.

"I heard he sold all his livestock last week and I know the farm's been listed," said Joe.

"He signed some loans for Billy and Billy took bankruptcy. All them fancy milking machines and now his dad's got to pay for 'em," said Tom as he struggled to keep up, the dead animal under his arm feeding a growing wet patch down the leg of his overalls. "Bob Carter said Billy had about $350,000 in loans and ain't gonna be able to pay any of it hisself."

They fell silent as they made their way through the brush to a gravel road. The dogs ran ahead, silent shadows chasing nothing down the darkening road. The Bluetick stayed close to Steve, but without that dependent posture most dogs take around their masters. His big head up, he was where he was because he chose to be, an elemental force as strong as the land's hold on the three men and their silent women.

"Six coons is a pretty good hunt," said Joe as he loaded three dogs into the box on the back of his truck. Tom opened the wire door in the box on the back of his truck and one at a time, shoved four dogs in as Steve opened a door to his truck and let his dogs climb in.

"Hey, Steve," Joe yelled as they began to get into their trucks. "You decide to sell that Bluetick, you let me know first."

Steve laughed as he climbed into the cab of his truck. "I'll do that," he said.

"The hell with him," Tom called out the truck window. "You tell me first and I'll trade you my new John Deere tractor for him."

Still laughing, Steve pulled out of the road ditch and with a wave headed down the gravel road. Joe backed up and around and took off the other way. Calmly waiting his turn, Tom pulled out slowly and drove toward his comfortable brick house, just down the road from his parents' old white frame house.

KAREN J. FOX

HOUSE GUEST

She lives in the back
of my mind and she
won't shut up!
She stands there
day and night . . .
Hands on aproned hips,
polyester knit pantsuit,
and fuzzy pink house slippers
beating time to some
imaginary rhythm in her
own head.
Her knife-edged voice
drones on and on,
grating my nerves
the way I grate up carrots
for salad.
She talks of her husband who,
God rest his soul,
died just to spite her.
Left her alone, he did.
She constantly reminds
me of my failures
and picks on my weaknesses.
Reminds me to water my plants
and to replace the lid
on the toothpaste,
bitches about dirty ashtrays
shoved under the sofa
and whines that she misses
her "shows" on TV because
I fall asleep when they
come on.
Oh, I've tried to make her leave.
Tried putting her out one time.
She got mad and the foot
tapping became faster
but the old biddy
stood her ground . . .
You know, when I get old
I might decide to like her.
That is,
if she doesn't drive
me crazy first.

VICTORIA GARTON

THE LAST TIME

New grass up through the old
urged me to some decision.

In slow motion,
our commitments ran as lovers.

Those other lives tangled our limbs.
We moved with no freedom.

Without joy, we could not bear
spring's green insistence.

Had we known this ending in winter
we might have held on.

GETTING THROUGH

No one but yourself
could get you through
that wedge of heat
compressing Kansas.

No one could slice or crumble
that solid oppression
or assure you
you would not suffocate.

There are times
when the salt of the earth
keeps in cool rooms
which are not open to you.

There are times when
the only salt is on your skin
igniting the wounds
as you go on blunt headed.

VICTORIA GARTON

GAMES WE PLAYED

We played a game called
"What I like best."
Saying "I like this,"
we could not let go of our lives.

I came to believe
that if one said, "I like this
and this," the last drop
could actually be savored.

In the name of fairness,
we played, "What I like least."
The game is like unmelted candy
going down the wrong way.

Yet, I came to know
that past the burning eyes
there is a surprising finality
to swallowing hard truth.

JOAN GILBERT

MISTER D

January 6. Mister D, Mary's old jumper, has stobbed himself. She just called, almost twelve hours after the fact, only now able to talk about it. They began a search at 5 a.m., out to do their chores before work, when he didn't come up to eat. He was standing at the edge of the woods in a pond of blood, a piece of tree branch protruding from his groin.

Mary said that as she ran in to call the vet she was physically sick, afraid she'd faint or vomit or be too hysterical to talk. "I thought I was probably calling to have him put away," she told me.

Her panic didn't need to be explained. For nineteen years, saving, juggling money, owning him was her major preoccupation. She wrote home about the saddlebred mix that gave him "pride of bearing" and "fluid motion." Later, when her dream was realized, Mary confided, "I think about him all the time. At work, with friends. . .I just keep thinking about getting back to him." Still later, lying in the hospital for five weeks with a broken pelvis (another horse had reared and fallen on her), she said, "It's not really so bad at night, because then I can dream about D, riding and riding, in the most beautiful places." And, to a coversation about what it must have been like in days when transportation depended on horses, her contribution was, "I know how people felt when they found a really good horse. I can feel D's strength and willingness coming up, when I ride him, as if he were saying 'I can go on and on. Where do you want me to take you?'"

They made many long trail rides together. They learned to jump well enough to win a lot of show prizes. They belonged, for awhile, to a hunt club. None of the many horses in Mary's life have been cherished like D, 16.1 hands, chestnut, whimsical striped face.

D has also been the continuity of Mary's life since college, and she told me she felt, this morning, that if she lost him, she would somehow be losing her past. D has lived with her in three states, seen her change husbands, seen her lose her father and most of her grandparents. These memories paraded by, she told me, during the long, dark and cold hour she waited alone (Dan had been obliged to go on to work) for the veterinarian to drive out.

By his pick-up's headlights, the doctor tranquilized D and pulled out a stick at least 12 inches long. "I couldn't believe it," Mary said. "It just kept coming. I didn't see how it could *not* kill D."

Bleeding increased then, beyond the doctor's ability to control with the horse standing. Mary made another frantic dash to the house, this time for something—anything—to staunch the flow. First at hand was a stack of bath towels, many of them nearly new, folded from the dryer the previous night.

"They were about as effective as tissues would have been," she said. D had to be anesthetized, but once down, his bleeding could be stopped, and the doctor could explore the wound by hand. He brought out a lot of wood, bark and leaf debris, but also some good news. The abdominal wall seemed to be intact. The stick had gone up a little sideways, damaging nothing vital. D had a chance.

However, he stayed down unexpectedly long. Mary, the doctor and his assistant stood by apprehensively as day broke, all of them blood spattered, all shivering with cold and stress, all trying not to look at the puddles of freezing blood that surrounded them and the pile of blood-soaked towels, taking on a grotesque, carcass-like shape of its own. (Later, Dan's mother and I, too frugal to be squeamish about horse blood on more than a dozen good towels, said we'd take them home to wash, but they mysteriously disappeared; Mary wanted no souvenirs of this morning!)

D had an injection of antibiotics and was, with difficulty, coaxed to the barn. Then the others left Mary to follow instructions about trying to get him warm. She stacked on his own blanket, one from the bed inside, and an unzipped sleeping bag. He continued to shake, standing among food and water she'd hopefully set within easy reach.

When she finally did go in to give herself some attention, Mary said she thought her teeth would never stop chattering, that she would never be warm again. After changing into clean, dry clothing, she had some hot chocolate and some soup. The rest of the day she spent running back and forth to check on D, each time expecting to see him down and dying.

Following the blood trail back into the woods, she found the grove of oak saplings D had fallen into. Spots of ice were left from the Christmas storm, and she saw that he had slipped on some of this, "roaring out," as she put it, in his usual fashion. Actually, he had moved quite a distance toward the barn in spite of his impediment. The stout stick must have moved excruciatingly inside him with each step. He had lost more blood than the veterinarian had had a chance to realize.

January 7. I have had my first look at D and feel little hope for him. He's in an "end of the trail" posture, nose almost on the ground. It's hard to imagine that he will ever again strike his herd leader pose on the ridge, neck tightly arched, mane fluttering, one hoof pawing. Mary bitterly regrets all the wonderful weekends that passed with no riding. Dispite his age, D has been in perfect health and full of vigor.

My main memory of this time will be the grisly little pink icicles forming along his belly where blood and fluid ooze from his wound. "He won't make it," I told myself. "Not with six degrees predicted for tonight." I will also remember the other horses gathered around D's space in the pole barn, right up against the fence panels that separate them. It is like a royal deathbed scene. Are they just curious, maybe speculating about who will be boss horse if D dies? Or are they concerned, perhaps easing his pain by empathy in some way we non-herd animals would not understand? What could an animal behaviorist tell us about this?

Dan showed me the huge syringe for the antibiotics they are to give, 120 cc in three shots. And that is supposed to change this wretched, shrunken creature back into the lordly D? One can only weep for them all.

January 8. Amazing as it seems, D is improving, terribly swollen on that side and down his leg, but Mary tells me he ate some last night and is drinking water as if aware that his fluids need to be replenished. I have just been over to see if he is still up and covered, so she can be reassured at work, for she had to go in today. He was up, blankets neat, and he looked around alertly as I approached. When he nickers at us again, then we can be sure his spirit is still safely inside him. The other horses have dispersed. Does that mean their help is no longer needed, or that they know there's no chance of promotion?

When we talked, Mary said that "getting stobbed" is the great fear held for hunters in the field. An unwise or poorly done jump could bring a horse down on something that would impale him. She said many fine horses have died this way over the centuries, victims of their owners' fun. It's one reason she got out of the club. Of course, nowadays, thanks to antibiotics, dangers are less. We compared D's chances, if they'd all lived 100 years ago. He would have bled to death with the stick out and died of infection whether it was in or out. How long would it have taken? How long, today, if he'd been a wild horse, or one of those unfortunates put on winter pasture and visited only occasionally by the owner? Lucky D!

January 17. He's had one backset, had to have another round of the medicine, but D is definitely recovering. The wound is still draining, but his swelling is going down and his appetite is almost normal. Mary takes him for a little walk each day, and soon he can return to his followers. He moves slowly, carefully, but determinedly. Less than two cupfuls of the magic elixir brought him back from the brink. That and the long accustomed magic of telephones which brought D help promptly. A few decades ago, it would have taken at least a half a day to get to town, locate the veterinarian and bring him out. The phone made constant supervision possible, even though the doctor never saw D again. Bills for the whole thing were only $50 in money, unmeasurable in every other way. . .as is our relief and gratitude that D is still alive.

If we were winding up with a moral, that would probably be something about sprouts in pastures, checking animals often, and never giving up without a fight. Mary adds another: "Never take them for granted. Don't plan to ride them later, or pet them when you have more time, or, someday, just sit down and watch them moving around. Enjoy them everyday, as much as you can."

ON COMPANIONSHIP

"Gad! It sure is *dark* out here! Like the back of beyond." My guest was a local newspaper columnist who had driven from town alone to speak to our writers' group. It's less than ten miles, but seems farther, because one goes from pavement to blacktop to gravel to narrow and sometimes rutty lane. On departure, she shivered and said, "And it's so *quiet* out here! Nothing but weird, lonesome wind in the trees. Aren't you afraid? How do you stand it?"

This is old stuff and I usually just refer to my nearby relatives and to my sizeable, mouthy dogs who would never permit anything unusual to happen unannounced. I also remark that an earth-sheltered house makes a person feel safe from almost everything but radon. There's just one door and windows are shallow and up under the eaves; only a contortionist could get in. Actually, I was much more afraid in town.

If critics have a sense of humor, I point out a sign relatives made for me which says, "A day in the country is worth a month in town." Dark and quiet are only two of the many reasons some of us feel this way. I look forward to restful dark and not just because work can be put aside then; there are special night-time restorations, some involving what my guest found "weird and lonesome." One is simply to sit on the steps, breathing delicious night air and listening to wind in the trees or the pond's residents (I love, especially, the insane chuckle of leopard frogs), or the coyotes, or whatever nature has on its program. The aerial ballet of bats, feeding around the security light, competes well with television. So do the light shows put on by fireflies.

They could be explained to that guest and many like her. Perhaps enjoyment is partly in our genes. I come from many generations of country people; all that I knew spoke fondly of what they'd sacrificed for profit or convenience. My father—in the forties, in a very small town—complained constantly about the annoyance of living too close to others. He would sometimes say mildly, "I miss the woods."

A thousand times I've regretted not asking, "Why, Daddy? What is so great about woods? Take me there and show me." Now I know, but would still like to be able to exchange specifics with him. Did he, too, notice that little bare black branches are lovely when wet and decorated with a few tastefully spaced crystal drops? These surely inspired the Christmas fashion for bare branches hung with tiny lights.

I'd like to ask whether my father ever hugged a tree. I have, and a friend of Cherokee descent told me that her people embraced their favorite trees in farewell when driven from their homes to the Trail of Tears. That would have interested my father. After a wearing trip to town, the woods can debrief me in half an hour, putting me back in condition for work. Was it the same for him?

Even without knowing, in the woods, I feel a companionship with

49

my father and all my forebears; there's companionship, too, with some of earth's better known people.

In storms I like to think of John Muir, climbing a 100 foot fir and clinging to its whipping top, experiencing wind as a tree does. When I hear the fearsome, sickening snarl of the chain saw, I remember his words: "Any fool can destroy trees. . .they cannot run away; and if they could, they would still be chased and hunted down as long as fun or a dollar could be got out of them." In spring, among the redbuds and many other blooming trees I cannot identify, I always recite to myself the conclusion of A. E. Houseman's tribute to the wild cherry:

> Now, of my threescore years and ten,
> Twenty will not come again.
> And take from seventy springs a score
> It only leaves me fifty more.
> And since to look at things in bloom
> Fifty springs are little room,
> About the woodlands I will go
> To see the cherry hung with snow.

I envy Houseman the fifty years he had then (though he probably wrote this in maturity, wishing he still had them!). A realistic expectation for me is 25, only a few of which, by the law of averages, will see me rambling over ridges and ravines. So I must hoard up the companionship of trees now, and all the other country things. When they are only memory, I will need every possible detail of those sights and sounds, the quiet and the dark.

JOAN GILSON

ANOTHER KIND OF POEM

Are all musicians that wordless?
The granola-crunching
boy piano player I know
who lifted Bach for
two hours
out of a solid black
Steinway grand in his
inherited tuxedo
with no missed notes?

Or a kid I know who can push
improvisations through
his trumpet
like cocking his tongue
behind watermelon seeds?

Do all musicians make
sidelong smiles,
swallow words,
knowing that words
can miss a beat?

BOOGIE CHILDREN

Little girl gymnasts twist, flip
Down red mats with the
Young rhythm of bone song
And the grace of Psalms
Balanced by hours' drill.
Strength spills in waves across
the stage.

When they turn to face us,
legs straight, palms
up, heads erect, and their
shining, shining eyes,
we clap, clap,
clap, amazed to be so
weak ourselves—
helpless before their muscular,
innocent sorcery.

JOAN GILSON

THE INHERITANCE

Yellow teeth grinning in a dying
skull my father left me
     only
a slick silk scarf the
color of parties and
300 bucks.

Just enough to
buy the second-hand upright
piano I found
lounging in shabby
style alone at
the back of the shop
in mid-town Kansas City,
a gift for my
little girl.

Bach splashing from
her fingers, harmonies in
     her bones, that baby slid
     smiling into now.
         And she casts melody
         across those yellowing
         keys in clear blue anthems
     while she grins
     a spell at me.

DIANE GLANCY

A CATFISH OR COMMON SUCKER

Why do you delight so unmercifully in your fishing?
Explaining with a jerk of your head
how the hook must enter the lip or jaw or better yet,
how the fish swallows it and the hook catches
in its gut.
I think of its stomach ripping like the fine silk
of my dress at this luncheon.
You have balls if anyone does.
What a relief there's your kind to offset mine.
Oh, life would be a teaparty with the fish, wouldn't it,
if I was all there was—
Let the fish come and eat with us,
set him a place at the table
with finger bowls he can stick his nose into
when he must suck water for his breath?
Let him hold it the rest of the time like we hold ours
when we are in his element.
Tie a bib around his fat neck.
Serve him insects in a silver chafing dish.
What lovely sleeves his fins make,
what stripes and speckles and spots along his dorsal!

But bayonets dance in your eyes.
You would slice him in two
while he took his first bite.
Where were you when they taught us to be women?
The razor blades jump in your fingers.
But I see the markings of the spirit world in his scales,
the eyes in his tail.
Hi yip, I would say—Fish, you are a friend
like the buffalo.
I thank you for your life—
and I would spear him quickly through the heart
while he thinks of his blessing from the Father,
while he thinks of the fine buckskin of his life,
and his mouth still opens and closes
like smoke signals let loose in the wind
which seem to say,
Tula, Tula,
though I can't be sure it's quite that.

DIANE GLANCY

LETTER TO MY FORMER HUSBAND

I didn't want to be with you
when you came to this.
I saw it long ago on the hill
in Krug Park
while I held two children
and you paced the gravelly road.
Back and forth
that Sunday before
you returned to your job.
Drinking left you scattered—
something like the birds
that flew over the park.
I could do nothing
but hold on to the leaves,
the trees,
the children.
You had something within you
in that distant day
that NOW
when you tired of flaying the sky
and fell
to the ground on your back,
feet kicking
wings twitching with frenzy.
And there would be no flight.
I was married to you
nineteen years
and then I let go of the emptiness
I would always hold.
You used to threaten
you'd drive the car into a tree.
You beat the walls,
hurt in your gut.
You'd clap your fists to your chest.
It was no marriage for me.
Even when you were in your
third floor office
and others envied your position
I saw your movements of despair
night after night.
I moved from your bed,
could not stand the beating wings,
the running feet
the pecking of your beak,
your place with those birds
over Krug Park.

DIANE GLANCY

ON CLIFF DRIVE

I have waited so long / mother in a flowered dress
soft hair for father now I / climb into the hill
with a squeak of the old bed / dusk in the valley
red / purple like tomatoes & beets at roadside stands
under propellers at night.
I have been locked in / woman of him
who turns up like a traveling snake oil show.
Old comforter—the smudge pots smoke
in cold vineyards.
The daughter's voice a butcher knife / the red & purple
bruise still calling.

VALERIE GORDON

THE BELLS TOLL FOR US, TOO

Nonchalantly, we black women sat by and watched as the Equal Rights Amendment failed to become law by midnight June 30, 1982. With the defeat of ERA, white males—and those women who think like Phyllis Schlafly—rejoiced as they congratulated themselves for their glorified abilities to legally keep a group of people oppressed in America.

While most white sisters mourned its death, black women uncaringly continued on with their daily duties. Ironically, and historically, we refused to realize that when the bells tolled for the ERA, they resounded—oh, so clearly, for us, too.

It's not the first time that ERA failed. It was first proposed in 1923, but its beginnings can be traced to 1848 when women first organized at the Seneca Falls convention. However, the priority concern there was not for a national amendment for women's rights, but a reaction to society's opposition against women publicly speaking out against slavery.

Famous white abolitionists and suffragettes, the Gimke sisters, were surprised by the outrage shown by both wommen and men when they approached a platform. Although slavery was "the" highly controversial and political issue, anger flared at the Gimke's audacity to assume that men actually wanted to hear what they had to say.

As the issue of slavery grew in controversy, women's organizations sprouted to refute its evil. At following conventions, male abolitionists like William Lloyd Garrison and Frederick Douglas were asked to speak on the topic and its affects on the nation as a whole.

It was during one of these conventions that embarrassed white suffragettes refused to let the compelling black abolitionist, Sojourner Truth, speak. Because of her deep voice and strong features, mocking white men questioned her womanhood. Standing proudly, Sojourner Truth ripped open her blouse to expose her breast and projected her deep booming voice with the conviction of 10,000 warriors shouting her famous speech, "Ain't I a Woman?"

Unfortunately, the union of the two oppressed groups was not made in heaven. Instead of squelching rumors that pitted one group against the other, members succumbed, debated among themselves as to which group, blacks or women, should receive its rights first.

Frederick Douglas argued that since slavery was more brutal and debasing, blacks had the more pressing need, while another historically significant woman's rights activist, Susan B. Anthony refused to let a "nigger" achieve rights before she did. Sojourner Truth rose to advocate rights for both groups. As a former slave she knew all too well the gross inhumanities blacks suffered from white masters and mistresses, but she also understood that black women would never be free unless women's rights were granted, too.

And she was right. Decades after the passage of the Fifteenth

Amendment and the Civil Rights Act of 1965 outlawing racial discrimination, black women still are the most oppressed group in the United States. Because we have always worked, there is a certain amount of independence felt among black women. But we black women make the least amount of money and hold the most menial jobs despite the fact that a high percentage of black women are the only wage-earners in their families.

Black women are the least represented in the political sphere and in the business world; they hold the lowest positions in just about every aspect of society. While white women make about .59 cents to every $1.00 men make, black women earn less than .45 cents.

Consequently, we black women need the passage of the ERA as much as or more than our white sisters. Although we suffer from the double whammy, any and every step made in eliminating any kind of discrimination—race, sex, age, handicapped or whatever— has to benefit us.

That's why we can't afford to sit idly by and with indifference watch the ERA fail again.

Valerie Gordon

Published 1982, *Northwest Dispatch*, Tacoma, Washington

PAMELA HADAS

LOSERS, KEEPERS: THE OPUS

OF WILHELMINA SCROWD

I. Wilhelmina's Opus on *Habeus Corpus*

Come on over here and tell me, Sweetheart,
why so shy and sneak-puss with your cattie birdcage?
I saw you snatch my pie from way 'cross the park.
Those long shots, Dearie, won't make either one of us famous.
Diddly-dot-dot-dot—a million indistincts to blow up.
Wilhelmina's not leary to get mugged, brought close and cornered,
for her arky pieprint to get smeared all over the daily blab ...
or is it some femme slick you're cocking your eye for?
Maybe your ambish is to take me for a fashionable bite
of the Big Apple, a sweet peek-a-boob slice
of some dodo rags in her nest of bags, her human interest—
so pleased to be a freak ... A nice song and dance
for the coffee table. Am I right? Left-minded?
You'd like a fairy godmother, no?
Some cracked phiz to filmize, then to take you straight
from your bath at home to your Lady Lenser Show,
your name up beside her, her finder, her keeper.
Ain't it so? ... Are you after the today angle?—
the bugs and slump of the me in general? Go ahead.
Kodak the kook, zap her in the soup, cook and dupe all you want.
But ... I won't be your sneak zoomed in on from away off.
Because, my Hocus-Focus Girl, at that distance of yours,
I am essentially ... invisible. But listen. Here's the deal:
I give this carcass to you close-up—all the pose and pluck
you'd ever want—plus wordage to go with. You bring me back
the snugglepup of a mention in *People*. Bring me your copy—
I could use it in my shoes. But, I'm nothing to know
without the talk, so ... so, next time, next time
bring your tape-O gizmo—got me?—and a heap of time
on your heart ... I'll usually be wherever you don't look,
so keep that third eye peeled ... and meanwhile, have a good life.

*

So, did we decide your plotto for me, Darling?
Am I your background, or your follow-up? Are we shooting
for a World's Homeless Series? (Ha! that's a good one—
you can quote me, it's yours.) You need some
hot-off-the-cuff-puff-biog for your ... Street Whoose Hooey?

Some because-whys, I-wherefores? Dissa and Data of my makings—
rambitions, curlicues to my ups and down-bringings?
And is it all for a moral lesson, or a wonder? Well, whatever.
To start: my mother thought this child was
absolutely bloody ... Christmas, she did, so there goes
your slush of early damages. Cleverness was always
my best stunt, and showoffable—better than any boyhunk,
my father used to say ... to cheer himself up.
What with being blue at birth, and thereafter
a first-rate factory for germs—a dicey child
from the word go—I seemed ... naturally ... miraculous.
In my gym tunic, my Minnie Mouse shoes—you should have seen me—
and Uncle Ratso's boater on my birdnest hair.
Oh, I wanted ribbons, but they struck my mother as ...
just too working class. Still, I made a gorgeous
lyrical affair of my thirteenth year—
what with Keats and bees murmurring in the immemorial and so on,
and a man who loved her ... pilgrim soul, and the very idea
of chaste kisses and passionate mash notes, and then my mother
leaving those oooey-gooey books all over the house—
what was I supposed to think—that the tooth fairy was having some
bookish afterthoughts? ... Like this soupy one:
showed a fishy cartoon bird stuffed up under
a line-drawing type mother's heart, and then some pipe-off
on the getting bagged with this bundle, made up
out of slipslop throbs, on the one hand, and the obsupifactuals
of an adding machine on the other, so I would be
in the knowing ... But oh, that summer I was
some jook organ gone nuts with honeysuckle.
We'd wail, "How dry I am ... " —my chums and me—
like ... sun-and-bird goddesses ... silly maiden egglings,
and all of us trollops at heart, in our tipsy balance,
thin-skinned, little radishes, hot and cool together.
Those days, I'd trim my hat with little posies
folded up and sewn from satin—remnants of coffin linings—
my father's business ... and with these tiny feathers
picked up off the ground. He used to take me
to bird-watch with him, Sundays, and this one day I asked him
please to climb up, and fetch me that brown thrush nest ...
and so that was when he fell, and his head cracked,
busted open, and with me standing there ... shocked
to see ... myself, in my own whole body, with my father's blood,
scrambled, with everything ... spilled out. And then it came to me,
but I'm not sure if in words it did: *A body can't be helped.*
No way, nosirree. There's no trimmings to cover up
the holes, the mess, the plain old felt grief of it—
nope, any frill is as much from sadness as no frills at all ...
You get the arpeggios ... or the silence ... a thrush
going nuts at night ... or nothing ... and it's all the same.

Can you make a movie of this, Duckie? Scenerize,
cook the old opera into something ... slicked-up and saleable?
We've anyways got our theme: the leper of today
becomes tomorrow's angel. No? Or, vice-a-versa. Yeah?
Sounds better than it feels. This arthritis, they tell me,
it's when a part of your body gets jiggered in a way
so its other parts—those that should know what belongs
to their exclusive-type get-together? —dont,
don't recognize you as themself. I think of it like this:
My bones are bored sick of this old bag they're stuck in ...
(no better than all the worser halfs I've been hitched to)
and planning to walk right out on me, ditch me, find a swell
repenthouse of their own, instead of this
drizzerable scratch-dive I am ... well, we'll see
about that, I guess ... X-rays ... read 'em and weep.
Am I skipping too much in the stories of my lives?
My marryings, bust-ups, harnesses and holidays?
It's enough to make a cat laugh, asking the likes of me
to date back, doll up and stack the skimble-skamble
of my very own and personal there-to-here. I'm so holey-minded.
I don't know but lots of the balled-up bygones
that come to mind this minute went by the truth
or consequences of somebody ... maybe I did, maybe I didn't, know.
In other words, Cutems, what I'm up against is
blankety-scratch, when it comes down to telling
what's from square one with Yours Truly,
and what's in there by way of a bughouse fable,
or slipped out kinda by chance from a funnygraph album
at some charity rummage. I just pick up things—
sometimes the music of what's going on, accidentally,
in everybody's heads ... it's like a radio jamming,
like rats laughing in the trash. Are you with me, Sweetie?
following my drift? ... Monte-rap artist, a switchblade ... waif,
a purple wedding dress, marmalade kitten, a Bowery arriviste ... .
Some days there's a pattern ... I also read ... in the dead leaves.

*

Now, I like the time frame of two days before
the day after tomorrow. There's no originality—
except for your refusals, maybe—no original threads
or combinations that don't get lost somehow ... in the telling ...
and memories ... are a kind of costume jewelry—now who
would want to drag out all her old fakements and what-have-yous
picked up here and all over for different lives, pretend
the clutter makes up a single person? Listen, I'm living
the real life of strip-downs and disconnections, being where
some parts of me forget the rest. Even your hand,

believe it, can forget its good name, and hurt ...
Somebody, going in, coming out of my mind, as I please ...
just as you are ... Voodoo Ruby ... Regina ... Thalassa,
or Blue Dahlia, especially ... sometimes Chief Itch-and-Rub, or ...
Chantilly ... the connections. But, today, my name is
maybe ... Cadenza ... I'm off now. You see,
the natural form of my life is exhaustion. It's organic,
an improv—it has its stops and some bottom lines,
but you can't tell beginning where, or if you're going to be
lucky ... or adjust exactly when ... to pick up, move on.
So. Your camera makes its own sort of sorrow, days,
but who listens to us in the night. Your crying
can kick off in any old chink of the carcass—
some little gangs of blood can start sniffing in tiny circles,
wanting out ... something terrible ... wanting the hell out of you.
It might take forever to get to your eyes, your mouth.
I mean, there is no way to tell. Maybe it is nothing to do
with you ... there is absolutely no way ... to tell.
So. It is often useful to forget who you are ...
I bump into friends like ... snowflakes ... splat down on water.
Like this one, it seems like forever I've called her
"Madame Anastasia Howdy von Hudson"—for short, for fun—
she has this cunning little house of crates—
wrapped up against the wickedest wind in Saran Wrap
borrowed from our Sweetie-Pie the Korean.
And, she has this pail with a fire in it. That never goes out.
It is an eternal thing ... but her fingers,
seven of them so far ... did fall off. Now her toes are
dried-up ... mangy ... pussywillows ... buds of soot,
and I guess about to go, the way all flesh goes. I suppose
most people like to find out about that from reading the papers.
Now, you ... Well, you can choose to go along
some of those tracks someday ... picture the traumas
of the haunts where even your ghosts give up their ghosts, or
you can go to where the gumptious bums roast stray dogs in the Square
—if that's what you want ... for your solace, or for make-do.
Or, you can just lay back and give the bloody wind a chance,
dreaming of a snooze with hot doctor's magic, or ...
of pimps with silver pencils and two-tone shoes.
Or, you can walk and walk yourself silly into a trance
of pitch-palaver, like I do ... 'til the loose
whispers start to go loud and nearly public ... I guess
that's my own favorite of all ... the heart's off-again,
on-again, off-off media ... but then, it's only one
of the many ways I know ... to solve the silence. Now,
you can go ahead and print that, Precious, as all I know
to say. Or, as one of all the possible combinations.
Make me your conversation piece. Dine out on me.
I don't mind at all being an imaginary person. Do you?

61

SHARON KINNEY-HANSON

TO LENI RIEFENSTAHL
From a Woman in Her Forties

While you are resting
     in your canvas chair
     aging near the edge
          of the jungle
do you fear
     some unexpected burst
     into the clearing?

     some target-bounding exotic
          ready to devour
          all you work and live for?

Here in the middle
          of suburban comfort
     reclined in plastic
          lawn chair
     reading for pleasure
I am no where
     (nearly) as safe
     from jungle disaster
          as you are.

Send for me.

Michael Buckner photo

Pamela Hadas

62

SHARON KINNEY-HANSON

MONDAY MORNING MISSOURI BLUES

Monday and reading the Sunday *New York Times*
and what's it to you
recovering from a two-week endblue
reeling of multiple
people who fall
into one
frame
after another
coffee-seeking poetry-reeking
Monday morning Missouri blues

FROM THE SANSKRIT

I shouldn't tell you
but this moon
    this cognac

        shake a woman
        up like hell

LINDA HATCH

LYSIS

Male spires of gold abuse the fluid sky—
Over the town the holy song gives flow;
The old nun retrieves her torch from the sacristy
While stone saints observe her prayer's glow.
Camelean boys attend the sacerdote
As women within the seminal words receive;
Men congregate in the piazza to smoke
Creating various worlds for all to believe.

It is natural to wish these forms to protect,
Dependent as we are on the celibate vestry,
But by this conserving can we finally expect
The unraveling in time of God's fertile mystery?
No. It will be in sharing the chalice
After all, that we endure the paradoxical lysis.

3rd Place Award 1985, St. Louis Women Writers Contest sponsored by the St. Louis Branch/National League of American Pen Women.

LINDA HATCH

COMPANY

The girl stepped onto the porch. The wind was quieter now, though it had worked hard all night dropping suggestions here and there, making sleep vague. *El Viento*, the locals called it, and it blew with the dry season, turning the area on the verge of its more lush cousin, the rain forest, into a near desert. *El Viento* threw sand in their faces and tossed their few words about so that some were lost, some you couldn't know their origin. Sometimes *El Viento* could keep people in.

In the morning now she could pull herself into her tree. She hung the bag full of books over one branch, and a greasy paper sack she punctured onto the stub of another. Cuddled there in the tree and fed from the bag, she would pass the morning reading.

This day the girl was unsettled, like the tree that rocked her in the wind, and reading was impossible. She had risen as usual before the others to steal time with her father. She had sat there opposite him, taking furtive glances so as not to intrude. The father stared frowning, turning coins over one another in his deep pocket, his feet crossed on the Ottoman, while the servant prepared his breakfast, always shirred eggs, stewed kidneys, mango juice. She pleased him with her silence and unobtrusive ways, and they sat, uneasy company, she worried about her pleasing, he frowning and turning his coins into the day ahead.

The servant brought breakfast and laid it on the stool, then retreated without a word. While her father ate, the daughter gathered a sheet of his discarded newspaper. In a moment the father would toss a napkin in the air and give her a reconciling pat on his way out. What she read in the newspaper choked her.

She uttered, "Daddy!"

"Yes, Sweetie?"

"What's this? They're talking about you. They're talking about the Company. What are they saying?" She was weeping, hurt for him.

He laughed. "Now, Sweetie, that's the Communist paper. You can't pay attention to that. It's propaganda. It doesn't have anything to do with me." He left then, and she had had to be quickly reassured by his quick pat.

With her own breakfast prepared now and stuffed in the bag on the broken limb beside her, she nibbled and gazed about the yard. She stopped at the wall and surveyed it. The wall was high made of stone and concrete. On top were embedded, as in a bed of nails, pieces of broken bottles which had once held drinks that people shared.

She had climbed that wall one time when someone had thrown some rocks over it. A rock hit her, and she had climbed to see who'd thrown it. She used a bush near the wall to lift her, and as she placed her knee at the top, broken glass ripped it. She fingered the scar now as she thought about the jeering faces of the boys who'd thrown the rocks.

The wall surrounded the entire Company compound like the body walling off an invading cancer. Here, at the manager's house, it turned the corner around the compound, so that the wall was on two sides of the house. Where it turned, there at the back of the yard, was another monolithic concrete structure. An empty well. It was built as thick as the wall and round. On the outside of the well, as it made its way around, were concrete supports. The girl could run up these, barely, climbing to the top, then walk around the well wall. There was an open space, an entry where once a massive steel door had been. Inside were brittle bushes and cactus-like shrubs. The girl could play there, throwing her voice against the concrete.

Beyond the well were the chicken wire cages of the pheasants and the tin roof of the laundry house where the servants idled in the slower afternoon.

The girl rocked in the tree and stared sporifically out that way. The wind placed some music from across the wall near her now. It was always music with words of love and death, or *cumbias* to dance to. She pictured the rutted dirt road beyond the wall, and, along this, the shacks of the brown locals between the road and the wide brown river. The dry season never changed the river, because it came from the rain forest. The shacks, and around them, were full of people. The men worked for the Company and the women for the wives of the men who ran the Company. The naked children played there, watched by the older ones who hung out rags to dry on tree limbs.

The girl had seen all this when she had cut her knee on the wall. The music brought by the wind came with the pictures she had seen when up on the wall that day, so that her experience of it now swayed like a mirage on a hot day.

Suddenly, the girl's sleep was interrupted by an incident which already had passed. A white something out in the yard by the well, and, here, in the corner of her eye.

She dropped out of the tree. The branches snapped back angrily, and the girl stomped into the kitchen. From the corner, the yellow boxer looked up from his dish of stewed beef and rice. The girl sat on the floor next to the dog and petted him as he ate. She stared at the servant by the stove, an Indian woman with black waving hair, dark skin in a green dress and white collar. The girl spoke to the woman in Spanish.

"Aliña, tieñes hijos?"

"Yes, I have one child," the woman answered.

"What's her name?" The girl switched languages too.

"Soñia."

"How old is she?"

"Six." The woman glanced at the girl by the dog in the corner.

"Don't you be eating that dog's food now!" she snapped at the girl.

"But you cook so good."

"That's not clean to do." The woman rinsed a spoon at the sink.

66

"Where do you live, Aliña?"

"What's this with all these questions? You go on now! I got to make lunch now. Shoo! Go on! A woman can't work with all these questions. Go on now!"

The girl shrugged and swung through the door into the rest of the house. The dog scratched the door open, followed behind her. She flopped herself down on the rug under a fan, and she and the dog settled against each other. The boxer licked himself while she listened to her sisters wasting time in the bedrooms. Darn, she thought. Company's coming tonight. She sulked as she recalled the bother of dressing up and watching her sisters behave foolishly with the boys.

A car entered the driveway. The girl's mother came out of the bedrooms and went into the kitchen to organize the servant. A second later the screen door slammed behind her father.

"Hi, Sweetie."

"Hi, Daddy." She smiled up at him, and he patted her on her head. He sat down on his chair with his feet on the stool and read the paper.

The mother called lunch, and the sisters came into the room arguing over who's-going-to-wear-what.

"Now, girls, we're not going to have this. Your father has had a hard morning at the office and needs his quiet."

The fat sister said, "Did you, Dad?"

"Not too bad, Sweetie."

"See, Mom," the sister jeered at the mother and kept on.

The girl took a deep breath and said, loudly, interrupting her sisters, "How much do we pay Aliña?"

The father looked up.

The mother said, "What?"

"How much do we pay Aliña?"

"Oh, shut uppp!" the tall sister said.

"We pay her as much as other women pay theirs," the mother answered.

"Let's give her a raise," the girl pronounced.

"There goes Miss Weird again," the fat sister said.

"Now let's stop this arguing!" the mother said. "We can't give her a raise because pretty soon all the women's girls would be wanting a raise."

The father turned to the girl. "I know what you're wondering about. Sweetie, what the laborers don't understand is that the marketplace won't take a rise in prices. In the meantime we've brought jobs and provided a better standard of living for them than if we had never come. The Company can't do everything for everyone."

The girl grinned triumphantly at her sisters.

"Oh, brother!" one of them said, scraping away from the table.

The girl idled the afternoon on the stoop of the laundry house, tossing pebbles at pheasants and listening to the occasional talk of servants in a dialect she did not know. The wind was stronger now, so that all sound was muffled, and her hair whipped at her face in small stings.

When the soda truck came, she watched the servants unload cases of pop onto the veranda. Then came the wooden yellow ice truck pulled by the brown mule. Kim Kim, the iceman, dropped blocks of ice into the waiting tiñas while the large yellow box creaked in the wind, and the mule shifted its feet.

She avoided her sisters until the last moment when she absolutely had to put on her dress.

"Comb your hair!" the tall sister snapped at her as she tried to sneak off.

At the party the girl sat on the porch wall, watching the dancing, and chipping at the ice blocks. The colored lanterns swung wildly in the wind, so that everything seemed to be movement. But the girl felt strangely sheltered from all that, held within herself.

The boxer came across the yard out of the darkness into the glimmer of the porch lights. He waddled up to her, and she saw that he was bleeding from his nose. She took him over to the hose spigot and rinsed his snout. There were puncture wounds there.

"Hey! Nipper's been bitten!" she yelled.

Several guests standing nearby gathered around the dog who wagged from the attention. The girl looked out toward the darkness and began to walk out to the well. She thought about the white thing of this morning. At the edge of the light, she stopped and adjusted her eyes to the night's own light. At the door to the old reservoir she hesitated, then entered.

The white dog growled and bit her swiftly on her sandaled foot. She winced, pulled her foot back. The animal stumbled, fell to the ground, too ill to move. When she ran into the house she was surrounded much like her dog had been, though for her it was an unpleasant event. She told her father what'd happened, and he dismissed the gardener to kill the rabid dog.

The girl's mother took her into the bedroom where she phoned the doctor. The girl lay exhausted and frightened on the bed, but listened to her parent on the phone. The dog must be examined. Yes, injections would be necessary. Twenty-eight of them? My goodness.

Her father entered. Now he was yelling into the phone. "Well, someone over there put that dog into our yard! I want to know who! Of course you better find out if anyone was bitten over there! They'll need the damn shots too."

The girl fell asleep; she could stand no more. During the night the injections began. The father held the girl as she tried to squirm away from the needle aimed at her abdomen. She shut her eyes against her father's worried look. Her screams were carried off with a purpose by El Viento — to be deposited some other place and time.

The injection was given.

The girl slept long past the time she was to have breakfasted with her father.

LUCY REED HAZELTON

MONEY SONG II

In an age which makes a state religion
out of euphemism, a realist will be
damned and demeaned as a cynic.
          —Michael M. Thomas, *Hard Money*

Poe once told a story of the rich
ensconsed in private splendour
dancing, drinking behind high walls
protected from offending plague
by water, wealth, indifference.
He wrote of death disguised in red
who came to dance and stayed instead forever.

One or two who read Poe's work
understood and I like to think
grew in stature, removed their walls;
One or two, perhaps you know them,
(said hello in passing) before you
closed the door. The poor are
not as lucky as you are.

In Washington they say guards
man the Whitehouse rooftops day and
night and in the Hamptons times have
changed. Chevy Chase and Georgetown
folks engage in talk of investment
banking, mergers; rearrange their
locks with regularity; eat Kiwi fruit
and Brie, Veal Oscar, Chateaubriand.
Dom Perignon flows like Niagara.

Somewhere protected the ladies
sit, members of the Eagle Forum,
decide which designer is right this
season. No El Salvador for their
sons but Communism must be
stopped; radio-active waste must roll
safely away from their neighborhoods.
Chernobyl is another place.

I like to think someone still cares;
Perhaps is still masked, wears red;
perhaps again will join the dance.
Perhaps I should be glad.

LUCILLE M. HEFT

PHANTOM POETRY LOVER

It all started when Aunt Elsie sent us a blue satin bedspread, single size, for our anniversay. I'm sure she meant to order a full size. We didn't want to hurt her feelings by returning her gift, so we decided to sell it.

My husband and I have found it very effective when selling something to advertise on the community bulletin board at our supermarket. I enjoyed creating an attractive ad that potential buyers will notice. I wrote the following advertisement:

FOR SALE
Lovely blue antique satin quilted bedspread
New, never used   Single size — $25.00
6938 W. Orange Dr. — 654-8123

After I prepared the card, I eyed it critically. Because there was some space left and also because I like the lines from Keats, I added at the bottom.

A thing of beauty is a joy forever.

I made a trip to the supermarket and thumb-tacked the card onto the bulletin board. We received many calls for the bedspread and sold it right away. When I returned to the supermarket to remove the FOR SALE sign, I was surprised to find printed on the card, these words from Emerson's "The Rhodora":

If eyes were made for seeing,
Then beauty is its own excuse for being.

I stood there smiling and exhilirated. Some person had a little exposure to the world of poetry. This was a challenge. I could not let those words sit there without an answer. What fun! Like a child with a new toy, I knew what my next "for sale" item would be—a table lamp that had been gathering dust on a basement shelf. Still in excellent condition, there were several years of good service left in it.

At home I printed the needed description of the lamp, phone number and address on the sale card, leaving ample room for Shakespeare's lines from *Romeo and Juliet*:

But soft, what light
Through yonder window breaks?

Back to the supermarket to put up this card. I glanced around at the midmorning shoppers who went stoically about their business. No

70

one seemed interested in the bulletin board.

We had a few calls on the table lamp and sold it within ten days. Up to this time, I'd kept the little game that was going on from my husband. Now I could keep still no longer and told him the story. He laughed and asked, "What'll you sell next?"

I hadn't decided, but I knew I could hardly wait to see if there was a poetry response to my last advertisement. At the supermarket a whistling black-eyed clerk was busily opening some large cardboard cartons piled in front of the bulletin board. Smiling, he apologized for being in the way and moved them. Expectantly, I eyed my FOR SALE card and was rewarded. In neat, small printing were the words from the Statue of Liberty:

I lift my lamp beside the golden door.

This was exciting!

My husband chuckled and commented, "Perhaps your poetry lover has been to New York Harbor recently. What's your next step?"

We had a bird cage on a stand in the basement which might be a good selling item. At home I made out the FOR SALE card with the necessary information and finished with Cervantes' famous words:

Birds of a feather flock together.

A week later we sold it. The FOR SALE card could now be removed. Back to the supermarket, and there it was, the same neat printing:

Her beauty was sold for an old man's gold
She's a bird in a gilded cage.

An old banjo was next. This time I added no poetry. Just a simple question:

WHOOOOOOOOOOOOOOOOOOOOO
Are you??????????????

We sold the banjo and returned to the bulletin board. There were two answers—the first one from Stephen Foster:

Oh, Susanna, oh don't you cry for me, for
I'm going to Louisiana wid a banjo on my knee.

The other answer was from Oliver Goldsmith:

Ask me no questions
And I'll tell you no lies.

He or she didn't want to be known.

71

Eventually I ran out of things to sell and put up cards with just poetry on them. I wrote Joyce Kilmer's "Trees":

> I think I shall never see
> A poem as lovely as a tree.

My poet friend answered with Ogden Nash:

> I think I shall never see
> A billboard lovely as a tree
> Indeed, unless the billboards fall
> I'll never see a tree at all.

This went on a few more months. It was exhilirating and fun. My husband became interested in the game. He and I spent many an enjoyable hour finding gems of poetry or prose we could use. It opened a whole world to us—not a new world, just a neglected one.

It was summer now and the month-long trip to California we talked about was to materialize. A week before it was time to leave, I put up a fresh card with Lord Byron's words:

> All farewells should be sudden.
> (We're leaving for California!)

My poet friend answered with Edward Pollack:

> There's something in the hour
> Which chills the warmest heart;
> Kindred comrades,
> Lovers, friends,
> Are fated all to part.

Just three days before time to leave, I put up one more card:

> Ships that pass in the night
> Speak to each other in passing.

We'd scheduled ourselves to leave at 5 A.M., but I talked an impatient husband into one more trip to the 24-hour supermarket before we drove west on the freeway. It was very quiet at this early hour as I walked swiftly to the bulletin board.

There on a large cardboard sign, leaving no doubt that it was my poetry friend, were two words:

RIGHT ON!!!!!!

As I was about to leave, my ears picked up a tune the lone checker was whistling. The melody? "I Left My Heart in San Francisco."

JULIE HEIFETZ

PARNASSUS APOLLO

"Only their feet were heroes."
—Arlene Blum, leader, 1978
American Women's Himalayan Expedition

With each step, she hated the mountain more;
the fog and wind, great walls of ice
dropping into darkness, improbable oceans
shifting to the inescapable rumbling of avalances
heavy in the air. Annapurna, cold and powerful,
thrusted higher and higher, indifferent to panic,
the dull pain of the body.

"Woman's place is on top," she'd said, and laughed.
That was 3 months ago, knee-deep in flowers
and the singing of villagers. Now she thought
"I don't belong here. This is not my place."
In the glacier light, flat, surreal, something moved—
white with red spots, falling like a pebble
from the pouch of a giant, sweet and musical.
Near her boot it rested, a god reclining in silence,
its limbs relaxed with dreams. She watched it letting go,
as though melting into perfect harmony with snow, then
fly away, inviting her to think of
something else, something soft but free—
something other than the power of the mountain.
She put a hand under her thigh
and eased herself one step closer to the summit.

JULIE HEIFETZ

BLUE MORPHO

*Braving the cameras which she has resolutely
shunned for most of the 3 decades she has lived
aboard Calypso, Simone Cousteau stands with her
husband to watch the reunion of their teams
after completing the 4,000 miles.*
                    Jacques Cousteau's Amazon Journey

Sailors and scientists, she's lived with
their seductive fascination; whales and sharks,
rivers and seas of 52 expeditions,
followed them into later life and this
superlative jungle.

Jean-Michel slips into the water, feature
for feature as though he sprang full-grown
from the head of his father. The river swells
with legends of pink dolphins and voices
in the branches.
She keeps no journal of face-to-face encounters;
no envelope of specimen collected;
offers no poem, no chilling realizations
of common sense conclusions;
no tape-recorded waterfalls, or sketches
of her favorite flower; no list
of things broken or lost, or forgotten.

"How many sons do you have out there?"
"They're all my sons," she answers,
waving to a distant yellow raft
from the prow of the ship, like a Morpho butterfly,
high and slow above the water, at the edge
of wilderness; an iridescent light,
welcoming them home.

Only this reference, like a loving dedication later,
"To Ma, who worried." And then she disappears
under the findings and photographs of heroes,
leaving the illusion of wings,
the illusion of light.

JULIE HEIFETZ

METAMORPHOSIS

What would she lose?
She'd seen the restless ostentation
of butterflies in elegant attire
at all the fashionable watering places.
Full skirts kicked aside to offer
a brief display of ankle or leg.
Wind-pudding and air-sauce, the lot of them,
their sylph-like figures curved
in coy sensuality, sucking sweetness.
They'd bought that Cinderella stuff,
hook, line and sinker, as though
a Fairy God-Mother whispered from the wings
it was their duty to beautify the earth,
so smile for the judges, honey.
Was that what all this struggle would come to?
A professional beau-catcher, impotent
as a bubble catching the sun's rays,
indulging in children and the love of dancing?
A dainty bon-bon in aimless emancipation?

She preferred bristle and slide,
the sure fit of her belly with darkness,
devouring the night, the earth firm in her hands.
She could make herself new again,
just by flexing her muscle,
or rear up like a dragon, grubby and glorious.
Give that up for a pair of wings,
a bit of rainbow silk and satin?

If she were beautiful, smooth and delicate,
would she see herself as others see her,
loveable and vulnerable?
Or as seeker, as hero, taking a stand
on green?

KRISTEN HEITKAMP

Excerpts from: "RIVER WINTER"

A treehouse view of honeysuckle, sumac, silver maples dancing from Rocheport hill to the river: rooftops, chicken yards, hogpens and alleys, abandoned Zion A.M.E., trailers and muddy trucks, rusting bedsprings, the railroad tracks and the slough. Willows raining saffron leaves, flash of woodpeckers: pileated, redheads and downies. A trio of pyramids. Johnson's sandplant and scales. A beached barge. Johnson's road, the levee, a silvery field, city park under a foot of water, ditto the revenue-sharing city tennis courts, Herb Coat's shack, and two monolithic maples. The field Fay Walker bought from Herb, intending to raise corn, that flooded and now constantly ebbs and flows. Hidden dunes. Then Moniteau Creek: herons, egrets, kingfishers, orioles, beavers, turtles, gar, woodchucks and possums, raccoons and red-fox-fast across the tracks where it flows into the Missouri.

Halfway up the windowpane are broad burnished fields, Monet's grainstacks, two ghost towns, a line of bluffs where River and sky share the heavens, diffused and disappearing.

WOLF MOON

It's a balmy zero degrees, sunny, no wind.

Walking down the tracks east of town, a strip of land between the high bluffs and the noisy river, shaggy dog running ahead.

We see a young eagle.

All we can hear is the *SWISH SWISH* and crunch of ten thousand floes on the water, bumping and grinding until the edges are round, like snowflakes or teacakes crowded on wing dikes and stranded on sandbars where the sand is packed hard.

We see a red-fox-fast across the tracks.

Icicles, seafoam columns hang from the cliffs, tasting neon and gritty from limestone. At the spring, green moss flourishes and the water is warm, tastes like sassafras tea.

We see the circling buzzards.

Eagle and buzzards parody the farm crisis, where on one hand you have the endangered species, the family farm, and on the other you have the carrion eater: the factory farm. To me it makes no difference whether this factory is sanctioned by national policy or by economic realities; the results are always the same. Foreclose on the family, and each of us loses the power of stewardship. Times have come hard on all of us. I have seen a greedy buzzard out on the spur, trying to lift the carcass of a black and tan hound, get creamed by a dump truck. Back in town a few diehards are watching Marlin Perkin's "Animal Kingdom" reruns. Where is the justice?

*

76

The land is a sleeping giant, unaware that she has just passed hands from the farmers to the forces of government and business that acted in collusion to strip her wealth; she sleeps as she slept under the glacier, yes as she slept when the great tribes built temples on her ridges and hunted in her hollows, yes as she slept through waves of civilizations born and conquered. Land that last stirred at New Madrid in 1811 and shook the continent. The land moved and the fertile Mississippi flowed backwards.

Missouri created and destroyed, recreated and inhabited, the land invaded by militia and guerrillas in a bitter and unconquered civil war—Missouri, where the forests change subtly, vanishing from East to West.

With Eden located slightly on the edge of the Ozark plateau, in the oldest river valley on the continent. Two fallacies tend to keep us from seeing it: one, that there is no wilderness left; and two, that there is no Eden. In fact both exist in every wasted, forgotten lot that blooms and goes to seed.

LATE WINTER

By February the stove is a constant. Each fire is considered, each piece of wood is chosen for its shape and age; the green and seasoned logs mix and spit, hiss and burn. The best time of day or night is the trip to the woodpile. In the morning, the sky lingers in the fog and slippers send sparks of frost onto the path. Woodsmoke from the valley carries smells of eggs and sausage, chili, long-suffering stews. At night the woodpile is a fortress and more than that a paradox, giving and taking: the work and trees and gas and oil all go up in smoke.

*

The car won't start. I dreamt last night that I had a huge zit on my chin and when I popped it an eye fell out. A blue and bloodshot eye. This morning I woke up in a fetal position. The fire had gone out. I could see my breath. The world was so still, in that gray breath before the sun rose, and when the sun rose all the trees started popping and cracking, and icicles wavered and fell from the eaves of the house.

That's when a woodpecker got a little frisky—it flew up and started drilling on the tinroof.

*

Beautiful day, at least the slice of it I saw from the car on my way to the office.

*

In the Rocheport sauna you sit on benches covered with towels as someone splashes water on the hot rocks. Someone throws succulent red cedar logsplits in the stove. Someone passes the springwater. Someone says I'm getting hot so you trade places, each person moving down the bench. Sooner or later you begin to sweat and it feels good when you stand in the snow and rub it all over, thousands of starbursts falling on skin, feeling electric and cool.

"The question is not: WILL I wear my longjohns? The question is: How many pairs of longjohns?" —Dean

The sun finally comes up, it sort of appears over Cochran's chimney like a shrouded flame, fanned by a mean wind that rattles the seedpods on the locust trees. Clear and dry and bright, it will be a good skiing day if I can get all the pine tar removed from the skis and fix the bootclamp which keeps working loose, improperly mounted (did I read the directions?) in the first place.

The drainpipe froze. I should have emptied the tub all at once, but no I let it drip and now it's freezing, drip by drip. It got down to 5 below and the woodpile's absconding—logs are actually rolling away, hiding in drifts of snow, the kind of drifts that make you think of igloos. I should have built an igloo, but no I had to ski through it, picking up clods and falling through the roofs of those fabulous drifts.

I looked at the bath tub filled with dirty sinkwater, and I think well when it unfreezes. . .for thaw is no word for the likes of freeze, froze, frigid.

*

Someone left a rabbit skin on the porch.

EARLY SPRING

White racing demon skies of Kansas clouds, gusts of maple squirts, wet woodsmoke (which is different than wet-wood smoke) that trails along like George's "fallout." "Yep," he declared last week, "Can't get in the garden noways, it's that fallout. Joe says it and I say too, it comes from the river and falls on the ground and you can't plant nothing."

Life in the Spring. You plant, you wait for rain. It grows, grows green. The earth turns over like a blacksnake and you're standing in the gumbo staring at the bluffs behind the sumi strokes of sepia trees. The sun falls over Tompkins Point.

Behind you, Pat comes out of her trailer with a paper bag. She skirts the black ruffles of the plowed garden and goes over to John Langdon's porch, where she drops an orange weekly paper on the step. The sky turns the colors of a Chinese fan.

THE BOTTOMS

Missouri continues to rise. Rocheport is cut off from the world at three of the four great "highways": the Missouri, the MKT, and old Highway 40.

Wednesday the river rose twenty-eight feet. Went wading into the garden and met a cottonmouth swimming in the peas! Began immediate efforts to salvage spring vegetables. We pulled a thousand green onions; we cleaned, trimmed, wrapped them and sold them to a grocer for eighteen bucks.

My armpits still smell like onions. It was horrible.

Thursday at seven in the morning the sky turned green. I waited for the locusts to bend over ninety degrees, and they did. The power went out and stayed out when a cable fell across the creek road. That tornado dropped into a hollow and cut down forty or so trees, mostly locust, and some walnut branches. We found a treetop lodged some fifty yards from its trunk.

*

Standing at the end of Tompkins Point, we had a good view of the ruined levee. Debris had stuck in the great hole (the old bay), and white-water marked the river's invasion of Rocheport. It was loud enough when we heard a greater roar. Part of the bluffs, a mile away, was rumbling and crumbling like a house of cards.

Later we took a boatride in what had been a soybean field. Captain John took a sounding at ten feet and then proposed that we waterski.

JUNEBUG

George and his girlfriend invited me to Sunday dinner, but something's come up. I walk over to his Airstream trailer, ducking under the clothesline that separates our lawns.

"So you can't come to dinner," George says. "You want Pat's number? Well, let's see." He pulls a wad of papers out of his overalls and carefully sets the pile on the porch step. "Gonna get hot today," he mumbles, "I heard it on the radio that it's gonna get hot today, well. Let's see here." George discards a folded scrap that reads *Country pork sausage 1.35* in his handwriting. He glances at another piece of paper, an advertisement torn from a newspaper, and puts that down. He fiddles with a plastic bag that still bears the trademark *Idaho Scalloped Potatoes* on it, unfolding the bag and sticking his hand in it. "Now, let's see here, Pat's number."

One of the neighborhood cats comes across the yard and nudges George's knee. Absently, George looks up at the cat, scratches his head and repeats, "Now, let's see here. . .Pat's number," while dumping three or four pieces of paper, as light as feathers, in his lap. One of them he unfolds several times, a big piece of notebook paper which bears his pencilled scrawl: *Pat gone til Wenesday* (sic) and a shopping list. "Gonna have to dust my taters," George mentions, "the bugs is all over them, but. . ." he looks up at me, "I can't dust them with that regular dust, cause of runoff you see I dust them with lime and ashes, uh huh."

"Um, Pat's number," he keeps repeating as he scans the page. "Yes," he nods to himself, turning the paper over in his hands.

Jan Ybloor wrote that Romanian gypsies wore and guarded such talismans, bearing important phone numbers; they were tokens handed down from father to son, soft and bleached and illegible. Ybloor wrote that he watched a patriarch pull something out of an embroidered bag and forthwith read off a ten-digit telephone number.

"Aha!" George announces, "Six Nine Eight—TWO...thousand! That's her number, 698-2000."

BLACKBERRY SEASON

Were you here last night?
The back porch was wet. Did it rain?
Two empty bowls, with spoons stained purple. There's pie for breakfast. You can hear the sand plant: wrroowwll chucachug Wrroowwll chuchuga.
Long sleeve shirt, overalls a straw hat and sunglasses. No underwear. Fill the waterjug. Collect the berry buckets. Whistle for the dog. Turn off the blacktop onto a back road, bump down a long hill, downshift, edge over a washout. They haven't graded the road since school let out. The hills, the woods are dark in the shadow of rising clouds colored berries and cream.

Gold and purple in the fields/ end of summer
Drawing near/ soon you'll be leaving the/ Valley

Sing to myself while the clouds turn as pale as the hayfields. The berries are choice if you get down under the canes and pick from inside the bramble. Boomer stops and whimpers at a snakeskin. There's a breeze, more berries under the sumacs and tangled in the trumpet vines.

*

He answers the phone, out of breath, wheezes that he's doing the laundry. "Sure," Joe answers, "bring them over."
I've got enough berries to fill two deep-dish plates dotted with butter and smothered in honey and flour to make the juice behave.
Joe's girlfriend Mildred lives up to Boonville and makes a mean blackberry cobbler. Her youngest daughter, he says, is a mess. Two hundred pounds and not more than five foot two.
He's hanging out the clothes on the west side of the house, out where the Sears wringer/washer sits on the porch. His BVDs, handkerchiefs, towels and sport shirts are brighter than sunlight. The trim on his house is painted baby blue.
The bucket's so heavy I have to put it down.
"I'll tell you a great place to pick berries," Joe lowers his voice and looks around in the direction of his brother Earl's house below us, and whispers. "But you just got to walk down to it, on the sunset side of the holler just past the first gate up on top of the hill where them boys cut wood thataways over the tunnel, know just where I mean?" And turns away, clamping a clothespin between his teeth, nodding at the Judas tree.

WOOD CUTTINGS

Went to cut wood with Joe Cochran this morning. I had agreed with some reservations. Joe is pushing at 65 and by his own admission has been stabbed twice, operated on thirteen times, and shot at half a dozen times, but he can still outwork a man in his prime. Joe said he knew of two black locusts that for his money were the best wood there was. He turned down the gravel road and off onto Herbert Coats' soybean field, which Henry Adams had just combined. The trees were on the fencerow side of the field. It was just getting sunny.

"Yeah," Joe said, cutting over the rutted clay tracks, bouncing the cup of tea in my hand. "I went up to see Margie last night. She called me, she said Joe, can you come over here tonight? I said sure, I can come over tonight, I'll be there. And she said, well I have somebody I want you to meet."

"And I got over there last night, and who the hell was it but old Herman! Why, he said, Joe Cochran you old so and so, I've known you for forty-five years, and what are you doing here?"

"Well, you see, Margie she's got herself this Herman as her other boyfriend."

Joe stopped the truck and pulled the water jug up from the floorboards. He poured some into the cap and drank it. Then he sighed and shouldered the door, got out and started unloading the tools in the pickup bed. He handed me an ax and we walked single file towards the trees.

"But anyhow. I said Margie. . .now you and him just go on there and have yourselves a good time. But Margie thought she was gonna get some kind of rise from me. That was what she thought! Why, I'm 65 years old, I don't want any young family now, though Margie bless her soul is as good as gold to me, she'd give me the shirt off her back. She's not like my other girlfriend Millie and her kids, that darn bunch of kids. It's this one up here, see it?"

He sized up the tree, a forty-footer leaning across an old roadbed. I wondered if it had been the old road from Rocheport to Columbia, the trace of the Boonslick Trail that sank ten feet in the soft loess soil, land eroded by countless wagon wheels and footprints. A woodpecker cackled. Joe's saw whined. I stepped back.

While I was doing "squaw work"—clearing the brush and piling logs in the bed of the pickup, he stopped for water. "See, now Margie thought she was gonna surprise me last night, but I just acted like well well, here's you and Herman, go have a good time. I said, Herman, you sure got yourself a good gal there, that's what I said, But Margie didn't like it."

"She said that Herman said he was gonna get her a washer/dryer. I said, honey, Herman can say he's gonna give you just about everything! Ain't that right? But she says that Herman can't do it *all*— you know, he's unable to oblige her. That's why Margie ain't gonna get serious. I doubt if he can, but I think he's just telling her that. She says, but he promised me a washer/dryer! And I said, Margie you and Herman make a fine howdy do."

He went to work, cutting down the second tree. It fell as if its knees had collapsed. Then he cut through the crown and sliced the trunk into logs, deftly, whistling to himself. "Foxgrapes," he said, turning off the chainsaw, pointing into the brush.

He watched me go after the grapes, and solemnly sat on a stump, his bad foot out in front of him. "Then when I was going out the door, she acted like I ought to kiss her, all puckered up. I turned aside and said goodby to Herman. Ha! Now ain't that something? Margie is as good as gold, she'd give me anything I want. But she sure ain't too smart."

Robert W. Dunham photo

Kristen Heitkamp

SHARON HIBDON

LATE NIGHT CONFESSIONS OF A COUNTRY WIFE

Lack of sleep does strange things to a person. I know this because I own a woodstove.

To those who have never experienced the nocturnal delights of "keeping the fire going" when the temperature plummets, I can only say that few things have tested my endurance so consistently. Long after my infant daughter relinquished her 2 a.m. feedings, I could still be found feeding the woodstove every two hours.

My husband and I belong to a vanishing breed, or maybe it's the other way around and we're part of a newly emerging status quo: rural dwellers. We moved from our home in the city to take up residence in the old farmhouse that is older than both our ages combined.

To those people who prefer trudging through the mire to pounding pavement, who find their solace among barn swallows rather than the corner drugstore, who forsake the conveniences of the city for the freedom of the country, I need elaborate no further. However, there are those among my acquaintance who wonder at a woman who lives in a house that has seen two world wars and several generations grow up and move on.

The decision to vacate suburbia came about through no difficult, soul-searching process, but simply a desire on both our parts to partake of what we had come to think of as the "good life." Naturally enough, this wasn't the consensus held by all. My mother, for one, thought I'd abandoned civilization for the Outback.

When asked by a close friend if ever I was "afraid to stay in such a big, old house in the middle of nowhere, all by yourself," I confess I was for a second speechless. This woman lives in the heart of a metropolitan city in an apartment complete with barred windows, a thrice-locked door, and a never-fail burglar alarm. The only reply I could muster was, "Aren't *you?*"

The middle-of-nowhere is in actuality a crooked, country road that is home to several families who are far enough away that we can luxuriate in our privacy and still be neighbors. Solitude, what most would assume to be the worst enemy, has instead become a faithful old friend.

No, as novice country folk our most nagging aggravation and biggest challenge lay in battling the elements and taming none other than Mother Nature herself. The elements we learned to hold at bay; learning Mother's nature took a little longer.

Upon arrival at our new homestead, we acquired a trio of ducks. Indeed, we raised them from ducklings swimming in the bathtub to adult hens and drake being escorted to the pond. A heart-warming sight it was to see us chaperoning our webbed trio to the nearest pond each morning and collecting them each evening. This was done in belief that they couldn't find their way there and wouldn't come back if they did.

Domestic ducks are very vulnerable animals, so it stands to reason that their longevity wouldn't be too long. Sure enough, their idyllic existence was permanently interrupted one bright afternoon.

My husband then determined to catch the varmint responsible for our ducks' untimely demises. A glimpse of the culprit one morning showed him to be a very large raccoon. To be precise, a very large, clever raccoon. A trap was set—a foolproof trap, I hasten to add—bait placed in it, and the stage set, so to speak. With morning came the assurance there had been an overnight visitor: the meat was eaten, the trap door unsprung, and a gift of the recycled variety received. This went on for several mornings until we grew tired of giving the old coon free room and board.

I've also learned other pertinent facts of country life. Such as: never wear a navy-blue-red-striped jogging suit in front of a Rhode Island Red rooster. I did this once in my own backyard and nearly lost my dignity before escaping the feathered felon. There's something quite humiliating about cowering before an animal whose brain is the last part of its body to develop.

Above all else, it's the abundant wildlife that holds us closely to the land. I discovered I need ony open my eyes and look around. Often I need look no further than my kitchen window. Standing there one morning at daybreak, I spotted a coyote bouncing across last summer's garden. Putting aside my natural apprehension for a moment, I appreciated anew the grace of his fluid movements as he cleared a fence. Although a nuisance to farmers, his instinct and cunning demanded my respect.

To see deer grazing with our cows is commonplace. But of all our backyard visitors, my favorite was an old gobbler who came calling the last day of turkey season. As the hunters headed home empty-handed (my husband included), he nonchalantly loped off into the woods, another Thanksgiving neatly avoided.

I can only conclude that there is a little of the pioneer spirit in both my husband and myself. For each inconvenience there is a greater reward. When winter thaws into spring, I am more than happy to shut the door on the woodstove for one more season. But if the truth be known, I wouldn't trade my feeling of self-sufficiency for a thermostat. It's hard work, but it feels like home.

BEV HOPKINS

NEIGHBOR

When I was eight, the Preacher
Held a pink rosary from the pulpit
And told us it was bad.
I never understood that evil—
Especially as I listened from outside the barn at Dick's
While Azaleah milked Ginger,
Fingering her rosary, mouthing prayers,
Near the front door of their weather-boarded two-story,
A cupped container held holy water,
And Pope Pius' picture graced a wall.
There were crucifixes, haloed Mary's
And kindnesses extended at my visits.
Tip and Jigs barked feeble warnings at my arrivals.
Dick teased me—
Let me drive his John Deere tractor
When I was only five.
He taught me how to shift gears
And let me sit in the big diesel he drove across the country
To far-away places like St. Louis, Chicago, Nashville.
When his career was building roads,
I would perch on the black seat of his yellow caterpillar
And pretend.
Azaleah fed me giant jelly rolls
Including dresser drawers.
She put up with my plunking on the old piano
And let me help her slop the hogs,
Gather aproned eggs, and crack black walnuts
By the back porch.
I guess the lesson across the road and up at Dick's
Made me doubt the evil of the rosary.

EDA HOWINK

BALLET

Only in ballet
is man willing
publicly
to place himself
in a secondary
shadow position
behind woman.

PAT HUYETT

I NEVER SIGNED LOVE TILL YOU DID

What'll it prove to say
I'm not like desperate others
who ache to take your name
or have you buy them
a refrigerator?
I got what I wanted:
More than once you unhooked my garters,
let me revel in a
sweet secret sleeve of skin,
left your smell on my pillowcase.
All that seems enough.
'Cuz honey,
If you can't slip it to your friends,
Who can you slip it to?

The only other thing I'd hoped for
was an August night in rural Alabama,
to straddle you in a swing
tied from a pecan tree,
the moan of the green branches,
the tightness of thighs,
the dip in the air,
the catch in the belly,
the sigh against rope and hair.

PAT HUYETT

DEJA VU

No cartoon light bulb appears overhead,
When your ragas for evening
anticipate June bugs
and the nighthawk's swoop.
No nightmare's recalled
with your cardamon coffee
and jokes about karma.
But Persian poems you read me
sound out the old ache,
unclog odd thought,
like a gem strayed back,
found in the rug.
Like these coffee cup rings
on the tablecloth,
a feeling seeps through,
permeates memory,
as we slide under muslin,
muttering of babies.
And my dull cup's cured,
the taste of it clinging
to teeth, to tongues.

JANE ELLEN IBUR

STRAY DOGS

I collect stray dogs. I'm a patsy for them. They sniff me out.

You know the kind. Old women who live alone in houses they were born in, reclusive old women, bitter but lonely, dwelling in the past and measuring their happy years by the lives of the dogs they've owned or taken in and rescued. Young men, diabetics, who hang out in bookstores and flirt with counter girls.

My dog accompanies me on my visits to the landlady and the dog is a bridge, a translator, for we all three talk dog language; it's what we have in common.

One of the first things I noticed were the two dogs on the floor by the ornamental fireplace. At first I thought they were alive, they had been captured in an active pose. They were so real. I touched them once when the landlady left the room. I was shocked at how stiff and unreal they felt. Each dog wore an apricot starched bow; at Christmas time the bows were red and a small Santa sat on the rug between them.

Old dog tales, that's what Florence, the landlady, shared with me. The one most often relived was about Topsy. Topsy was a small wire-haired mixed breed, mistreated, beaten, found outside shivering in the winter. Florence took him in, wrapped him in a blanket. She lived in the house she was born in, where she had spent her life caring for her father, her two maiden aunts, and finally her sister, till all those who depended on her were dead.

Topsy was mean to everyone but Florence. She bit the aunts, the sister, especially the vet. To Florence she was sweet and grateful.

When I knew Florence, she was alone, left out in the cold. Like Topsy, she was mean to everyone. I took her into my life, wrapped her in the warm blanket of concern. I lent her my dog.

That began when I would be at work for the day; I would leave Cody with Florence so neither would be alone. Later, whenever I put Cody in the yard to go, Florence would let the dog in her house. When I went to the basement to wash laundry, I would hear Florence above me, talking to Cody. She would call the dog up on the bed, and the two would lie there and watch t.v.

When Florence later went to the hospital, confused, dying, she asked why I wouldn't let Cody come to visit her anymore. I tried to explain, but it was fruitless.

Cody and I gave three extra years to Florence. Before, she was waiting to die. Old people sometimes adopt an old dog. But young people don't adopt an old person, and you can't just give them a shot to put 'em out of their misery. Often they just starve themselves to death, starved of love, affection, attention, companionship, eating dog food from a can.

Like the dog who sleeps on a favorite blanket, Florence has her special chair by the front window. When she was gone, I sat in that chair. It was the stiffest, most uncomfortable piece of furniture I ever paused on.

When I clerked at the bookstore, a stray dog came in, and I talked to him, friendly like, as I talk to all my customers. It was like throwing a hungry dog a bone, that bit of courtesy, and he came back every night after that, stayed until closing, insisted on walking me to my car, sat in it with me while the engine warmed, and chewed my ear off.

His life was a disaster. Being diabetic and going blind was, in some ways, the least of his problems. For someone who needed to be on a strict diet, his food habits were incredible. Every night he came into the store eating a double dip ice cream cone from the Baskin Robbins next door. He had talked himself down to five teaspoons of sugar in a cup of coffee. Physically, he was always close to the edge, sugar dipping and soaring from one extreme to another.

He was desperate, begging under the table for scraps of affection. He wanted to be adopted by me, someone to control him, someone to train him. But I couldn't. He wasn't housebroken.

Mutts make the best dogs. They're the sweetest and most loyal. Just like real Americans, with a lot of mix from the past, mutts are complex, yet gentle, not a stuck-up breed like Dobermans, the English Terrier or the French Poodle.

There was a drunk lady on Arsenal, walking in circles, muttering to herself, a black eye I could see a block away. I doubled back to rescue her and ended up driving around for an hour trying to figure what to do with her. Nothing she said was coherent. I guess I thought that she had just been beaten up and kicked out of her house. Maybe just a cat fight. But probably she was just a drunk who ran into a wall and was standing in front of her house. Who knows. What did I think I could do for her? I should have just called the Humane Society and had her picked up and taken to a shelter. What I did was take her to a senior citizen place and get her some hot coffee. People there talked to her, trying to identify her and where she lived. She was totally uncooperative. We ended up calling the police and *they retrieved her,* dropping her at a shelter for the night. I was two hours late for work. They loved my explanation.

I was walking down Taylor Avenue one summer toward the Child Guidance Clinic. Across the street was an old woman, singing to anyone, wearing a cotton dress so thin you could read her bones through it. Her dress was buttoned askew, her hair wild. I crossed the street and she spoke to me, some disjointed conversation I couldn't follow. I told her I had a meeting and had to leave. "Will you come visit me? I live in that," she pointed to a basement apartment. I told her okay, just to keep her from following me inside.

But I did pause on the way out, and something pulled at me to go see her.

At the door she didn't seem to remember me, though only an hour had passed. She invited me in anyway. It was like entering a rank cave, a place where a wild dog lived. A place jammed with junk. There was no color, no air in the hole. Here or there I could distinguish a table and two chairs, a kitchen table, but everything else blended together brown. I followed her to a kitchen overrun with hundreds of roaches. She offered me a piece of cake from the table. There were bugs in the cake. I declined. With a dish towel she smacked a roach or two as they crawled up the wall. I was nauseated. I was overwhelmed, I felt like I was suffocating. She was the dog who collects everything from all over the neighborhood, and buries the prizes in her secret place.

We sat on the two chairs, which she told me folded into beds. She asked me to stay the night. I said I couldn't. She showed me throw rugs all over the place, on the floor or piled on a table. She had made them all from used nylon stockings.

I left with my tail tucked between my legs.

Knowing my history, it's not so weird that I picked up that dog tonight on 12th and Park. I didn't have enough going on in my life; spouse sick at home, and me spending half the afternoon caring for my eighty year old Nanny who is desperately ill. The dog trotted up to me the minute I parked the car. He was not a puppy, but young, a year at the most. He had all his teeth. He had a cute face, short ears, medium snout, stub tail. Definitely no Shepherd or Collie in that dog—snout too short. He was an American dog, you know, mixed breed.

I played with him for ten minutes and then went in the building to take care of Nanny. Two and a half hours later when I was leaving, he appeared again, biting at my shoes and dancing around me in circles. I sat on the ground for a minute and petted him. I started the car; I looked back at him. It was a cold night, starting to rain. I got back out and sat with him and cried. The world is such a cruel place; someone dumps a dog on a cold night. I couldn't bear it. I went in and called ten people to see if one would take the dog. Everyone declined. My spouse was getting upset that I was not home yet. I didn't want to just leave the dog in the rain. Nanny said, "If you're that upset, take the dog home." I did. I had to coax the dog into the car, but we were finally on our way.

I drove through the alley and put the dog in the back yard; I knew I could not take him through the house, what with my dog and two cats. I parked in front, walked through to the back, and took some food and water down to the basement. It was about five minutes before the dog trusted me that it was okay to come into the house. Then he ate. I put him back outside for awhile. He would throw himself against the door until I opened it. I could hear him upstairs at the other door, crying, while my dog sniffed the door.

The dogs played together in the yard, though my dog was pretty rough, and the little one never barked. I figured that was the reason the dog got kicked out; he had no bark. I called more people to take the dog. No luck. I felt worse as the night progressed. I assumed the dog was not housebroken, so I could not bring him in. Besides, my spouse did not want to see him at all and also get attached. I could not leave him to cry in the basement or scratch at the door all night. I had to take him somewhere.

The Humane Society said they would take him in the morning to Rabies Control where he would be held for three days and then put to sleep. The Animal Protective Association said they would hold him for five days to see if he was claimed and try to adopt him out. That seemed like the best bet. I loaded both dogs into the car and drove, smoking after I had been trying to quit, out to the prison. I felt like a jerk. Maybe someone had just set the dog out for a while and he was originally only a couple of blocks from home. Now I was taking him half way across the city. Was it the right thing to do? At least he was out of the weather, not going to get hit by a car.

I feel like a bitch.

JANE ELLEN IBUR

CAT NAP

My mom said I looked a little sleepy.
Perhaps I should curl up and take a little cat nap.
I was surprised by this.
Why couldn't I take my own nap?
Why should I take a cat's?
Wasn't that taking something
that didn't belong to me?
Should I get the cat's permission?
Or take a kitten nap,
which would have made more sense.

And why a cat?
Why not a dog,
or a tiger's nap?
Was this cat nap a better kind of nap?
Was it a reward?
A punishment?
Was this a one-time thing,
or would it become a custom?

What expectations would follow
this kind of behavior?
Would I have to use a litter box?
Would I claw up the furniture
and have my nails torn out?
Would I purr and blink slowly?
Would I make bread constantly
and become terribly particular,
taking only tiny bites of my dinner
and then walking away?
Would I pursue bits of paper around the house?
Would I hiss?
Would I do finger spreads
and take lots of baths?

I was horrified and suspicious
of this stranger in whom I had
placed the safety of my life.
And these thoughts were not unfounded.
Even now she is preparing fish for dinner,
and last night we had liver.

And what about this cat
whose nap I was to steal?
What about when it got sleepy?
Would it take my nap,
a kid nap,
and isn't that a real crime?

LYNNE JENSEN

TELLING TRUTHS

I have read the research, and I know
a cat must shift her eyes
to continue seeing
what is in her line of sight.

You are reading this and know
a different truth.
Unlike the cat, my eyes are still.
I seek the place in you
a woman's never asked for.

BEE NEELEY KUCKELMAN

CACTUS JUSTICE

One June evening in the Arizona desert
a man drunk on Margaritas
mistook a Saguaro cactus for a tall woman
wearing a green pleated dress
and white and yellow flowers in her hair.
He slurred, "How about a little lovin', Sweetie?"
A soft breeze swayed the cactus slightly;
he thought she answered "Back off, Buster."
In a tequila rage he fired his shotgun.
Birds and an elf owl fluttered from her pockets.
She wobbled and fell, covering his body with hers,
as in the embrace he had hoped for.
She tickled him with a thousand soft needles
just before she crushed him.

GRANDMA SAID

that we should never ever
walk upon the top of the little cave out back,
because we might fall through the ceiling.
but she didn't say we couldn't run,
so when Grandma wasn't looking,
we raced across the hump.
One day the hand of Grandpa's wall barometer

pointed right down to the floor.
The sky turned green and black,
and we went down in the cave.
We sat in wicker chairs
and watched the jars of peaches
flicker in the candlelight.
We stayed inside til Mrs. Pitts
hollered through the heavy door
that the storm was over.

Grandma also said
that we should never ever walk upon a grave.
When I accidently stepped
on the edge of Grandpa's grave,

Grandma gasped and groaned, "Oh, my!"
I felt the ground begin to sink
before I jumped away,
afraid I'd fall into his cave
and find him sitting in a wicker chair
eating peaches and perhaps
he'd ask me if the storm was over.

---

published 1986, Harbinger

MARILYN LAKE

AN AMERICAN MALE ENGLISH SAMPLER

American Male English is a language quite apart from standard American English. If you are a single woman, interpreting what a man says to you in terms of standard American English can lead to unhappy results. Increasing your awareness of many variations of meaning in American Male English can help you make it through your single years.

This sampler will increase your awareness of the most common statements and their American English variant meanings. Occasionally, a little advice on how to respond is added.

1. *I'll call you tomorrow night.*

Everyone knows this one. It's used at several times in a relationship. Most often it's used at the end of an evening or the end of a phone conversation.

Do not sit by the phone and wait for this call. Do not give up any other things you want to do to wait for this call. Especially don't hold your breath.

The probable meaning is "I'll call you within the next week or ten days." "Tomorrow night" in American Male English generally means after tonight and not more than ten days later.

2. *I'll call you sometime.*

Especially don't give this a moment's thought. The key word is sometime. "Sometime" in American Male English means never. Men never say never. The letters must make them choke.

Other variations of this phrase are "Let's get together sometime," "Let's go to dinner sometime." You know a few, don't you?

3. *I never lied to you.*

This is the exception to the rule, one of the only times men ever say never. The probable meaning is that he never told you the whole truth, but he never lied.

For example, he tells you he's divorced and you later find out he's married. He says, "I am divorced. This is my second wife." As far as he's concerned, he's never lied to you.

4. *My wife and I are separated.*

Probable meaning: his wife is visiting her mother for three weeks.

5. *I'm tired. Let's not go out tonight.*

He will do everything he can to get you to the bedroom where you will find out he's not tired at all. Believe me.

6. *You decide. I love just being with you.*

He'll moan and groan all evening if you don't guess what he wanted to do.

7. *We'll talk about marriage the next time I see you.*

Usually, this phrase is used when the subject of marriage has come up in a phone conversation, or anytime he can have a reasonable excuse to put the dicussion off. Perhaps the end of a date or in the morning when he's on his way to work.

96

You will interpret this phrase to mean he is thinking about marriage, but there isn't time to talk about it now. He probably is thinking about marriage, years and years from now.

Two possible meanings are: He doesn't ever intend to talk about marriage. He intends to talk about marriage, but about why he can't get married.

His reasons why he can't get married are interesting too. They may include the fact that he already is married; you may not have known this. Or he has been hurt too much. Maybe he can't support both you and his exwife. An old standby reason is that he can't marry you because he isn't good enough for you. The most often used reason is that you don't really love him.

Unhappily, the key words in this phrase may be "the next time I see you." Often there is no next time he sees you once the subject of marriage has come up.

8. *You know I care about you.*

This phrase is the mainstay of American Male English. To him, this is a variation of "I love you." A safe variation. A man who says this doesn't say I love you and seldom does the little loving things that show affection.

The meanings for the phrase "You know I care about you" run into the myriad, but here are a few:

You know I love you even though I don't tell you.

You know I love you even though I don't do loving things.

I have a deep feeling for you that I am afraid to call love.

I have a deep feeling for you that isn't love, but I can't
tell you that.

I don't know what I feel.

I want to keep seeing you but think you won't let me unless
I make you believe I care about you.

I will miss you for a week or so after this is over.

I don't want you to think this meant nothing to me, even
though it meant nothing to me.

You are important to me, but not enough to give up anything
really important, like football, or Thursday night
with the guys.

He may someday use this phrase as a way out of the relationship by saying "I never lied to you, I never said I loved you. You know I care about you though." There is that never, no choking when he says I never said I loved you.

9. *I love you.*

The most misunderstood phrase in American Male English. This last one has the greatest variety of meaning, all known only by men. I mention it because you need to realize that this phrase seldom means what you mean when you say it. Enjoy hearing it, and wait to see what he does. It all cases, what he does will show you much more than what he says!

DORIS LANDRUM

THE STATE OF GRACE

Grace woke just before six as she always did and turned off the alarm before it sounded, in order not to disturb her mother, asleep in the next room. She wrapped a bathrobe around her thick, middle-aged body and tip-toed across the hall to the bathroom and then to the kitchen where she filled a percolater and plugged it in. When she returned, she moved mechanically about the bedroom to make her bed and get dressed for her job as fourth grade teacher at Stanley Lower School.

In the mirror of her old-fashioned dresser she checked her image and was satisfied. Her dark skirt was lint-free, her white blouse immaculate. She patted the rigid waves of her greying hair and powdered her pail face, smoothing it into an expression of serenity.

I am in the hollow of His hand, she thought. It was not His will. Pride made me want to accept that promotion and now I have risen above it. Mamma was right last night. My duty is here and she can't be asked to move away from this house where we have lived for forty years. But oh, what shall I tell Mr. Cox? He seemed so elated yesterday when he told me the job was mine.

"God, help me! Help me through this day!" she entreated aloud. Immediately, ashamed of her weakness, she revised her prayer to, "Praise! All praise to Thee for this opportunity to serve." Pastor Bird had explained to her how miraculously one could tap the power of Eternal Love by maintaining a constant spirit of Thanksgiving.

"Question not, petition not," he often adjured her. "Only continually offer praise for what is."

She looked around the bedroom to be sure all was in order before she went into the kitchen and put breakfast on the table. Just before she called her mother she gave the table a critical glance. All ready were juice glasses, pats of butter, muffins in a napkin-lined basket, a bowl of jonquils in the center of the tablecloth. Mamma liked things nice.

"I can see you didn't sleep well last night either," she said as her mother drooped into her chair. "Here's your coffee all ready for you, sugared and cooled." Mamma had a delicate appetite and had to be coaxed to eat even the small amount her thin inactive body required. But she only looked with distaste at the table and slumped over her plate.

"Now, Mamma, let's start the day right with a good breakfast. It's a new day and a new start. We'll put last evening behind us and get right on with our life as it's always been."

For the first time the old lady looked at her hovering daughter. "What in heaven's name are you talking about?"

"Our decision last night, dear. I can see it weighs on you. I want you to know it's going to be fine. Mr. Cox will keep me on as fourth grade teacher as long as I want."

"Well, I should think as much! You're a Sipes and a Pruitt and there's never been a word said against either side of our family."

"Yes. And I'll tell him I don't want the promotion. I'll tell him I prefer to stay here in this town."

"Oh, that! Why I never gave another thought to that flighty idea of yours. Moving to Oak Lawn! You know good and well I can't leave my home, this town, my church, and the cemetery and all."

Grace was silent during the rest of their meal and while she washed the dishes. At a quarter till eight she gave her mother a goodby kiss and left for school. She would be back at noon to prepare their lunch and listen to her mother's account of the television programs she had watched. Each day was much like another.

"The simplicity of your life is a beautiful thing," Pastor Bird said repeatedly. "Would that I could order my days so well, but routine is a luxury out of reach of a minister at the beck and call of his flock."

Six little girls met Grace at the entrance of the schoolyard and walked in step on both sides of her, arms linked. "Oh, Miss Sipes, I'm glad you wore the blue scarf." "Miss Sipes, I got all my homework." "Can I sit by you at assembly, Miss Sipes?"

Their fawning made little impression on her, although she smiled benignly down into the upturned faces. Secretly, she preferred her ten-year-old boys' blunt honesty and was charmed when they invited her to umpire a baseball game or to admire a handmade birdhouse. She thought that if she had married and had children she would have hoped for sons only. Mamma like to say, "A son's a son till he gets him a wife, but a daughter's a daughter all of her life." Mamma's right, she told herself. When does a daughter ever become a person?

She and her little admirers parted at the door because children were not allowed inside the building until eight-thirty. She slipped quietly past the open door of the teachers' lounge and hurried to the fourth grade room. She had to write the day's inspirational poetry on the chalk board. It the early years of her teaching she had put a Bible verse on the board and led her pupils in prayer. Now she enjoyed circumventing the Supreme Court's interference in her religious ministrations by using poetry with a spiritual allusion. Today she used Browning:

> All service ranks the same with God,–
> With God, whose puppets, best and worst,
> Are we: there is no last nor first.

They won't understand it, she conceded, but some day it will come to them.

By a great effort she made herself seem composed when she was interrupted by the entrance of Miss Tucker, the elderly principal.

"You look half-dead," was her sharp greeting. "Don't tell me, let me guess. You've decided to refuse Cox's offer. Your mother put her foot down, didn't she?"

Grace willed herself to exude warmth and compassion toward the acerbic old lady and told herself, A soft answer turneth away wrath.

"Oh, Grace, please don't pray at me," scolded Miss Tucker. "You and I have known each other long enough to talk straight out without any detour through the Divine Presence. So! You're refusing the promotion to principal of the Oak Lawn school. Grace, that school needs you and your talents. You're sentencing yourself to a life-time job here because your mother doesn't want to bestir herself from that house where she became a bride. And you won't even go to AAUW meetings because you're too busy going around cleaning the corners with a rag on a little pointed stick."

"Mother was always such a good housekeeper when she was able. She values a nice house," replied Grace with a determined smile.

"A-a-ah! She drove her hired girls ragged! I remember if you don't. The only way she could have found scope for her capacities would have been to run a a cotton plantation before the Civil War." She strode to the window, looked out at the swarming playground. When she turned around, her lined face was as severe as ever but her eyes were wet. She came to Grace and put an arm around her. "I'll tell Cox for you," she said. "He said he'd be over this afternoon to see you, but I'll call now and tell him." She left the room.

When her thirty pupils burst in, Grace was ready with her customary calm. She was a good teacher and she knew it. The day went well, but she was drained of energy at dismissal time. She stood at a window and watched the stream of children flow across the playground, dividing into lines to board the buses and into little groups to walk to nearby homes.

"God bless them," she murmured, smiling. The usual after school paperwork kept her busy for an hour. Then she hurried down the silent halls after everyone was gone except the custodian.

"Good night, Mr. Dawes," she said cheerily, trying to whisk past him. But as usual he wanted to talk.

"Been a long day, Miss Sipes."

"You're right. But the laborer is worthy of his hire, you know. We can go to our rest now."

"Well, not yet. Them kids and their dirty shoes. You know how that is." He leaned on his broom and panted. "My God, Miss Sipes, I don't know why every woman in this country ain't dead."

"It is hard. And don't think your devotion to duty isn't observed, Mr. Dawes."

"Thank you, ma'am!" he beamed with appreciation.

With another pleasant "Good night" she escaped. He didn't understand that I meant that the Lord seeth and knoweth, she said to herself. How I pity people who have not that consciousness of Him that comforts me.

When she came within sight of her home she saw Pastor Bird's car parked in front of the house and she began to pray fervently for strength, knowing what might be facing her. She knew that whenever the minister came calling, Mamma confided in him all her concerns

100

about her daughter's shortcomings, the recounting of which intensified her irritation at them. Grace was much relieved when the two of them turned to her with smiles when she entered the living room.

"Welcome, welcome, Mistress of the culinary arts!" was the man's genial greeting and Mamma said, "I guess you don't remember that I told you the pastor was coming for dinner this evening, do you, Grace? And he has to eat right away because this is his night the youth group meets."

Mamma was skilled in the technique of launching a strong attack when she was in the wrong. Grace covered her surprise and graciously excused herself to go to the kitchen. No time for the meat loaf she'd planned. She crumbled ground beef into a skillet and browned it while cooking an onion in butter in another pan. Then she combined these ingredients with some green pepper, herbs and tomatoes, all products of her garden. While they simmered she set the dining room table with linen place mats and Mamma's Haviland china. She got everything ready before she started the spaghetti so she could give all her attention to timing it.

Pastor Bird always appreciated her meals. His plump jowls quivered when he laughed teasingly at her attempts to make it a party.

"The best crystal goblets," he said, holding one up to the light. "I could almost believe she'd serve me wine. But she knows her pastor doesn't defile his body with strong drink. Ah, this girl of yours is a wonder. I'm surprised some man hasn't taken her away from you."

"Oh, she's never cared about the men," Mamma responded comfortably. "Seems like it was just meant to be that she would stay with me and be an old maid schoolteacher. You know how some girls are cut out to get married and some aren't. I don't know. I set her a good example. I married at sixteen and she was born the next year, and I've given my life to being her mother."

"Ah, but this girl," intoned the minister, mopping up his plate with a piece of crusty, homemade bread, "this girl is one of God's own mothers. All day she cares for the little ones of others."

Grace stepped out of the room to get the dessert. They didn't seem to notice. She rolled scoops of vanilla ice cream in coconut flakes and put them in Mamma's glass sherbet cups. She heated the chocolate sauce, then poured it over the ice cream, just a trickle on Mamma's but quite a lot for Pastor Bird, who liked rich desserts.

"All praise to Thee," she murmured as she placed a cherry on each mound.

SHIRLEY BRADLEY LEFLORE

POEM FOR THE BLK WOMAN

–dollie, mildred, ottavie, henrine, emma

I house the legend of mutima
The heartbeat of the earth
The offspring of the moon and the sun
Thrust from the energy of afrika

       i am the blk woman

The symbol of love
The channel of creation
The vibration of peace
The anger of storms
The suffering in pain

       i am the blk woman

I have seen the first rains
And the las fire
I am the seasoner of soul
Many are my tales untold

My womb stretches across the mouth of the universe
To create nations and rhythms
My body's borne witness to birth
My spirit the taster of death
I have seen the 13th month
The 32nd day
The year 3000 before
The year 03

       i am the blk woman

I have cradled the newborn's cry
and the ole man's moan
rocked the smiles of aging nature in my arms

I am the other part of god
I am the other side of man
I am the spirit of life

       i am the blk woman

ELIZABETH LEXLEIGH

PRAIRIE

Exquisite the tall and tapered
Prairie grasses lush
Green and gold they glisten
With the sun they drink
And whisper earthy secrets
As they nod their heads
To the chant of the wind.

A verdant sea billows, rolls
Runs twisting and swaying
Far out far away to join
Seamless the iridescent light.

And I to wander it, musing
Yeasty aromas, pungent twangs,
A soft snap underfoot, I go
As if it were not a wonder.

published 1986, Gypsy Compilation Book

SHARON LIBERA

WHAT I TELL MY FRIEND

We all approach it. Only you have the chance
To shape yours. Everyone is watching you
And trying not to show it. Even me.

The more you insist on having lunch,
And phoning, and buying books, and running,
The more we forget the parenthesis around you.

Pound says, "Trees die & the dream remains."
But already I cannot picture the branches
Of a black oak felled last summer in my yard.

Designs in sand are lost because the grains
Slide down. The space you take is here,
The color written on everyone around you,

Not to be taken away but grain by grain,
As, in a century, a circle is disassembled.

SHARON LIBERA

A SONG FOR TWO VOICES

Bring me a woman who lives lonely
On her land far in the hills,
Who sold her children to the peddler
And is grieving still.

There is no woman living lonely
In the strange place you say.
There is no woman who has bargained
Her infants away.

Bring me a woman fair and lively
Who paid a call on Death
And told her venture in a fable
That robs' the breath.

There is no woman fair and lively
In the strange place you say,
No woman who has written more
Than a letter yesterday.

Bring me a woman once foolish
Who loved with her whole will.
Ah she, she lives not far from here,
And is grieving still.

THE CHOICE OF SUBJECT

What weakness this is,
My words tied to people, so that
If they disappear, my words circle
Their absence.
I would like to know about birds,
To paint tiny buildings and haystacks
In a vista over there. My eye is relieved,
Receding into that world.

LYNNE LOSCHKY

JUST PASSING THROUGH

"East Africa's black rhinos
Can sprint at 35 miles an hour.
They have been known to charge at trains
Passing through their territory."

East Coast establishment white matrons
Can stroll at the rate of 3.5 stores per morning.
They have been known to charge at Macy's,
Credit cards passing through kid-gloved hands.

East Ethiopia's brown-skinned masses
Can crawl at 35 fatalities per afternoon.
They have been known to beg for mercy
From food trucks passing through their misery.

Eastern mystics, meandering wisemen
Can amble purposefully for weeks, months, years.
But they have been known to drop their presence
At a passing-strange stable housing one humble Lord.

JANET LOWE

ADDRESS TO AN EARRING THIEF

Forget about my sadness,
that the silver filagreed earring
wedded me to three generations,
embroidered the ears of all my women.
Forget.
But know this about the earring you fold in your fist:
You'll wear it not knowing of my grandmother's hazel eyes
or her penchant for brooches.
No sound of the cuckoo will tick against your ear,
no tint of Maxfield Parrish blue shade your eyes as it did hers.
The smell of the winter closet in the dayroom
will not rise in your breath when you hold the earring,
nor will the warm tissuey feel of an old woman's skin
haunt your fingertips.
Thread it through your ear with caution:
It won't throw the light in prisms for you
or drop from your ear weightless as a gypsy's charm
but droop black and heavy as her curse.
My curse, more cruel than hers, will leave you wishing
the bauble never found your hand,
lay lost in leaves in needles
till plucked for anchor in a nest.

JANET LOWE

ODE TO A GRAPEFRUIT

She wanted me to eat it
out of love, I know.
She gave me choices:
    with sugar
    with salt
    peeled
    portioned
    squeezed.
At five, ten, and fifteen
I refused her fruit.

Twenty years later
I take it pure:
    Each morning I cup a yellow
    world in my hand,
    split it, revealing
    the pastels of Monet.
    Delicately carve round the rind,
    dig into the pearly pulp,
    scoop till it gleams,
    white, veiny,
    clean as a communion cup.
    Tip, drink the juices
    of the empty world
    dribble down my chin.
If she were here
her hand would catch
the tears.

EDITH MCCALL

UPHEAVAL ON THE MISSISSIPPI

A keelboat trip could be dangerous, people in St. Louis told the
English botanist, John Bradbury. He had nearly completed his American
studies in December 1811, and was in the fur-trading village arranging
for transportation to New Orleans. Friends warned him of treacherous
snags that, in very few minutes, could send a keelboat to the river
bottom. Nevertheless, Bradbury arranged passage with a French crew
carrying a cargo of lead.

Had he known that much greater danger lay ahead, he might
not have been so eager to leave St. Louis. The boat's embarkation was
just before the beginning of the New Madrid Earthquakes, greater in
magnitude than any in the history of North America, including the San
Francisco quakes of 1906. They were named for a village Bradbury would
pass early in his voyage down the Mississippi, in an area of southeastern
Missouri known as the "bootheel."

The first shock came December 16, 1811, about two in the morning.
Scientists today estimate it to have been of magnitude 8.6 on the Richter
Scale. The next severe shock came January 23, 1812, estimated at 8.4,
and the most severe of all at 8.7 occurred February 7. Casualties were
few because these awful tremors occurred on what was then the sparsely
settled, United States' western frontier.

Tremors and aftershocks registered all the way to the Atlantic coast
and continued for months between and after these major shocks. Reports
flooded in, reports of cracked plaster in Richmond, Virginia, of church
bells ringing without a pull of the bellropes in Washington, D.C. But
along the Mississippi and in river towns, the earthquake did much more
than crack plaster or ring bells. People reported that they thought the
end of the world had come as land and water became uncontrollable
enemies of all living things.

Viewing the year of 1811 through the magnifying lens of hindsight,
people felt convinced that 1811 had held many omens of disaster, and
was a strange year throughout. Spring floods filled the rivers from bluff
to bluff, spreading for miles over the lowlands. Much sickness followed.
When summer came, a heavy stillness hung over the lower Ohio and
Mississippi valleys. That summer was remembered as a summer without
thunder in times of storms; instead, a "subterranean thunder," a rumbling
deep in the earth.

"A spirit of change and recklessness seemed to pervade the very
inhabitants of the forests," an observer commented later. He told of
"countless multitudes" of squirrels making their way southward to the
Ohio River and plunging into the water, many drowning in the murky
waters. The sense of foreboding increased late that summer when a
comet streaked through the sky nightly— a sure sign of trouble to come,
frontier people said. When the comet disappeared late in the autumn,

time was rife for disaster.

Despite this talk, John Bradbury embarked on his voyage to New Orleans. On the evening of December 14, he and his crew reached the village of New Madrid, located on the north bank of the Mississippi on a loop known as Kentucky Bend. Bradbury thought it a disappointing place, with only "a few straggling houses, situated round a plain of two to three hundred acres in extent. There were ony two stores, which are very indifferently furnished."

His crew set off about nine o'clock on the morning of the 15th. Since a keelboat moved faster than the clumsy flatboats in which most frontier produce was transported to market in New Orleans, Bradbury's boat passed at least thirteen such vessels as it proceeded downriver that day.

About thirty-five winding river miles below New Madrid, they passed a settlement called Little Prairie, where Caruthersville is today. Farther downriver, they approached "The Devil's Channel," a difficult passage to navigate, and decided to leave this task until morning. They tied up to a tree on a small island five hundred yards above the "devil's" entrance.

"After supper we went to sleep as usual," Bradbury wrote in his journal, "and in the night...I was awakened by a most tremendous noise, accompanied by so violent an agitation of the boat that it appeared in danger of upsetting." The crew—French speaking fellows—cried out, "*O mon Dieu! Monsieur Brandbury, qu'est ce qu'il y a?*"

Bradbury hurried to his cabin door to see an agitated river and the noise? "inconceivably loud and terrific," he recorded. "I could distinctly hear the crash of falling trees, and the screaming of the wild fowl on the river." But his boat held safe to her mooring, although rocking violently. The men, who had built a fire on a large flat stone on the deck near the stern, hurried to extinguish it, although the shock had ceased.

"But immediately the perpendicular banks, both above and below us, began to fall into the river in such vast masses as nearly to sink our boat by the swell they occasioned," Brandbury wrote. The most terrified of the boatmen was the "patron," the one in charge. He was no help in advising Bradbury on what to do, crying out, "*O mon Dieu! Nous perierons!*"

Bradbury checked the time. It was two in the morning. He gathered his valuable papers and money and went ashore on the island. By candlelight he saw that the earth had split open, and found "the chasm really frightful, being not less than four feet in width, and the bank had sunk at least two feet." The chasm was at least eighty yards, and at each end of the island the banks had fallen into the river. The crew's lives had been saved because they had moored to a sloping bank and not a perpendicular one.

Lesser shocks continued. About four o'clock, Bradbury examined the banks again by candlelight. Using a compass, he noted that each shock came from the same point, "a little northward of east, and proceeded westward."

"At daylight, we had counted twenty-seven shocks during our stay on the island.... The river was covered with foam and drift timber, and had risen considerably, but our boat was safe. Whilst we were waiting till the light became sufficient for us to embark two canoes floated down the river, in one of which we saw some Indian corn and some clothes. We considered this as a melancholy proof that some of the boats we had passed the preceding day had perished."

Just as Bradbury ordered the crew to embark, another severe shock occurred. The Devil's Channel loomed ahead, now so full of driftwood that passage appeared to be impossible. Bradbury, with an almost useless crew of terrified men, decided to give them time to pull themselves together and found a sloping island bank at which to tie the boat. He ordered his men to go ashore and prepare breakfast. Three more shocks came before they readied again to embark and attempt the channel passage. He fortified each man with a "glass of spirits" to help drown their terror.

And so they set out, forced into speed by the swirling waters and having constantly to switch course in order to avoid collisions with fallen trees. Bradbury wrote, "Immediately after we had cleared all danger, the men dropped their oars, crossed themselves, then gave a shout, congratulating each other on our safety."

About eleven o'clock another violent shock came, augmented by sounds, earthly and unearthly. Terror seized the men again. But then and afterwards as they moved downriver, Bradbury and his men felt safer on the turbulent river than on land. They feared the falling trees and the sudden dropping away of ground beneath their feet.

They had another uneasy night as shocks continued at intervals. The next day, a group of about twenty people standing outside a log cabin hailed "captain" Bradbury. He stopped to talk with these people and learned they had gathered to pray for deliverance instead of fleeing from the area as their neighbors had done. They told him that a sandbar opposite the bluffs opened, that as it closed, water rose to "the height of a tall tree," that back from the river the earth had opened in several places.

One man had an explanation for this. He said that the comet had two "horns," and that the earth, having rolled over one of them, was now lodged between them. The shocks were "occasioned by the attempts made by the earth to surmount the other horn." If the attempts failed, the end of the world would come. Bradbury and his men experienced shocks three more days before their voyage reached a more peaceful end. On the 25th (a Christmas day that apparently was ignored) a friend from St. Louis overtook them. He had been just above New Madrid when the first shocks occurred, and said that the village was in ruins. The ground sank, he said, leaving the townsite under water, and residents left for higher ground. This report proves to be inaccurate. New Madrid was not flooded on December 16; it was completely submerged later, after the January 7 shock.

But in New Madrid that first great shock was not easy to live through. Eliza Bryan, a resident there, wrote of it in 1916, remembering the "hoarse and vibrating" thunder, the cracking sounds of trees splitting and crashing down, the roaring river; the smell of sulphur in the air, frightened people crying out and running about in the darkness of the night.

Another New Madrid resident, unidentified, wrote of the tremendous noise that awoke him at about two in the morning, and said, "the house danced about and seemed as if it would fall on our heads." His family went outside, only to find it difficult to stand, for the earth rolled in waves. The New Madridian also wrote of the change in the atmosphere: "At the time of the shock, the heavens were very clear and serene, not a breath of air stirring; but in five minutes it became very dark, and a vapour which seemed to impregnate the atmosphere, had a disagreeable smell, and produced a difficulty of respiration." The writer comments that about six-thirty in the morning when he attempted to go to check on his neighbors, "The motion of the earth was about twelve inches to and fro...the earth seemed convulsed—the houses shook very much—chimnies[sic] falling in every direction. The loud, hoarse roaring which attended the earthquake, together with the cries, screams, and yells of people, seems still ringing in my ears." Panic prevailed, and some residents fled, never to be heard from again.

The animals also behaved strangely. Cattle sought open ground, but "finding it convulsed, threw them into confusion, they ran about bellowing as in the greatest alarm and distress, seeking the camps of people..." Birds appeared to lose the power of flight and perched on houses, boats, and even on people's shoulders.

Little Prairie (nearer to the epicenter of the first shocks than New Madrid) was completely wiped out by daylight of December 16. Nearly one hundred people arrived at New Madrid on Christmas Eve, having gone northward, hearing there was less damage there. Among them was a miller, George Roddell, whose mill tipped over and house had "sunk down considerably." Where swamp had been across a bayou, now it was dry land. Miller and family tried to run across a field, but a large crack in the land stopped them so they turned toward woodlands. Another shock came and there seemed no place to go. Within fifteen minutes they found themselves standing in water, waist deep. A Philadelphia newspaper reported, "As they proceeded, the earth continued to burst open, and mud, water, sand and stone coal were thrown up the distance of 30 yards—frequently trees of a large size were split open, fifteen or twenty feet up. After wading eight miles, they came to dry land."

Detailed accounts of damage from the second major shock (on January 23) do not appear, but between it and the February 7 earthquake, waves of lesser shocks are noted. Mrs. Bryan wrote, "the earth was in continual agitation, visibly waving as a gentle sea." Another person described the activity between greater and lesser shocks as constant trembling, "like the flesh of a beef just killed."

By February 7, the epicenter had moved northeastward, near New Madrid. Most residents had abandoned their homes and had set up camp or built "light wooden structures" on higher ground. This proved fortunate, for the February 7 shock toppled even sturdy log structures and shifted the river channel, leaving the old town underwater. The damage to soil was greater this time than before, with craters reported at 12 to 50 feet in diameter and 5 to 10 feet deep "from the surface of the water."

Just prior to the first earthquake, the "New Orleans," first steamboat to descend the Ohio and Mississippi rivers, waited at Louisville for the river to deepen so that she (125 feet long and 42 wide) could be piloted over the Falls of Ohio. Once over the Falls, she docked briefly to drop off the falls pilot. Before her engine was restarted, her timbers creaked and shuddered. It was December 16; the first quake's aftershock had reached Louisville.

Aboard the "New Orleans," with its steam engine pistons and gears and side paddlewheels making so much noise and vibrations, occupants couldn't tell if another shock was in progress. More frightening were two incidents as the craft puffed down the Ohio. This huge blue steamer, making unearthly sounds, shooting out sparks—a mysterious menace to Indians—was pursued by two war canoes until it outdistanced them. And passengers had to save the steamboat one night when a fire broke out in its forward cabin.

A pilot's skills were well tested, especially upon entering the Mississippi River. Old landmarks disappeared and new driftwood snagged or blocked the way. The most difficult part of this voyage came during the night when "New Orleans" was tied to a tree on an island just below Little Prairie. Although "New Orleans" was still tied to the tree in the morning, the island was gone. The skillful pilot charted them on safely to New Orleans, arriving January 12, having good fortune in an arrival well ahead of the second and third major shocks.

A bit of justice appears in a tale told by Captain Sarpy of St. Louis. He and family, carrying "considerable money," tied up on the evening of December 15, 1811, on an island known as Number 94, not far from Vicksburg. Sarpy discovered, however, they shared this island with a gang of river pirates. Under cover of darkness, Sarpy moved his boat a little farther downriver where he and family felt some earthquake traumas that night. When daylight broke, the captain discovered that Island No. 94 had disappeared, presumably taking the unsavory characters with it.

Vincent Nolte, a New Orleans merchant arriving at New Madrid February 6, rested in his keelboat cabin when the greatest quake of all showed up about four o'clock on the morning of February 7. While other captains ordered their boats cut loose, Nolte risked remaining moored. He wrote later that the Mississippi was "driven backward for several hours, consequence of an elevation in its bed." When the waters rushed back, "boats, then floating on its surface, shot down the declivity like an arrow from a bow, amid roaring billows and the wildest commotion."

A result of this upheaval: creation of two sets of falls, one about a half mile above New Madrid, and the lower some eight or nine miles downriver. The roar of the lower falls could be heard in New Madrid; going over them was frightening to those in boats caught in the pull of their current. But the action of the river itself leveled the falls in a few day's time, although the always hazardous snags multiplied, increasing the dangers of river traffic. Where the river spread over its banks in reverse action, the water's force cleanly cut groves of young cottonwood trees as if done by human woodcutters, and set them afloat.

Timothy Flint visited people at New Madrid, after it was all over, and wrote of this reverse action in *Recollections of the Last Ten Years in the Valley of the Mississippi,* 1826. "A bursting of the earth just below the village of New Madrid, arrested this mighty stream in its course, and caused a reflux of its waves, by which in a little time a great number of boats were swept by the ascending current into the mouth of the Bayou, carried out and left upon the dry earth, when the accumulating waters of the river had again cleared their current."

It was after the "hard shock" of February 7 that the greatest upheaval on land, as well as on river, occurred. Where there had been ponds, land drained; new lakes and domes of land appreared. The largest and most evident of changes evolved in extreme northwestern Tennessee, where a forest sank and Reelfoot Lake emerged with trees still standing in lake depths of five to twenty feet. Reelfoot runs eighteen miles long, five miles wide.

In those early times, amateur scientists experimented to detect earthquake movement and added knowledge of the geographical extent of the New Madrid Earthquake shocks and aftershocks. In Louisville, Jared Brooks constructed pendulums to measure vibrations and he found they continued well into May, when his record stops. In Cincinnati, Daniel Drake kept detailed records of shocks in that area. These, and other men concurred in finding measurable vibrations throughout 1812. Reports from Louisiana, Arkansas, Mississippi, Missouri, Tennessee, Kentucky, Illinois, Michigan Territory, Indiana and points eastward to Massachusetts and all down the Atlantic seaboard as far as Georgia were given. One hundred seventy-two years have passed since the last major shocks of the New Madrid earthquakes. But all has not been quiet in that interval. On March 25, 1976, quakes measured a magnitude of 5, centering in Marked Tree— a few miles west of the Mississippi in northeastern Arkansas. Microquakes of 1 magnitude occur in that region, and with frequency increases in the 1980s.

Studies now show the causes of the New Madrid earthquakes, the probability of a recurrence, and the probable effects of another series like those of 1811-12. These studies are part of the work of the United Geological Survey and, specifically for Mississippi valley area, by the New Madrid Seismotectonic Study Group, based in St. Louis University.

The fault lines of this region are different from those of the San Andreas Fault in California, which is a plate-boundary region. Earthquakes along that line are principally from vertical slippage, while the Mississippi valley's are both horizontal and vertical. Three fault lines map the New Madrid area; embedded rather than on the surface, they are detectable only with modern seismology instruments. In lay terms, quakes occur with interaction between sections of the earth's crust and an old, rigid, immobile, underlying section (known as a craton).

Will another great "interaction" quake the Mississippi valley? Yes, inevitably, say scientists, but none will predict *when.* As to effects, this is a matter of enough concern that commissions actively prepare for them. The area is far different from what it was in sparsely settled frontier days, and likely more serious damage will result than would result from a major California quake. The city of Memphis is most vulnerable, but many other urban centers would be affected. Additionally, today there are utilities, pipelines, bridges, highway overpasses—a multitude of structures that did not exist in 1811-12. But such is the nature of humankind, that people have God-given strengths to endure and rebuild, should such a disaster occur.

And what of New Madrid today? A visit there gives no impression of anxiety. The town of about 3000 is peaceful and quiet, its back turned to the river that once was its lifeblood as well as its enemy. Beyond the levee, the Mississippi flows, dark and silent, giving no hint of the terrible violence of which it has proven itself capable.

Reprinted through the courtesy of Historical Times, Inc., publishers of *American History Illustrated*

PATRICIA MCCARTY

PINKIE

I saw her today
at yoga class
when I stretched
on polished oak
pretending to smell clover
and cut grass.

She slipped around
the corner of my mind,
ran through zinnias
stiff as painted wood,
orange and pink and purple.

Now she hides,
sits cross legged
like a buddha
where flowering almond
willows down to build a cave.
Her Easter chick
grown to grain-filled hen
rests warm in the nest
of her slender legs.

She watches summer
wind washed
and pegged to a clothesline.

I'd call
but she's too far away to hear.

ELLEN GRAY MASSEY

CATALYST

Jaundice dozed in one of the empty wheelchairs parked on the concrete veranda in the shade of the building. He had made himself comfortable in the hollow of the slightly worn cushion, fitting his body perfectly into the depression. He was curled up into a tight ball, turning his head and neck so that his eyes, whiskers and nose were hidden. Even his ears and long tail were indistinguishable in the soft ball of long yellow fur.

Up and down the long veranda two elderly men were moving slowly with the aid of walkers. A nurse encouraged them on. They reached the farthest point of the veranda, turned around and shuffled back, staying in the shade thrown by the brick wall of the rest home.

"My, you're doing fine today!" the nurse congratulated the man who was most feeble. "You're walking this distance so much better today. Don't you think we could do it again?"

"No, I can't do it," the man whined.

As the trio made their way back to the chairs, the nurse continued to encourage the feeble man. The other man was moving easily and cheerfully.

The feeble man slumped over his walker, looking at the ground and his feet as they inched their way along the walkway. When he reached his wheelchair, he raised his head with a sigh of relief. The other gentleman had already turned around to take another turn.

The feeble man saw Jaundice comfortably snoozing in his seat. A smile flitted across his face. The strained lines between his eyes from his continual frown disappeared as his pursed mouth spread out into a toothless grin. He watched the cat for a moment and then, straightening his posture just slightly, turned around with more energy than he had heretofore shown, shuffling after his companion. "Can't disturb Jaunie," he said aloud to nobody in particular.

By the time the men returned the second time, the morning sun had reached the chair seat. The big tabby cat uncurled, stretched and jumped up on the arm of the chair out of the hot sun.

"Ain't he a caution?" the feeble man asked, as the nurse helped him into his seat. The cat didn't jump down. As soon as the man was seated, Jaundice walked back and forth rubbing his head, first one side and then the other, against the man's bare arm, purring loudly.

"How ya doin', Jaunie, old boy?" he asked, fondling him.

Jaundice luxuriated in the attention a few minutes before jumping down and running into the building when a nurse came out. She caught the door just before it shut to keep it from slamming on his tail.

Jaundice trotted through the lobby to the left hall. He moved purposefully, his long thick tail held high, his shiny fur rippling in rhythm. He passed two open doors before turning into the third room.

He jumped up on the first bed. The emaciated woman lying there had been immobile, staring up at faded ceiling blocks. The instant she felt the mattress give just slightly to the cat's weight, she moved her head to look at him. Attention returned to her vacant eyes as she zeroed in on his big yellow eyes staring straight into hers. She lifted a blue-veined hand to stroke his silky fur.

"Hello, Jaunie-boy," she murmured in an almost inaudible voice. "I thought you forgot me today."

Jaundice made two or three soft throaty sounds. The lady half raised in bed and turned to see the big cat better. She mumbled something again. He responded with soft meows and stretched out beside her as she fell back on the pillow. The invalid stroked him slowly first with one bony hand and then the other. The cat rolled over, necessitating her moving in bed to reach him.

All the rest of the morning Jaundice was in and out of rooms down that hall. In one room he became playful when he found his plastic ball with a bell in it, dribbling it across the tile floor as the occupants laughed merrily at his antics. He jumped on the beds of some bedridden patients and on the arms of the chairs of those sitting, but he never walked on anyone or sat in their laps.

Just before noon he settled down at the foot of a talkative bedridden woman who was propped up with pillows. She watched with interest, smiles wreathing her sallow, wrinkled face, as Jaundice gave himself a thorough bath, and then settled down for another nap. The patient and her equally ancient roommate shared tales of Jaundice's latest escapades. When they exhausted their fund of Jaundice stories, they chatted on endlessly about other cats they had known in happier times. The yellow tabby would twitch his right ear occasionally.

"See that? Jaunie knows we're talking about him, the little dickens." The two ladies admired him for a few seconds before continuing their conversation about cats.

They were soon interrupted by visitors. The administrator of the rest home and three official-looking strangers—two men and a woman—marched in without knocking. One man held open a black book. He occasionally marked in it as if he were checking off items from a list. The woman took copious notes on papers fastened to a clipboard. The third man seemed the least officious of the three. Smiling pleasantly, he greeted the two ladies.

"This is a typical room," the administrator explained to his visitors. "You can see each patient has her own closet, her own dresser and little whatnot table. The bath is. . . ." He explained all the desirable features of the room. As he passed the foot of the bed where Jaundice lay, he petted him without pausing in his recital. Jaundice raised his head in response.

The notetaking woman held her pencil in midair when she spotted the cat. "The cat's got to go," she said in distaste.

"By all means," the man making the check marks agreed.

The pleasant man looked at the yellow tabby with interest. "How beautiful! What's his name?" He leaned down to observe him more closely. Jaundice looked back at him with equal interest.

"Jaunie," the owner of the bed replied promptly and proudly picked him up and held him protectively in her arms.

"Most everyone calls him Jaunie," the administrator said and then chuckled. "His name is Jaundice. He showed up here a couple of years ago a scraggly bag of bones encased in fur."

"The cat has got to go," the notetaker repeated.

The pleasant man smiled at the patient who was clutching the cat tightly to her as the group left the room to continue their inspection tour.

By late afternoon Jaundice had made the rounds of the other halls, eaten his dinner in the corner of the furnace room where a place is fixed for him, and was once again napping, this time in one of the big arm chairs in the lobby. The lobby was comfortably full of ambulatory men and women sitting in small groups, waiting for time to go to the dining room next door. Two men stood by the grand piano, another sat on the hard bench. None showed interest in the instrument—they were there because there was no other place to sit. No one disturbed Jaundice.

Some of the residents looked anxiously toward the administrator's office which opened onto the lobby. The three officials had been closeted in there for two hours studying ledgers, figures, plans and statistics about the operation of the home and proposed improvements. The door finally opened and the three stepped out, all carrying brief cases. Their faces had the look of another job completed. The administrator appeared. His look was one of relief. Inspection was over.

Some people in the lobby looked up as soon as they stepped out. The grapevine quickly informed that the late morning visitors were from a governmental agency to investigate the home for a possible grant for improvements and expansion of patient care and comfort. The money was not a matter of whether the home continued or not, but, as the administrator explained to the residents months before when he applied for it, it would greatly improve the home, making their lives more pleasant. The grapevine kept them informed all day of the officials actions and comments until they disappeared into the office. With much interest and concern, the residents studied the faces of all four people to try to read the results of the inspection.

The check mark man said, "Everything seems satisfactory. You meet all the specifications."

"It's a cheerful home," the pleasant man said. "The morale of the patients is positive."

As the officials walked slowly to the entrance, passing by Jaundice still asleep in one of the lobby arm chairs, the notetaking woman agreed, "Yes, everything seems in order, but that cat has to go."

The pleasant man paused in front of Jaunie. Sensing that he was now the center of attention, the cat opened his eyes and looked at each of the three officials in turn. Then he raised up slowly in the middle of the cushion and arched his back. Then he held his head high, wrapped his tail arund his right side, neatly tucked the tip behind his front paws, and sat down.

With much dignity and self-esteem he sat there. The man couldn't resist petting him. "What's the harm?" he asked her.

As if she were talking to an imbecile, she said, "A cat in a rest home? It's unsanitary. He'd get in the medicine room. He'd get in the kitchen and into the food tray. Unthinkable!"

"No he doesn't," the administrator said. "He only goes where I tell him. He does what I say. If I say, 'Don't go in the kitchen', he doesn't go there. If I tell him not to go into the medicine room, he doesn't go there. He never goes near any food."

"Humph" she grunted.

"Here. I'll show you," he said. "Jaundice, get out of the chair."

Jaundice jumped down from the chair and trotted toward the hall. "No, Jaundice," the administrator said sternly, "don't go there."

The cat stopped and then turned to the door to be let out. Instantly two patients were at the door to let him out. Through the glass doors everyone watched Jaunie lope across the lawn.

Once again the woman affirmed, "The cat's got to go."

"The cat stays," the administrator said. "Even if it means we lose the grant, the cat stays."

The elderly patients who were listening to every word clapped. During the conversation more ambulatory and wheelchair patients had appeared from the halls spanning out from the lobby.

The woman looked at him with disbelief. She let out another exasperated sigh and walked out. The man who carried the check mark book looked undecided for a moment, then he, without a word, followed.

From the hall of the bedfast patients came a muffled clapping as the news of the administrator's decision spread to them. There came a clatter of metal spoons banging on metal bed rails from the emaciated woman's room.

The pleasant man looked at the backs of his departed colleagues through the glass door. He glanced around the room crowded with grinning old people; feebled cheering still drifted from the hall. He shook the administrator's hands and said so softly that only those very close heard, "I'll see that you get your money."

LESLIE ADRIENNE MILLER

THAT BOY

Leslie Adrienne Miller

I doubt if there is anything
I can teach that boy
beyond the way to touch
a woman, or the way
to hold his fork, though
he will forget these things too
as easily as he forgets
the marks on his buttocks
where I held on too tight.

He doesn't notice the way
my slip straps slide down
or the smell of powder in his sheets.
He looks out the window
to avoid the spectacle
of my body here with him
though he never turned away
when he saw a man drop
from the flight deck of an aircraft carrier
to a perfect instant death.

When shortly before dawn he clutches
the sleepy rag of my spine
it isn't really lust
that makes him hysterical
and sad. The prison dogs
have him by one lean ankle
and God or the Devil
is telling him
they'll never let go.

Then he loves me briefly
because I might be the fence
those dogs pried him from,
something made for holding onto
even if it is part of a trap.

He won't admit that anything
of his life has made differences
but he is young yet,
too young to spell cities' names
on my bared breasts, too young
to believe that I am
a difference making itself in him.

published 1982, 13th Moon 6:1-2

121

LESLIE ANDRIENNE MILLER

AMERICAN SUMMER

And didn't you sit on somebody's breezeway
with your skinny legs over the arm
of someone's abused porch furniture,
handing a candy Lucky Strike on your lip
before you snapped the end off?

And didn't you go out in the yard at dusk
with the stolen butcher knife, the big kids
telling you "hide" telling you "shush"?
And didn't you creep into the open yard
and see Casey's floodlighted body face down,
the knife in his back? And didn't you scream
or run, did you?

And didn't Casey tell you the next day
he'd kill you if you touched his sting-ray,
and didn't he go on matching the end of his rifle
to pigeons in the eaves of Schott's Grill?

And didn't somebody's mom look out at you,
her hands in dinner dishes, saying,
"Do they learn cruelty from each other
or is it bad blood. . .Harry. . .is it bad blood?"

And didn't somebody's day keep his eye
on the newspaper, knocking his pipe
in the rim of an ashtray three times saying,
"They stick the knife in their armpits,
Christine, all in good fun"?

And didn't Pete take you down
in his fort with all the 7th grade boys
and tell your little sister she could talk
on the phone if she'd pull her pants down.
And didn't she do it? Didn't she?

And you never told on Pete,
did you?

published 1982, Northwest Review 20:1

LESLIE ADRIENNE MILLER

RED COWS

They're called *limousines,*
says a man I know,
but he could be wrong,
or lying because he likes
to think I'll write it down,
get, if not his whole self,
then this one, possibly flawed,
part into words for him.

Someone else told me about how
the cows are carted up here only
for the few summer months the mountains
give, how the rich alpine grass
reddens their hides before they're
crowded into trucks and pointed home.
It is significant that I do not
remember who told me about the grass
and trucks, while the man who first
called them limousines, still
has a name.

Before I go back to Denver myself,
I'd like to have a picture
of that field of russet rumped cows.
From the road they seem
a showroom of sofas, expensive
and carefully displayed against
high valley blue and plush.

So much for lies. Those cows
really are limousines, while that
bowl of mountains around them
won't stay in my prairie girl's head.
I weigh a little more
than I did in June; the back
of my neck is richly browned;
and I have been loved,
anxiously, occasionally, stupidly,
but loved. Come September,
we'll all go down towards Denver,
cows, children, me, fair weather, all,
of course, except for the man
whose best and only gift to me
was what to call those red red cows.

123

MARLENE MILLER

THE SWING OF THE EARRING

It's complicated, the way life goes on.
The feet keep traveling across the dance floor,
the earring keeps swinging against the cheek,
charms on your bracelet keep time with the drummer
as they hit against the open palm of your hand.

The only thing slow in this room
is the sweat that is crawling like a snail
down the length of your backbone, though inside
you are oddly chilled and your mouth is a tight line,
clearly not as it should be.

It's like going down the highway at a smooth clip.
Then the car in front of you smacks on its brake lights.
It's not what you had planned when you set out that day,
and tonight you feel your feet too frenzied on the dance floor,

and you're busy staring down at the different shades of wood,
when you should be smiling.

THE PAISLEY SCARF

When you die,
all that remains
is packed up in grocery cartons,
a few belts flung over a foot stool,
some favorite books stacked on the wash machine,
furniture piled in dark corners of the cellar,
your two favorite chrome end tables
on top of your peach velvet chair.

Everyone argues over who should get
your oak colored paisley scarf
(the one you brought from Monte Carlo)
and they all say what a pity that
your sweaters were size — small.

So this is how it ends.
Just a few valuable remains,
some giveaways, some throwaways,
and your silk scarfs weeping over the
blue edge of a laundry basket.

124

Marlene Miller

CHARLOTTE NEKOLA

BEFORE HER LIFE

What does she wait for?
No boats wait behind these brick houses.
The noons hiss sumac and weevil.

She plays chords on the piano,
thinks they are Moscow, Kiev
and presses one key afterwards:

mute thud, cat's paw on a windowpane.
The Enterprise Flour Mill juts ghostly
from its dark field.

At night she points to red stars, blue stars.
The man standing next to her says no,
you imagine that.

One day she buries a pine cone
and looks in through her own front window
as if she were a neighbor's child.

The trains haul corn, beans, seed.
"Evil weevil, evil weevil," her children cry
as they run from door to door.

It is red fish, river, sea,
she says, over and over in her sleep,
red fish. river. sea.

CHARLOTTE NEKOLA

FOR DAUGHTERS

My mother said, "Don't read those stories."

I want to watch the streets of a city
turn their hands up at night.

My grandmother said, "In California
I moved my breadboard next to a window."

They cut the feet off a girl in red shoes.

This is my father's story
of a woman he never forgot:
"She stood on a ferryboat
wearing a mauve dress."

I want to sleep with rivers.

My aunt said, "I made Edna a skirt
with 104 pleats, once."

A mermaid sold her tongue for legs.

My grandmother said, "I went to school until the eight
year; then my knee was lame and I had to go home."

I have run at night from streets and rivers.

But now I am making a promise:

I will write a story
where women can walk.

HELEN PATMON

FLYIN OAN ORANGE 'N' BLACK BUTTAFLY WINGS

Gentle snores echo as dreams whispered all that was too treasured to speak for everyone except me. So much silence. So much darkness. Only Jesus—shining in the night—on a cross—on the wall. Would this night ever end?

"I must sleep. Sleep, I must sleep."

Big teeth and claws propped my eyes open as I pleaded, "Not monsters again. No lions, please, Jesus-on-the-wall, please."

As quickly as I had said the savior's name, my old friend sleep and I embraced. Closer and closer she held me—warmed me— cuddled me. We drifted further and further away from claws of fire and fear. With the ease of an eagle we glided through darkness until birdsong danced with my face and air fairies bounced in my hair. Endless ocean waves cuddled my ears and shadows of palm trees crooked across my face. I was safe now.

"This must be the land of milk and honey. I will live off the fat of the land and stay here forever. I can sleep here, sleep forever."

The soft gentle strokes of the sun began to fade and strange red streaks slashed my face. The chickadees grew still and ocean waves became thin air. When I turned around to see if my palm trees were still there, all I could see was the dark escaping figure of my oldest sister as she slipped out the bedroom door. My throat clutched for air and my heart leaped through my bones. I patted the bed from bottom to top but no Sue, no Rose, no Bea? There was nothing to be done. There was no denying that, yes, morning had come.

Downtrodden and forlorn, I went to the window and pulled the shade and there dazzling in full brilliance was the sun. I was the last one out of bed. No greater shame hath a farmer's daughter. No greater burden to bear hath she.

"You ain't outta that bed yet girl?" Mama cannoned.

"I am! I am! I'm up," I declared as legs and pants and shoes and socks and shirts and "Oh, my God underwear" struggled for supremacy.

"She ain't up, Mama."

"I am too up."

"She ain't up, I'm lookin right attha and she's layin in the bed," said my younger brother as he switched away to the kitchen.

I do not know why my mother had my little brother. What good was he? He told everything and couldn't play anything.

"See, Mama. I'm up," I said as I snatched the soda and my toothbrush and scuttled into the kitchen to face my accuser.

"Well, she wadn't up wholla go."

I looked at him with lightening eyes as he danced through the kitchen. Out came his tongue and "Naaa, naaa, na, na, na." I dashed in front of him and violently kissed him with the screen door as I leaped

127

on to the porch. With every tooth in my mouth I proclaimed "Goodie, goodie, goodie," as King Louie fell in defeat to the kitchen floor.

Morning was a much better deal than night. Making night made about as much sense as making my little brother. A dragon wouldn't dare mess with me in all this light.

"So much sky. How could God make so much sky? How could he get way up there and put them clouds there? God must be able to fly."

"If you want somethin' ta eat, you betta hurry up," said ol' Louis, making a desperate effort to recover.

"You eat all my breakfast and I'll knock yo head off!"

Knowing very well that Louis' threat was real, I applied the soda, rubbed my teeth, raced to the kitchen and not a moment too soon. Louis had the last biscuit headed for his lips.

"Gimme that," I said as I snatched the biscuit. He laughed and strutted toward the door. I had a full day of playing ahead, so I ate quickly.

"Whatta ya wanna do today?" questioned my older brother Sandy. Now, Sandy was a brother a sister would want to keep. Sandy played Man, and Cowboys and Indians, and Dolls with me. One time he even beat up Clyde, The Midget, because he called me a "yella pie-face." He knew all kinds of things. He could draw paper dolls just like real people and even make cars for them.

"I dunno, what you wanna do?" I scarfed down breakfast and began to pack a lunch of raw sweet potatoes.

"You wanna steal some of Grummo's fruit?"

"Naa, gotta whuppin for that yesterday."

"Wanna play Man?"

"Naaa played that last night."

"Hey! Daddy's makin a garden. Lets us make one." With sweet potatoes in hand, out we went.

The first thing we had to have was good soil. Black dirt was the most fertile soil, Daddy had always said. The old Blackjack tree shaded our favorite playing ground. Many an ant had met its Maker under that tree and many a grasshopper stumbled one-legged to his defeat. It also had really black dirt. So this had to be the place.

"Hey, there's a lotta beans in the dirty clothes house, so lets us plant beans," said Sandy.

"Yeah, Daddy plants beans too," I added.

Planting beans was more than a notion. The stupid black clay argued with every chop of the hoe and how rocks got that deep in the ground I did not know. Sandy said the dogs put them in there. Working in Oklahoma sun is serious business. The heat is dry and always there. Sweat seemed to fall from every pore. The only hope was ol' Blackjack. Even under ol' Blackjack I could feel the constant pressure of the sun. I prayed to Jesus-on-the-wall for relief but not a breeze came. Where was that stupid Jesus-on-the-wall now anyway? I guess he only worked at night. I was determined to be a farmer, so back to the ground I went.

"Now, you get the rake and smooth out the part I dug up," said

Sandy. Raking wasn't anywhere near as bad as digging, so I accepted this assignment with joy. All day we dug in the ground, turning over rocks and Big Boy's bones and even a nickel. We stopped only for our lunch of sweet potatoes. Finally, as the sun became less of a threat and ol' Blackjack's arms grew wider, we finished the plowing. The ground smelled sweet and looked like millions of broken up pieces of chocolate cake. The broad Oklahoma sky seemed to smile at us for a job well done.

"You figga God made this dirt?"

"God made everything."

"You figga God can fly?"

"I figga God can do most anything he wants to."

"Daddy say farmin close to God we goan get." I paused and gazed into the sky. "God sho must be somethin."

The next task would be to plant the beans. The beans were kept in the dirty clothes house, which was really more like a shack than a house. There were as many holes as there were boards in the dirty clothes house but Mama said it was a house so it was a house. As we opened the door all we could see was a multi-colored rag mountain but not beans.

"They must be in here somewhere," said Sandy as he began to fling clothes hand over fist.

Finally in the back under the diapers we found the can with the words "USDA BEANS." As I raised the lid, I was greeted by millions of eyes all seeming to say "Pick me! Pick me!" As I stood paralyzed by indecision, Sandy progressed to more challenging tasks.

"Can you do that?" he questioned as a bean zinged in front of me. "Take a bean and put it in ya mouth and then do ya lips like this," he said as he bugled his lips. "Then blow out."

I took the bean, savored it, and stretched out my lips. Just as I sucked in my breath, up walked Louis.

"Whut ya'll doin? I'mmo tell Mama ya'll out here messin in these clothes."

The bean shot down my throat causing me to gag until I though my throat would come out my nose. The air around me grew black and I could feel my knees turning to jello when a crash to the back sent me mangled to the ground. As shapes began to reappear, my first sight was the sun reflecting off something shining and then nothing but teeth: Louis.

"AhhhHaHaHaHa! I'mmo tell! I'mmo tell!" he screamed as he barely missed my advancing fist.

"Go ahead," challenged Sandy, "an I'll tell Mama you peed in the bed."

Louis skidded to a halt, gave a hurrumph and stomped away in defeat.

"C'm oan Hellin," said Sandy as he walked away. I grabbed a random handful of beans and ran to catch my hero.

As we neared our garden plot, I looked up once more in wonder at the brilliant orange sky.

"You think God got wings?"

Sandy stopped and with one hand on his chin replied slowly, "Could be, could be."

"You think His wings like buttaflies or grasshoppas?"

"Buttaflies, buttaflies orange as the sky and black as the dirt."

As we began dropping beans onto the ground I imagined God soaring through the sky with orange butterfly wings dropping clouds as easily as we were dropping beans.

The beans looked like Louis' uncombed head: rows of little, black settlements neatly and distinctly placed on a brown smooth background. The hard lumps of clay were my friends now. I placed each bean in its bed and eased them under blankets of earth. All we had to do was to water them. Water and wait.

Each and every morning we eagerly checked the progress of our children, watering and oooing and awing at each new floor. At the first sight of what we thought was a weed we brought out our hoe and slayed the enemy. Our babies repaid us by growing quickly and strongly. Soon beans hung like long plaits from each and every plant.

"Tomorrow we can pickem," announced Sandy proudly.

As night arose, I tossed and turned in anticipation. As the monsters came I called to Jesus-on-the-wall, but he didn't do anything. Finally, I forgot ol' Jessus-on-the-wall and began to think about the sky and Daddy and Sandy and the next thing I knew it was morning. It was picking day. Today I would be a farmer! I snatched on my clothes and skidded through the kitchen. Just as I placed my foot out the screen door, a hand snatched me blind.

"Where you going' gal?" bellowed Mama.

"Uhhhhh, brush my teeth."

"With no sodee?"

Why would I need clean teeth to pick beans? I thought but knew much better than to say. Dragging my toes I picked up the soda and went out to the faucet to wash. In the corner of my eye I could see our little darlings waving good morning. I waved back and went to the kitchen to eat breakfast.

"You spose ta wash them diapas today."

"But Mama—"

"Don't you back talk me."

All life left my body as Sandy quietly whispered, "We'll pick the beans later." My face felt like melting silly putty and my feet as heavy as rocks, but I had no thoughts of disobeying Mama, so out to the dirty clothes house I went.

The lifeless mounds of diapers did not seem eager to see me and I most definitely did not think they were cute. Yet, each one thanked me as I released them from prison with soap and water and set them flying through the air on the clothesline. For awhile it seemed like the mountain grew, but gradually I came to the last stinky diaper.

The sun was high overhead and Sandy was gone to play baseball with Junior down the street. So I patiently waited under ol' Blackjack checking every few minutes to see if Sandy was coming. Finally, I saw him and I took out running and screaming, "Can we pickem now? Can we pickem now?"

"Yep, but first we got to go eat and then get a bucket."

After choking down my lunch, I began to search frantically for a bucket. At last we were doing it! We were going to pick the beans! We would be farmers now for sure. As we cornered the house, we saw ol' Blackjack, we saw the black dirt but we did not see one solitary bean. My heart tried to jump from my chest, but my chest kept beating it back. My face tightened as I fought back the tears of disappointment. Where are they? Had the dogs ate them? Did the grasshoppas carry them off? We would never be farmers now. We both sunk to the ground and lay our heads in ol' Blackjack's breast. Streams of tears burst from my face and Sandy was still and silent. As I sweeped my face, what should I see but one lone bean lying on the ground. Buckets of tears poured from my face as Sandy assured me we would plant another garden.

Just as we were about to go steal some of Grummo's fruit, we saw Louis and Sue coming from around the house arm in arm. There dangling from the hands of a four year old were our precious beans, stalks and all.

"See what I gave Sue for Mutha's Day?"

"Mutha's Day. This ain't no Mutha's Day."

Sandy covered Louis like a blanket, as Sue missed the ground by one step. Dirt and grass and Louis and Sandy were one, twisting and twirling like a tumbleweed. When all was quiet, Sandy got up and dusted off his pants.

"C'mon Hellin, lets us go play."

It was times like this that I loved Sandy the most. He had saved my honor. Defeated my enemy. He was my hero and my friend.

We were't farmers yet, but someday, somehow Sandy would find a way.

JUDY RAY

MIDDLE EARTH

Down under farm fields
of this middle earth—
beneath pock-marked mud,
rows of burnt straw, and
one black Hereford
bull standing belly
deep in a small pond—
sit ordinary
young men, two of them,
two voluntary
hostages to a
midwest minefield of
missiles. These clean-cut
young men are programmed
to turn together
upon command
two keys in a red
metal box just as
the computer is
programmed to give them
that brief command for
Armageddon.
        But
now our helpless trust
must rest with just one
young man, George, who
expects one day to
have to turn that key.
He has to be careful,
calm, and conscientious.
His buddy, after
all, has just been court-
martialled for turning
a submachine gun
on a dog.

JUDY RAY

FOR SAM: LOOKING BACK

Far down the lane
a fence leans
and you lean on the fence.
A wood thickens dark
behind you.
The sleeves of your
plaid shirt are
elbow rolled as always,
and you look back this way.

You look back this way
with that smile that is
snowdrop—shy and wistful
despite your rugged stance.
In photos we've often
caught you laughing,
sunflower-bright:
you falling in loon-haunted lakes,
glistening from an after-sauna swim.

If this were a photo—
the fence leaning
and you leaning on the fence—
I would enlarge it
to bring you closer.

We would bring you closer
if this lengthening lane were not
a ribbon of sadness.
We would lean beside you,
say what will always
be unsaid although
we say it daily
to rocks,
to wind,
to pillows,
to altars where candles
keep the words burning on.

JUDY RAY

THE SHOPLIFTER'S CONFESSION

Why do you always want to know *why*?
It was January, after all,
Winter inside and out, and my coat
Had no pockets. I had nothing warm
To hold except a cup of tea
(I paid for that) in the steamy station
Cafe where I could sit and pretend
I had somewhere to go.
New Year's Eve, or the End of the Year,
Had been just that—all draining away
In the blood of what should have been new.
Have you noticed the mirrors in that
Department store? They're like a fairground
Funhouse showing fat and thin, stretched necks,
Dwarf legs. Everything there is offered
In a myriad of nameless colors.
The gloves were simple, though, the simplest
I could find, just navy blue.
Don't you see? My hands were cold!
Everything I touch turns cold.
No, not *gold*! No-one would question that.

Yes, that's my pen. Did I steal that too?
Perhaps I borrowed it from someone
And forgot to give it back. After all,
Your pencil there says DUMP TRUCK PRODUCTS,
ELLSWORTH MOTOR FREIGHT LINES, INC.
And you're using it for doodles.
I thought I would write a letter,
Then think of a friend to send it to.
I've written twenty-seven now,
All to a lover far away
Who left no forwarding address.
I'll mail them in the river
To be washed and eddied out to sea.

When I found the clock I was really
Trying to get back, to be on time.
Everyone was busy in that shop,
Selling to be busy, buying
To be busy—hardware, furniture,
Practical stuff. I wanted to ask
About the alarm—would it be a

Raucous buzz to jar me from nightmares?
A gentle chime so I'd stretch and always
Think it Sunday? A cuckoo that would
Cuckoo thirteen times? I lugged that clock
Up and down the aisles, but no-one
Had time to listen to my questions.
I suppose you think that's clever,
To suggest that I was stealing time
Because I stood at the precipice
Edge of a decade, or sought a
Time bomb ticking towards punishment.
But I just wanted to wake up,
To find a job to wake up for.
We frame our lives with time
And I had none to frame.

Why is your tone more serious now
When you turn to my square of russet
Carpet? Perhaps because you see no
"Extenuating circumstances" of need?
Because it's bigger? I didn't slip
That in my bag, you're right. I made a fuss
About how to roll it up, left all
Confused, and walked out brazenly. I
Wandered for miles with that carpet under
My arm like a giant baguette,
Thinking of the flaming echo of
Autumn leaves on fiery palette.
At the museum I had to leave
My package in the coat room, of course.
These other things that seem to bother you
Appeared when I unrolled the carpet
Scrap, my prayer-mat, if you like.
A hunk of cheese, some dates, a loaf of bread,
A leather collar for a dog
(though it's too cold for a picnic
and my dog died in a ditch,
hit by a car), and this paperback,
Down And Out In Paris and London.

No, I'm not forgetting the statue.
That's what everyone has screamed and scowled
About. Is it because she's a goddess?
How am I supposed to know if those
Are really rubies and emeralds
At her neck, in her hair? They should be
If she's a goddess. Have you followed
The grain of the wood that curves with
The turn of her head? I've sat for hours

Wondering if she's cold too.
Despite her beauty, and the love
There must have been at her creation.
You're going to take her back now, right?
What's so outrageous about my
Respectful contemplation?
"A thing of beauty. . ." you know,
And "for ever" might not be long.

Why do you always want to know why?
Don't you see that nothing plus something
Often equals nothing?
When I challenged the Funhouse
Mirrors they showed me nothing.
No lover listened, or dreamed
Of fishing in blood-red oceans for
Twenty-seven muddy letters.
And everything I touched and took
Back to my room turned cold.

Judy Ray

MARIA A. REED

ADULT EDUCATION

Why think,
after this long decade
of that first formal encounter
with self and expression?

We sat close at the table
paint and paper placed before us.
I marvelled at your ease, your flair,
for motion and hue,
the colors flow from your brush,
while I panicked at the vast
expanse of unmarked white
seeing only irrevocable commitment,
brush poised between opportunity
lost or gained.

We were to paint the evening sky,
clouds violet, rose, gold
billowed across your page:
I despaired;
mine never would change
once caught within the confines
of paper, paint and frame.

IN THE GARDEN

*"Of temporal man, who
can say, This is . . ."*

Veracity held tight the bough
before the serpent's goad to
taste the select fruit:
Will juice-stained
lips speak truth
besot with ambiguity,
to name the tree,
the clay, the clouds
of that one God, who
tempt the ignorance of grace
with
ripeness?

MARIA A. REED

APPLE HARVEST

The last apples lay in the bin
soft, misshapen, out of season.
I smelled them in the cool
darkness of the cellar and gathered them
to the gray drip of a reluctant spring.

The peels spiralled beneath my fingers
exposing a crushing winter's bruises,
tender, translucent flesh netted brown
where pressure and time had weighed heavy.

Salvaged slice upon slice
fell into the spongeware bowl.
Juices melded
(lemon, sugar, spices)
within the fragile crust
till steaming it emerged:
heady scent of autumn,
ripe season of our love.

C. A. RHOADS

THIS END UP

I was standing in the south kitchen door with my hands full of paint brushes and sponges and the like when Ma's old '49 Chevy pulled up to the gate. Buck Barr, having heard the engine drone as Ma shifted to second to take the last, steepest part of the lane, had already slunk away, back to his pickup truck and his bottle. Remembering his hands on me, the smell of his alcohol breath, and the feel of his sticky beard stubble, I wondered why Ma was always attracted to that kind. But Ma with Buck Barr wasn't the only puzzle. There was a violent trembling in me, and a heat like I'd never known before. Yet, here I was, for all the world, trying to act normal. To act like there wasn't nothin' on my mind but getting us moved into a new place.

Cissy and Caleb piled out of the Chevy and raced past me without a glance. Through the huge country kitchen with its sickly, pale green wainscotting they went, nary a glance at the oversized cookstove that reminded me of nothing more than a monster spider out of a "B" movie. But they stopped short in the tiny front room. It had no electricity; therefore, no light. Squeezed between two flanking bedrooms, it seemed like a pinched bird's breast, trying vainly to support out-sized, energy-sapping wings. But it was wallpaper which had arrested Cissy and Caleb. White wall paper, it was, to make up for the lack of light. And on the wallpaper, in bright red serapes, little Mexican boys attempted to jump over bright green cacti by the hundreds. They all—those Mexicans— fairly jumped off the walls. I 'spect it was the most colorful room Cissy and Caleb had ever seen.

I watched Cissy as she spun slowly on the heel of one scuffed penny loafer. Both of her socks, gray with overuse, had crawled down her heels. Her heels were lookin' gray, too. Gangling arms and legs angled from the too-small hand-me-downs. Thin as slats, they were, and freckled and sun-toughened as a peach during a drouth. At eleven Cissy still had not learned to manage her limp, flaxen hair and it hung to her shulders in a tangle.

Caleb snuffed a drip up one nostril and stared around in wonder. Excepting the fact that he was only three and barefoot, he was Cissy's exact male counterpart.

Mostly them two were called "the kids." Sometimes I was counted in on that, sometimes not. It depended a lot on whether Ma wanted me to shut up and mind my manners, which made me a "kid," or whether she wanted me to tackle a job she didn't want to be bothered with, which separated me from her two little ones.

Cissy and Caleb discovered the patch of sunlight that was a screen door opening onto the west porch at the same time. On silent cue they banged through it. I joined them at the porch railing, enjoying the long, sloping view which ended half a mile away with a line of trees bordering the west side of Hiway 65. Presently I heard Ma giving Granny the grand tour. They were in one of the bedrooms. "There's twice as much storage room as in the old house, Mom," she said in her too-gay voice. It was the voice she used when she wanted to convince us we'd never before been so well off. The voice that said, You'd better like it, because this is the way it's gonna be.

In each bedroom one whole wall was given over to "built-in" closets and storage cupboards. Although the rooms were newly papered and scrubbed clean of sixty-odd years of other people's lives, there was something of shoddy workmanship in the wafer-thin closet doors. Covered with matched wallpaper so that they might disappear into the wall when closed, the doors were warping away from their moorings. I heard a closet door slap shut.

"I suppose it'll be alright," came Granny's soft answer. Nothing from Ma then, and in my mind's eye I could see her heavy face settle into a grim, defiant attitude. When Ma spreads enthusiasm about, she wants enthusiasm back.

Avoiding the bedroom, I made my way back to the kitchen to look for something to open the gallon of gray floor paint Ma found on a pantry shelf. Out in the sunlight—beyond the weedy green of the fenced-in yard with its rusted well pump, "the boys" leaned against a dirty pickup, companionably sharing a bottle of wine. Sometimes boy friends passed into and out of Ma's life without my ever meeting them, so it wasn't strange that I didn't know these two. One was Buck Barr, Ma's new boyfriend; the other was Hoover Casson, whom Ma called "a harmless wino." Since, together with Ma, they both put in a tolerable good day sucking on the exposed end of one brown-sacked bottle or another, I wouldn't have known which wino was which if Buck hadn't told me, "I like *all* the women in the Warren family."

There's gonna be a lot of gray around here, I thought, bringing my gaze back to the paint.

"We're gonna take care of this here linoleum," Ma said, pointing her toe at the worst of the faded areas. The boys were finishing up with the first load of furniture. We were standing in the empty kitchen. "This is Armstrong linoleum. It'll last years. Best there is. No use spending good money on another when all we gotta do is paint over the old design." Her voice climbed into that fake cheerfulness and her green eyes were shining with her own cleverness. "Ha-ha." The last 'ha' was practically a lilt, "that's how the Armstrong people do it; no reason we can't beat them at their own game."

I looked doubtfully at the old linoleum. I didn't think the design was painted on at all. But I didn't know for sure, and I knew I couldn't argue Ma outa the idea. You couldn't argue Ma outa anything.

Footsteps. Some plotting, others more purposeful. A deep slow drawl said, "I gotta take a leak." That was Hoover. His plodding footsteps faded as he descended the west porch stairs one at a time. Buck Barr— I still didn't know who he was then— came into the kitchen.

"Let me see your knife, hon," Ma said to him.

Dutifully he pulled a grimy Barlow from his jeans pocket, taking

140

more time than necessary to fetch it away from his groin and staring me up and down speculatively all the while. It wasn't the first time. He'd been watching me every chance he got; but, maybe because of all the booze he'd guzzled, he was getting more bold as the day wore on. The other one, he'd taken to watching me too, but never said anything. Not even with his eyes. Eyes can tell you a lot, but not his. It gave me the willies.

Ma, busy with her thoughts, didn't notice Buck. She tested a blade and then began to cut off the corners of the three sponges, turning their rectangular shapes into diamonds and circles and squares. "Sissors would work a lot better," she mumbled. "But God only knows where they are."

"Got the bedsteads all set up and ready for action," Buck said. He ran his hand over Ma's rump in a slow, possessive way. And while he did it he stared right into my eyes. Ma looked slightly annoyed, but pleased at the same time, knowing I was right there, but not wanting to discourage Buck's affection. She moved away from him a bit and he let his hand drop to his side. I felt my face go red. Buck chuckled. "That's all. This trip."

"See," Ma turned to me, "after you get the floor painted with the gray and it has had time to dry, why then you can dip these into tins of red and black paint and set them down on the linoleum. You won't have to move them around or anything, they'll leave a design all by themselves. Okay?"

"Yeah," I agreed, trying to ignore Buck's smirk.

Ma put her arm around his neck, then, happy-go-lucky like said, "You boys think you can get the last of the furniture this trip?"

"Don't know why not," Buck replied, nuzzling her neck and brushing the palm of his hand over her breast, "if the other half of this movin' firm ever gets done pissin'."

"Mom'll have the last of the boxes packed by the time we get back to the other house. We'll put as many as we can on the truck and that way I can bring her and the kids with me in the car. It'll save that much gas."

The other half of the moving firm, as Buck called him, put a booted foot on the sill of the porch and leaned against the doorjamb. The day was hot and bright behind him, but his face was in a shadow. "Anything left in that bottle?"

Buck grinned, headed for the door. "Out one end and in the other."

Ma tossed her head, making her thick red hair, drawn up in a pony tail, look all the more horse-like. "We won't paint til later. Carla, you stay here and unload boxes. Get things put away. Won't be room for you in the car on the way back, anyway."

She was walking away. Going, the way the day was going. "Are you gonna get the kids' fireworks?" I asked her back.

"Oh, for God's sake!" She spun on me. "Fireworks, fireworks! That's all I've heard all day long. First from the kids, now from you!"

"But it's the third. If you don't get them today—"

"I know what day it is. If I get 'em, I'll get 'em. If I don't, I don't."

Ma went on out, hurring as she neared the pickup. Men were Ma's fireworks; her candy; her wine. I saw her throw her head back and laugh when Buck turned a bottle upside down and waggled it to show it was empty. The three of them, Ma, Buck and Hoover, talked for a few minutes and then climbed into the two vehicles and drove off.

"The firewords are important!" I said aloud. But there was no one there to hear. There never had been.

I knew how disappointed the kids would be if Ma didn't get a few sparklers, at least, or some snakes for them. It was alright for me— I was older and I'd had plenty of chances to learn how to stand up to disappointment. Trouble was, I wasn't old enough to do anything about it. Sixteen and useless, that was me. I looked down at myself, at strong suntanned arms and legs, slender but sturdy body. Useless, I amended, except for doing chores.

But somebody had to do something. Granny wouldn't be any help. I bent over one of the boxes she'd packed. Packed frantically and in stunned silence. Strange the way Granny took orders from Ma—not as if she were totally dependent upon Ma, though she was—but more like she were just one more harrassed kid. Ma had grand contempt for all the millstones that pulled her down and kept her from the wonderful life she wanted to live. The kids and I felt that contempt often enough, but Granny kept things close. I wondered how it was doing damage to her.

Ma had come racketing in this morning after being out all night, tossing cardboard boxes into the middle of the front room and calling us all sleepy heads because she found us still in bed at five o'clock. "Why, it's the shank of the morning," she'd said, mouthing a string of platitudes, "half the morning's been wasted; it's the early bird gets the worm." Remembering put a sour taste in my mouth. Even from across the room I could smell the liquor on her, see her eyes were bloodshot. But she had been steady on her feet—so not drunk—and any tiredness she felt was hidden in the determined excitement of the moment. She had kissed Cissy's forehead and given Caleb a perfunctory hug and then announced: "We're movin', kids. To a new house." Then she'd thrust her jaw out at Granny and challenged, "It's all set."

The kids began bouncing around, chanting, "We're gon-na move, we're gon-na mo-ve."

Granny's eyes dropped to her flannel gown, threadbare and too large for her, and too hot to be wearing in July. But it was all she had. "What about—"

"*Every*thing's been taken care of," Ma cut her short. Her eyes warned Granny not to say too much.

It wasn't a matter of keeping anything from us. The kids were too young to understand and I already knew what Ma had in mind. Two months behind in the rent, and what with the fourth coming up, our landlord had left town for a long weekend. When he returned, his rental property would be empty. The trail two days cold. One situation almost begged the other, didn't it? I knew as well as Ma that he probably wouldn't bother to track us down, even though we were only a few miles distant. He'd simply be glad to be rid of "that Warren bunch." No, there hadn't been anything to hide. No shame was involved, not on Ma's part. She just hadn't wanted any argument. She hadn't gotten any.

All Ma and Granny's clothes—moved on hangers—were hung away. I'd made up beds and stood on a chair putting extra blankets in an upper storage cupboard in Ma's room when I heard the noise of Buck's truck coming up the driveway.

No doubt there'd be more boxes on that truck, and furniture too, that needed carrying in and putting to rights. But I felt in no hurry to meet up with the boys, so I closed the two doors— one that led up to the front room and one that let out onto the north porch—and determined to keep quiet and out of the way until Ma showed up. She'd not be bashful about calling me help.

It wasn't such a smart idea. Buck must've made a beeline for the house. And for the bedrooms, when he didn't find me right away. It wasn't no time before I heard his mocking voice. "Well, well, you've got this lookin' real nice. Real nice." Though he wasn't a big man, he seemed to fill the room. And though he made no move that could be considered threatening, when his calculating eyes moved from bed to me and back again, I was afraid.

And I felt something else. There ain't no use to deny it: although Buck was sweaty and had more than one day's growth of beard, and though he had on him enough alcohol stink to make my stomach lurch, his presence, the fact that he looked on me as an object of desire— well, that excited me. His black, curly hair and black eyes—probably considered good looking to some, I reckon. To Ma, for sure. There for a time I didn't know if I was scared because something might happen or because it might not.

"Where's Ma?" I asked and watched him grin.

"Why, your Ma is gonna be a little while. Said she had to run to town before it gets too late."

"She's getting the kids' fireworks?"

"Well, I dunno. Could be." He came toward me, reached out and touched my chin. "You're just as pretty as a picture, know that? I like hair cut in a bob like yours."

"Don't you think that other guy might need your help?"

He looked me up and down again, for maybe a dozenth time. "Could be," he said, his mouth pulled sideways wistfully. "Could be *I'm* the one who needs the help."

It was right then we heard Ma's old Chevy drone. Buck dodged over to the window to look. "Damn." While he was there, cursing under his breath, I ran from the room.

I had time to pick up the paint brushes and sponges, time to get as far as the south porch when Buck caught up to me and in one swift motion shoved me roughly against the wall. I might have done a better job fighting him off if I'd the sense to drop those things. As it was I shoved him with elbows and knees which didn't do much to stop his hands from touching me where nobody ever had before. He clamped

143

his mouth on mine, seemed not to find any satisfaction in that and then buried his face in the crook of my neck. Then he staggered away from me, groaned and grabbed at his swelled crotch. I didn't want to look but I couldn't help myself. He saw my gaze and seemed to shudder. Rocking drunkenly —but not from drink—his eyes bored into mine. "It'll happen," he said, "it'll happen."

The sound of Ma's car shifting down for the hill sent him slinking away. It took maybe a whole minute for me to realize that my thighs, my whole body was aching strangely.

So much gray. I didn't know how long I'd been there on my knees staring at that blasted paint can, day dreaming, but it was long enough for the kids to lose interest in swarming over and around the porch steps. They blasted into the kitchen, skidding on their knees beside me like a couple of airplanes coming in for a landing. It always did me good to see them in such a state of happiness, even when it took so pitifully little to please them.

I chucked Caleb in the ribs. "What's up?"

Caleb giggled and looked at Cissy conspiratorially. Cissy leaned close and whispered, "She got 'em."

"She did? Where are they?"

"In the car. In a box on the back seat."

"What kinds?"

Cissy shrugged. Caleb, her mirror image, shrugged too. "They was in a box with a lid," Cissy explained.

And so they didn't dare look for fear of angering Ma.

"Where's Ma now?"

"She stinks," Caleb quipped. Cissy giggled.

"That's what *she* said. She said, 'I'm gonna take me a bath. I been workin' so hard, I stink.' "

"Shoot! What's she done, except drive the car and drink—"

"Huh?" Cissy asked.

"Nothin'. Where's she takin' her bath?"

Cissy pointed to the closed door leading to the north porch. "Granny dragged the tub out there and fixed her water. But Ma ain't in it, yet. She's ironin' a dress." The towhead nodded knowingly.

So Ma figured on going out again tonight. With "the boys." It was going dark. Both vehicles were parked beyond the gate. No sign of the moving crew.

"You two hungry?"

"Granny fixed sandwiches," Caleb said. "At the other house."

"And there's one for you, Carla," Cissy remembered. "In a sack," she shrugged apologetically. "It's on the front porch. I guess I forgot."

"That's alright. If you two want to split it, I'm not hungry," I lied, knowing that they were always hungry as pups.

As soon as they'd banged through the screen door, I slipped out to the car. Nothing stirred except a few june bugs. There on the back seat, just like Cissy had said, was a box with the flap lid obscuring its contents. It had a number stamped on it in two places and the words "Pleasantvl, MO." Nothing else except "This End Up" with two arrows.

I eased open the car door and reached in.

Booze. That's what I found. A six pack of Falstaff, two bottles of cheap wine, and a half-pint of Old Charter. I let the lid drop back into place. Should've known, I told myself. There were stands every few miles, all up and down the highway, if she'd been going to buy fireworks. But the only liquor stores to be found were in Pleasantville.

"So, that's what you like." It was Buck's sardonic voice. I tried to scramble out of the car but he pinned me against the back of the seat. He snaked one hand into the box and brought out a bottle of wine before backing out of the car and pulling me out with him. "I'll be glad to share with you," he whispered. I saw Hoover over his shoulder, staring at us with eyes sleepy from too many drinks; he drew the back of his hand across his lips in a hungry gesture. Buck muscled himself between my legs. Slowly, methodically he thrust his hips forward. Once. Twice. Three times. "I want to share everything with you," he rasped. I pushed at him, my breath became ragged, too. Abruptly he stopped and half turning tossed the bottle to Hoover, who caught it as if rehearsed. Now, both hands were free. He grasped my buttocks and lifted me from the ground, pressing tighter and tighter.

I had the heels of both hands dug into his chest, but as strong as I am, it was futile. "I ain't trying to steal your booze," I said, "I just wanted to see if Ma got the kids their fireworks."

"Is that what you want?" his chest was heaving. He stopped again.

I made myself look him in the eye. "Yeah," I said, I could see he was thinking.

He dropped me and stepped back, frowning. His eyes never left mine. "There's a stand not a mile away. I can be back inside of fifteen minutes."

I swallowed. "Not if you pick out a good selection."

He said nothing for a moment. "Twenty, then. The damndest bunch of fireworks you ever saw." If he was waiting for me to say something he was disappointed. Finally he spun on heel and leaped into his pickup, opening and closing the door in one smooth motion. "Get in, Hoove," he ordered.

Hoover was still trying to get his door shut when I lost sight of the truck. For all my trembling weakness, I made it back to the porch before Ma came out to see what was going on.

"Where'd they go to?" she asked.

"I dunno," I lied. I was getting good at it. "They must've run out of cigarettes or something. I heard them saying something about Camels."

"Camels? That's funny. Buck smokes Kools. And Hoover'll smoke anything he can bum."

"Oh."

"Did they say they're coming back?"

"Yeah."

"Huh! Well, it'll give me a little more time for my bath. I sure wish there was at least a tea kettle of hot water to put in it," she sighed. "But your granny can't think of where to find any wood for the cook-stove. And we can't set up the kerosene range until you get that

145

floor painted. I do wish you'd manage around here without me showing every step of the way."

"You want me to try to find some wood?"

"Nah. It's too dark now. You better geta start on painting that linoleum, though. It must be getting on for eight o'clock. You don't want to be up all night." She yawned at the thought, and then laughed at something only she could see, her eyes showing the strain of being awake so many hours. She let herself sag for just a minute and then stretched the weariness away. Jaunty of step, she closed the porch door behind her, shutting herself away from our dreary lives.

I let myself out of the house again, thinking to call the kids to me and tell them about the bunch of fireworks on the way. Instead, unnoticed, I sprawled under a hackberry tree and watched them chase fireflies.

My mind was a jumble over the predicament I'd gotten myself into. Buck thought he'd struck a bargain. Down on the highway strings of lights filed by, mechanical fireflies, they were, that no kid could hope to catch. I wished time to stand still or to rocket forward, past this night. It did neither.

It was velvety dark when a pair of headlights slowed and made the turn into the lane, bobbing up and down torching the way for the speeding pickup. I waited. The gravel crunched. The racing of the engine before the ignition is cut. Doors slamming. And finally, the rattle of a grocery sack near my right ear. The man had the homing instincts of a bat.

"Hey. Kids!" Buck called. And they came running. Obedient and anticipatory, with large eyes zeroing in on the bag stuffed to overflowing. "It's the fourth of July," Buck crowed. "Time to celebrate."

"Not 'til tomorrow," Cissy meekly disagreed. How painful to see her anxiety, wanting the fireworks, not wanting to do anything to cause this generous Santa to withhold them.

"What?"

"It's not the fourth 'til tomorrow. Sir." Cissy added hastily.

A scowl formed on Buck's face, then disappeared. Almost. "Well, there's enough here for both nights." He held out the sack.

Cissy turned to me. "Is it okay?"

I nodded. "Only the sparklers and smoke bombs and such. And be careful of the matches." I gazed at Buck as I spoke. "You brought matches?"

"I didn't forget nothin'," he snarled.

Letting out a whoop, Cissy took the sack from his outstretched hand and sped away. Caleb ran fast after her.

Buck gripped my arm and jerked me to my feet. "It's time we did a little celebratin' of our own," he said thickly. "Let's go sit in the pickup."

"—no!"

"What?" he demanded, anger rising in his tone.

"Let's don't go there. Let's. . .let's go to the bedroom." I pointed toward Ma's room.

A slow smile came to his face as he put his hands on my shoulder, kneading gently. "Anything you say, baby." He took my hand and pulled me through the black night into the darkened house. I felt dazed. It was, suddenly, like being in another dimension where time avoided its own rules. With a quick sense of alarm it occurred to me that events might be moving too quickly. Maybe it hadn't taken as long as I'd figured for Buck to fetch the kids some fireworks.

I must have been hanging back because when we reached the bedroom Buck's patience snapped. In seconds he'd thrown me down on the bed and fell on top of me, springs squalling in protest. His laughter was loud but he whispered, "So, you wanna have a little fun on yer Ma's bed, huh? Well, that just makes it all the sweeter for me."

His hands, moving between us like hard knots of wood, unzipped his pants. Then he began groping for the zipper in my cutoffs. I guess I kinda yelped, for he lifted up.

"What the hell?"

"Wait. . .you're going too fast." I couldn't get enough air and my heart was thudding wildly. "I'd. . .I like it to be slow."

He propped himself up on his elbows. "Get under me, square, and spread your legs. Like this," he grunted impatiently while I dallied. "I don't never hafta show yer Ma. . .but that's alright, I'll play teacher."

Buck slid his hands down to my rump again, pulling me against him. He grunted softly at each deliberate thrust of his hips. I tried to count them, but kept losing my place. "I've heard of women who like to be dry humped," he murmured, "but you're the first I've had."

My breath was becoming harsh. The strange ache I'd felt earlier was back. I wondered where Granny was. Was she already asleep? And Ma? Ma was taking an awful long time with her bath. Awful long.

When Buck moved in order to fumble with the buttons of my blouse, I adjusted my postion so that the feeling wouldn't go away. Nothing else seemed to matter, then. Not the fuzzy stupor I felt, not the fact that he was ripping my blouse in his haste, not the fact that he was accomplishing what he wanted all along.

Of course, that was the moment Ma chose to open the door and flip on the light. She'd come back to her bedroom, just like I thought she would.

"Sonofabitch!" Buck roared, his eyes which were kinda glazed over took on a quick, wary look when he saw her standing over us, wrapped in a towel and looking about as stunned as I ever hope to see her.

Even though I'd planned it, I admit I was plenty scared. We both scrambled to our feet, tugging at our clothing. I could see that he was thinking hard, trying to come up with some kind of explanation, wondering what tact to take with Ma.

And Ma showed him the way. She stepped across the floor to get at me, slapped me on the side of my head, very nearly knocking me down. "You slut! You little slut! And *you*," she whirled on Buck, "just what in the hell do you think you're doing?"

"Oh, baby," he soothed, "you don't understand. . ."

I left them to it, slipped around Ma's back and out the room, out of the house, and down the porch stairs to the welcome blackness of the night. The air felt cool and good on my burning face. A lot of things would be different in this new house, it occurred to me then. Out of pure cussedness, I crept close to Ma's window to listen to them threshing out their differences. I had no doubt that they would. It was the means they used to adjust themselves to this snag in their relationship that interested me.

"—come on, now," Buck was saying in a cajolling voice. "You know me better than that! Why, I got kids of my own her age. But, God Almighty, when she just kept waggin' it under my nose. . . I'm only just a man, after all."

"She's too young for that sort of thing," Ma said. But I heard the doubt in her tone. So did Buck.

"Too young, hell!" I heard his zipper screel. "Look at this! She's a pretty little bitch, is all," Buck went on, "and you know I've been needing you all day. Why, if you'd been there instead of her, I'd have been doing some fine work with this. But as it was, I was *tryin'* to hold off. I knowed it wasn't right."

"Don't you ever touch Carla again."

"You kiddin'? When I got a real woman to take care of me?"

Silence. He'd be kissing her, I supposed. I heard the bedroom door shut and saw the light go out. I supposed right. In no time there came a rhythmic squealing of bed noise.

So that was that. Ma enjoying her fireworks. The kids theirs. And me, I still had the kitchen floor to paint. I took one step and ended up in Hoover's arms.

If a person's heart can flutter to a dead stop, mine did then. Out of the frying pan. . .

Hoover took a clumsy step backwards. "You okay?" he asked, laying a palm against my still stinging cheek. Slow words, slow movements; everything the man did seemed to require deep concentration. I couldn't find my voice so I just nodded when he asked me again. He swayed alarmingly backward as he twisted around to look in the kid's direction and back at the darkened bedroom window. As if suddenly remembering where he'd left it, he let his hand fall to his side.

"You gotta be careful of fireworks." So painfully slow.

"They can hurt you. . .if you don't watch." He blinked sleepy eyes at the darkened window again. Then he staggered away.

PHYLLIS J. ROSSITER

STONEY LONESOME

She sat bolt upright in bed. Across the hollow the sun gilded the rounded pate of the mountain known for a hundred years as Bald Jess. For all but a dozen of those years, she had prided herself on catching Bald Jess each dawn still in its gray-green nightshirt, before it blushed in the sunrise.

"Mary Rebecca Bird, you're gettin' plum dilatory in your old age," she chided herself, then remembered that she had resolved not to speak aloud unless the dog was present to provide an excuse. No need to give folks cause to think she was addled just because she was old. For that matter, there was no reason save habit why she should rise at dawn. Except that she needed to store up all the beauty she could against the day those two old men, who called themselves her boys, would make good on their threat to put her away in that so-called rest home.

She exchanged her muslin nightgown for a dress made by her own hand of chicken linen and watched as the morning light likewise transformed Bald Jess. Unbidden memories came to mind of the day her man Coy had cut that window into the logs so she could see the mountain of her birth. She slid a hand—could that gnarled claw really be hers?—along the sill he had fashioned and shook her head. Though gone these 25 years, he was more and more on her mind of late.

With the efficiency of long practice she smoothed the feather tick on her bed and tucked the faded cover around it. Her first quilt, pieced when the stiff old fingers had been clumsy young ones. She sighed. These days the recollections seemed nearly as real as the warmth of sunlight.

She fingered the comb her man had fetched all the way from Joplin, slid it through her long gray hair. No need of the looking glass to tell her of the face now as craggy and marred as the bluffs above the river. Every glimpse of it surprised her, for in her heart she was still Becky Bird, the pert young slip of a girl who sang at all the play parties, the bride of the neighborhood's favorite fiddler. They had met when she was 15 and cook to the crew that lumbered the Devil's Elbow. She twisted the lank of hair into a bun at the back of her neck and fastened it with tortoise-shell hairpins. Felled, the fiddler was, by a lifetime of slaving in the timber and the zinc mines and the marble quarries though he was born to be a fiddling mountain man, pure and simple.

She heard the dog on the door rock shake himself and scratch, his leg thumping now and again on the cabin wall. With a smile she called, "Breakfast in a jiffy, King James." He was right; time to shake off the dreams of the night. The dog gave a low growl, an almost inaudible rumble that swelled to a snarl. "What is it, James?" Becky hurried to the door and threw it open. The clearing proved as empty as she'd expected. "Come on in, feller. I got a biscuit for ye."

149

King James barely glanced her way, wagged a brief greeting. Head high, sniffing the air, he stalked a few steps into the yard.

"Why, James, never knowed ye'd to turn your back on a biscuit. . ." She shaded her eyes and peered into the forest. The freshly greened trees pressed in closely all around, but they were friendly. "I declare I don't see a thing," she told the dog. Just the same, he was doing his job as he saw it. "Mought be a hunter in the holler," she muttered.

The sun was not yet high enough to warrant a sunbonnet. Becky hefted the half-empty water bucket from its bench inside the cabin door, and made for the well house at the edge of the yard. Though most of her neighbors had water in their houses— right there in the kitchen— she thought it a pure pleasure not to pack water all the way up the hill from the creek. Her man had chosed this home site for the cold-running spring behind the cabin. For almost half a century it had furnished her with water a few steps from her door. But now, after years of running only in wet weather, it had dwindled to a mere trickle. Her sons had arranged for the drilling of the well while home for their paw's funeral. She could count on the fingers of one hand the number of times they had returned since. She sighed. And then to fret with her about moving to that old folks' home.

King James' nervousness unsettled her. She scanned the sky. No storm clouds gathered, no wind. Head cocked, she listened to the mountain's morning. "Hush, James, be still so's I can hear." The dog fell silent and pressed against her legs. With his fur all puffed out he seemed larger, more menacing. Becky breathed deeply of the spring-scented air to calm her shakiness. She thought the young leaves trembled, too, and the forest was strangely quiet. Missing was the rackety birdsong, the murmur of creatures in the underbrush. Not even a blue-tailed lizard sunned himself on the door rock. A change was on the ridge though she could not guess what, she shivered. Seventy-two years she'd lived on this hillside—most of them safely alone—and never a morning like this one.

"Come on, James." She stepped smartly toward the cabin, the dog at her heels. King James would protect her from all but the wrath of God. And why be scared of such things as could not be helped?

But always there was the fear of being forced to leave her mountain— of being locked up in the city with others past their usefulness and attractiveness. Her sons had prophesied it. A day would dawn, their rare letters threatened, when someone would come to take her away to the nursing home. And what could King James do to stop that?

The restless dog declared himself vigorously now, his earnest bark riddled with growls and snarls. He stood in the middle of the clearing, stiff-legged, the hair bristling on his back. Becky paused in the doorway. The woods crowded the cabin harder now than they had when she and her new husband had come here to take up life together. She was 16, he 17, and Grandpaw had given them these few acres off his homestead. She smiled to herself. Now it was all hers—Grandpaw's land and Uncle Dub's and even her step-paw's. And a lot more that Coy had killed himself to pay for.

She heaved the filled water bucket back to its bench. The hardest job of the day, it was always the first. She called the dog inside and fastened the door. The box of cook wood was nearly empty, but she hated to venture outside again just yet. She laid a fire in the cook stove and dipped water into the tea kettle.

King James had joined her in the cabin willingly enough, but he stood on his hind legs at the window and stared at the clearing. Becky busied herself making their breakfast and talked softly to the dog as she worked. Fond of him, she was, but she had buried so many loyal companions in 88 years that it seemed senseless to make a fuss over one more. To be sure, he was still young—and a right good watchdog. And no doubt she was a sight safer here than in a town where folks were murdered and poisons spilled into the roadways and rivers. Leastways so she heard on the radio.

At the thought of the radio, she started. Perchance there would be news on that contraption that would explain the strange tension on the mountain. With the tail of her apron protecting her hand, she wrestled the cast-iron skillet of potatoes safely onto the warming shelf. Once she had nearly burned down the cabin by forgetting her cooking. She might be hard pressed, at times, to argue her fitness for remaining in the hills alone. But she learned from her mistakes, as she had all her life—and she knew her limits.

She fetched the ancient radio and placed it in the middle of the round table. The cord barely reached to the electrical outlet dangling with the bare light bulb from the ceiling. Becky perched on the edge of a chair and twisted the dials impatiently. "Dang thing's but a nuisance," she told the dog, resisting the reverie of memories attending the ugly box.

King James greeted the first squawk from the radio with a crescendo of barking.

"Hush, James, you fool dog, I can't hear the talking over your noise." She knew her voice lacked conviction for she was no fonder of the thing than he. What need had she of the world beyond her ridgetop? But she was puzzled by the charge she sensed in the air. And a known danger was less to fear than a shadowy dread.

Station after station offered only the loud noise they called music. Becky turned the dial slowly until the more familiar and welcome chords of a gospel song filled the cabin. She lowered the volumn to a harmonious murmur and leaned back in her chair, breakfast forgotten.

The dog exploded into a frenzy of warning and hurled himself against the door. Becky pressed a hand to her chest to calm her thudding heart and crossed shakily to the window. She squinted into the sunlit clearing, almost afraid there would still be nothing there and that the mysterious morning would never end.

But she spotted the man at once—crouched near the well house. He seemed to be watching the cabin, though now and again he darted a glance into the trees behind him. "All right, James, I see him. Good dog. Hush now." The dog quieted and joined her at the window, pressed his nose against the glass as though it knew the secret of the stranger's identity.

Becky stared at the figure in the yard. She chewed her lip and pondered. If he had business with her, why didn't he come to the door? If he was up to no good, it hardly seemed likely he would be so open about it. "I declare, James. You've got me so spooked I plumb forgot my manners." She flung open the cabin door and waved. "Morning! You had breakfast?"

King James dashed into the yard, his tail waving a greeting, his bark one of welcome. The figure by the well house stood erect. When the dog did not attack, the man took a step toward her, then another. James glanced at Becky and paused, careful to stay between her and the stranger.

She studied their visitor as he approached the cabin. He wore bibless overalls and a plaid work shirt, but she did not know him. Under a felt baseball cap, his face was wide, his pale eyes far apart. She was satisfied that they met her gaze without wavering. He had the straight back and high cheekbones of an Indian, but his skin was chalky white. And he was no mountaineer, for his shoes were made of cloth.

A few steps from the door rock, he paused. "Good morning, ma'am." He nodded to Becky and offered a hand to King James. His doffed cap revealed rust-colored hair. "I smelled your wood smoke."

Becky smiled to help put him at ease. He seemed no more than a boy. "I'm afixin' breakfast, lad, and ye be welcome to partake with me."

"Thank you, kindly, ma'am. I am hungry." He bared his teeth in what Becky took for a smile. "But I'd be happy to earn my meal, if there's something you need done." Citified, his speech was.

"Why as it happens, I could stand to have a jag of cook wood split." She marveled that he had found his own way so far back into the hills—and wearing such flimsy shoes. As she turned back to the cabin, she saw that he rolled up his sleeves and headed for the wood pile. It would be a wonder if he knew one end of the axe from another.

She smoothed her hair and returned to the skillet of half-fried potatoes. For the first time in a long while, she was aware of the plainness of her two rooms—the coffee-can canisters, the scarred wood floor, the curtainless windows. She poked up the fire and added more coffee to the steaming pot. Whatever could bring a young city fellow so deep into the hills?

There could be only one answer. She had known it from the moment King James first warned her. The stranger had come to take her away to the old folks' home—when there could be no home for her but this old rackensack cabin. She pushed some canned meat around the skillet and studied about what to do. Every tub must stand on its own bottom, her man used to say, and she was not yet ready for someone else to do her thinking.

Her guest sidled through the door with an armload of wood. Becky watched in surprise as he properly loaded the box beside the cook stove. And cleverly split, the sticks were, belying his fragile appearance.

Cuts and scratches webbed his bare arms.

"Appears you've tangled with the bramble bushes," she observed. "There's a wash pan yonder in the well house."

"Yes, ma'am. Thank you. I helped myself to the wash pan and some water earlier, when I wasn't sure if you were up." He nodded his head in a little bow, stood uncertainly near the door, his gaze flickering over the radio with something like alarm. "Do you have a telephone, ma'am."

Becky shook her head. "Nobody I know left to talk to." She motioned him into a chair at the table. "Though the health nurse said she'd try to get me one for to call help if I need it. Well, I warrant you're ready for this," she said as she slid half of the fried potatoes onto his plate and forked the meat beside them.

"I am indeed, ma'am, and I thank you kindly." He rubbed a faintly red stubble of beard and eyed the food like a hungry dog. Even so, he waited until she filled her own plate and fetched the biscuits and coffee.

Mannersome too, she thought, and a puzzle for sure. She sat stiffly, wondering when last she had shared a table with a young man. Sitting on his haunches, King James took up his post between her and the boy. The dog was watchful, but seemed unworried. Though it might turn out to be the sorriest day of her life, nothing would be served by going hungry. When she picked up her fork, her guest began to eat hungrily.

"Do you live here alone?" he asked between mouthfuls.

She nodded. Surely the rest home must know all about her from her boys. Maybe he meant to test her. "Been widowed these 25 year, but I'm still lively as a tick in a tar pot." She was pleased by a real grin on his face. "I raised two of the meanest boys these hills ever spawned right here in this cabin," she told him. "But they never pay me no never mind. And now I have great-great-grandchildren I've never set eyes on."

He forked another biscuit. "My name is Matthew."

"I was born Mary Rebecca," she said slowly. "And known as Mary Beck for short til I was 6 year old. Then my maw married a man who already had a girl named Mary, and since the new Mary was the oldest, she got to keep the name. My step-paw wanted to call me Becky, but I would have none of it. I answered to naught but Rebecca. Then when I married, my Coy tuck to calling me Becky Bird, and the name just stuck, despite my frettin'." She paused, afraid he would think her rattled. But it was such a comfort to have someone to talk to. "My step-sister's long buried under the graveyard trees on Jackson's Knob, but Becky Bird I'll be until I die—and that not far off, judging by this laziness asettin' in." She flushed. "My, how I do run on. But I don't often have someone to listen, save King James there." She nodded to the dog.

Matthew smiled at them both—a genuine gold flash that warmed his eyes and seemed to fairly light the room. She wondered how he could bear to snatch folks away from their homes.

"But I take extra care," she hurried on, "and as long as I don't fall and break a hip or get forgetful, they've got no call to take me away."

"But it's so lonely here." He searched her face. "Wouldn't you rather live where you'd have somebody to talk to all the time?"

She shrugged. "I have King James and the lizards and my chickens. And sometimes I even talk to the rocks if they get in the wrong place in the garden."

He smiled again. "I would be terribly lonely living way out here by myself."

She drew herself up straight in the chair and shook her head. "No, Matthew. It's all I know. You can't go back on your raisin'."

Matthew stared at his plate. The cook stove cooled and popped. The radio between them sighed a favorite hymn, and Becky began to hum along absently.

A burst of telegraphic clatter shattered the song. Becky started, recognized the breathless voice of the station's newsman though it faded in and out of static. She struggled to understand ". . . Search . . . all law officers . . . major manhunt . . . that the man is armed and extremely dangerous. . . ." She glanced at the boy across the table and was shocked by the pain on his face.

Static filled the cabin, the hoarse voice like a whisper beneath it. "People in outlying areas should be especially alert . . . survival training and can exist in the woods for weeks or months if need be. I repeat, all rural residents should be on the lookout for this killer. . . ."

Becky reached a trembling hand and switched off the noise. The silence seemed nearly as loud. She squinted at Matthew. "So you aren't the man from the nursing home?"

The flicker of surprise on his face did not erase the pain. "No, ma'am." He met her gaze.

"Then I guess you must be that . . . guy they're lookin' for." Strange, she did not fear him; but he had shared her breakfast and she had seen him smile.

"Yes, ma'am. But I mean you no harm." His voice wavered but not his eyes.

She nodded. "I reckon I know that. Is it so? Did you kill somebody?" She fingered the hem of her apron.

He propped his elbows on the table and, dropping his head into his hands, shook it miserably. "I guess so. I don't know . . ." A sound like a muffled sob. He raised his head; tears glistened on his cheeks. "I didn't really realize what was happening. He had a gun. I thought . . . I panicked."

Becky closed her eyes and sighed. She wondered about the one who had died; no, she did not want to know. She and this old mountain had seen so much suffering. And now this terrible waste of such a young life. Poor Matthew. Maybe somebody hexed him, or he got ahold of some of those drugs the preachers rave about.

With a hand on the table she pushed herself erect. The boy sat with his head bowed, King James' nose on his knee. Now that was a pure wonder; but, to be sure, she liked him too. She banked the dying embers in the cook stove. "I declare that sun's so warm I don't believe we'll need a fire toward evening." She turned to the table. "Will you

154

"have some more coffee, Matthew?

"No thank you, ma'am." He lifted his head and smiled the golden smile. "Mrs. Bird, I wonder . . . There's not even a road up here to your place. How do you get supplies?"

She shrugged. "I raise most of what I need. And I get a lot of the rest of it in the woods and out of the creek—nuts and and rabbits, greens and yarbs for my remedies, crayfish and cats, if I'm lucky. King James here, he helps out now and again with a 'coon or 'possum." She smiled at the wonder on his face. "I've always worked hard, boy, and when you've done things all your life it ain't hard to just keep on. And there's some nice folk from the town that comes up ever few months and brings me flour and coffee and a mite of sugar. Don't take much to keep a Bird alive."

He laughed with her at her little joke. "But don't you have trouble cutting wood? Why do you still cook on a wood stove when you have electricity to the cabin and could have an electric range?"

She clucked her tongue. "Now, lad, wouldn't a body be a plumb fool to pay for electricity when she's got 500 acres of timber to cut for free?" She began to clear the table. "And most always one neighbor or t'other is willing to cut my wood on shares."

He rose and carried his dishes to the work table. "Five hundred acres." He shook his head. "No wonder they want to put you in a nursing home." He sought her eyes. "A person could live up here for years and nobody would know."

"You mean hide up here?" She shrugged and chewed her lip. "Once you could . . . But now, things a changin'. There's more hunters and them motorcycles or buggies, or whatever they call 'em." She shook her head. "It's not as peaceful on Stoney Lonesome as it once was."

His eyebrows lifted. "This mountain's called Stoney Lonesome?" He gazed across the hollow.

Becky nodded. "As far back as I can remember, that's what folks have called it. Never saw no call to change it."

He ran a hand through his rusty hair. "No, I can see why not."

She sighed and turned back to the table. No way a city fellow could understand . . .

King James gave a low growl. Becky turned to him in surprise, but she heard the new sound briefly before the dog's barking overwhelmed it. She whirled to Matthew.

His eyes seemed haunted. "Helicopter. They're looking for me." Even as he spoke he flattened himself against the wall near the door.

The roar of the machine swelled until Becky could no longer hear James' fury though she looked straight at him. She made for the door, but the cabin quivered as if shook by an earthquake and she put out a hand to the doorjamb to steady herself. The vibrations pulsed through her. She must behold for herself the thing capable of rocking a house. She opened the door.

A blast of tortured air from the helicopter jerked the latch from her hand and slammed the door against the wall. King James bolted through the opening, brushed against Becky's knees and knocked her off balance. She struggled to keep her footing; her left foot slipped off the sill and landed jarringly on the rock step outside. She flailed her arms to catch herself from falling but knew it was in vain.

Matthew shot out an arm and encircled her waist. The force of her momentum pulled him away from the inside wall and he swung lightly to the door rock with Becky in his arms. He drew her to him briefly, made sure she stood steadily before he released her. At the edge of the clearing the helicopter dipped away from the cabin and moved slowly down the side of Stoney Lonesome.

Matthew drew a quavering breath. "That was a close one."

Becky nodded, wondering whether he meant her rescue from the fall or his escape from the searchers. Neither was she sure if his arm had gone out to catch her or to keep her from running into the sight of the helicopter pilot and possibly giving him away. But by saving her, he had left his hiding place.

He held her elbow and helped her to the bentwood chair under the eaves on the south side of the cabin. As always when she sank into that chair, she thought of Coy. He made it for her when she was expecting their first son; he said she needed more rest, and she had laughed at this. She leaned her head back and looked at the sky where the helicopter had disappeared. King James loped up the hill from that direction and drank noisily from his bucket near the door.

Matthew squatted nearby and studied her face. "Are you sure you're all right?" The concern in his voice seemed real enough.

She nodded. "But I must admit it. I just can't turn off the work and worry like I used to." She smiled into his nearly colorless eyes and wondered about his family, his mother.

He dropped his gaze and fingered some stones at his feet. James nuzzled his hand. He smiled and hugged the dog to his side. "Can I ask you something? What will you do when you can't take care of a garden and chickens, or fish or tramp around after greens and such?"

She shrugged. "Well, sir, I'll allow I've given that some thought. But the Good Book says not to worry about tomorrow. The Lord blessed me with the strength to do what I've had to, and in His kindness He may let me live out my days on this old Stoney Lonesome."

A wisp of wood smoke curled under the eaves and wrinkled her nose. An owl hooted. She frowned; it was a bad omen for an owl to hoot in daylight. The sun slid over the hills and crept over Stoney Lonesome. She closed her eyes against its brilliance.

When she awoke to the sound of an axe chopping wood, King James lay quietly at her feet. She sighed. The helicopter had not come back. Nor would they ever find him on Stoney Lonesome.

The chopping stopped. Through half-shut eyes she glimpsed the figure of a man disappearing into the woods. She stiffened. "Matthew?" she called.

He hesitated, then pivoted on his canvas shoes. In a few strides he stood before her. "Good-bye, Becky Bird. Thank you for giving me this time to think, to decide what to do." He clasped her hand in his. "No matter what ever happens to me, I'll never forget you or your kindness—or Stoney Lonesome."

She shook her head. "You saved my life, lad. At my age a fall like that . . ."

He jerked his chin skyward. "If it hadn't been for me, you wouldn't have fallen in the first place."

"Oh, but you're wrong," she said with a smile. "The helicopter would've still looked for you, and I would've still wanted to see it. And broke my hip and laid there and died."

He squeezed her hand. "If it hadn't been for you, I would've gone on running—probably got killed. I'm gonna turn myself in, Becky. You know what you said about not going back on your raisin'? I don't know why I killed that man, but I sure don't want to kill another." Tears welled in his pale eyes.

Before she could speak, he was gone. She stared into the trees long after they had swallowed him, listening to his progress down the side of Stoney Lonesome. King James whimpered and crowded her legs. She sighed and heaved herself from the bentwood chair. "You know, James, I dare say I've a great-grandson about Matthew's age." The dog licked her hand and trotted at her heels into the cabin. She donned her sunbonnet without looking in the mirror. "I'll allow there may be some poke salat just waiting to be my dinner. Won't take a handful, just for one."

Across the hollow the sun began to silhouette the fringe of trees on Bald Jess. Shadows deepened in the corners of the cabin and for the first time in twenty-five years, it felt empty to her. For the first time in twenty-five years, Becky was lonely.

She clucked her tongue. "You know, James, maybe it wouldn't be so hurtful to just take a peek at that rest home. One of these days . . ." She shrugged and gathered up her greens basket. "Like my Coy used to say, a mountaineer *always* will be free."

BETTY COOK ROTTMANN

DEPENDENT

Outside your quiet room the winter rain
Keeps weeping vigil as you lie again
Among the gleaming maze devised to hold
You here, though in a white-spread world of pain.

Your heart, whose faint throb lifts the spread, declined
To bow to bitterness, instead refined
Into a patient courage. I am ashamed
Because I suffer less, yet am less kind.

But I am strong, and promise, as you start
On this new road of trial, to play my part.
Lean heavily upon my strength, for I
In turn must lean on your valiant heart.

Betty Cook Rottmann

published 1959, *New York Herald Tribune*

SYLVIA SWAIN RUMMEL

THE BEAUTIFICATION OF MELBA LOU BURRY

There are tales that are queer from L.A. to Tangier,
From Shakespeare to "Days of Our Lives";
A history text leaves a student perplexed
From the Pyramids through Brigham Young's wives.
Whether history or fiction conveys more conviction,
That's a judgment I'll leave to a jury—
The tale queerest of all began in Blake Hall
When we beautified Melba Lou Burry.

Melba Lou Burry, from Dark Holler, Missouri—
From a pig farm that had no TV;
Her legs grew thick hair like a Kodiak bear
And the warts on her chin numbered three.
Her dishwater tresses and hand-me-down dresses
Covered skin that was lifeless and rough;
God wasn't kind when He had Mel in mind—
On others He used His best stuff.

But He gave Mel a brain when He made her so plain
And a wit that endeared her to us;
The warts on her chin, she said with a grin,
Made her look more like Lincoln—more studious.
Her dishwater hair caused her little despair,
She said, "It's not beauty I crave;
As for the leg hair—it looks healthy down there
And just think of the razors I save."

But we girls in Blake Hall weren't happy at all
When we thought of her prospects with guys.
We knew she was swell, but they ran like hell
When the vision of Mel filled their eyes.
She had one blind date with a jock from Penn State
Fixed up by our Housemother Moore;
He yelled, "What the Heck!" and broke his big neck
In his headlong retreat for the door.

So after that mess, we gave up, more or less,
And let fate concoct its own stew,
Till one fall when the Hall had a really big ball
And we vowed to include Melba Lou.
We'd use high-tech cosmetics and even prosthetics
To aid in the desperate cause;
And if we should fail—could they put us in jail?

159

We were just camouflaging her flaws.

So we yanked Mel from her studies, then ripped off her cruddies,
And yelled, "We're transforming your bod!"
She said, "I'd as soon be parboiled at noon
In a cannibal pot on the Quad.
I'll look like a goose—Oh, please turn me loose!"
But we were relentless that night.
We shaved and we tweezed, we tinted and teased,
We threw piles of clothes left and right.

We loofah'd her hide till it glowed from inside,
We covered her warts with Erase;
We Clairol'd her well, daubed her down with Chanel
And Max Factor'd her body and face.
A fiber-filled Bali, a Lanz gown from Sally
And Capezio slippers from Sue,
And Claudia Searles threw in cultured pearls:
These completed the new Melba Lou.

We were vastly impressed as we went to get dressed.
Three stayed on guard till the dance
Lest she fling off her finery, flee to her swinery,
And screw up her only big chance.
But we needn't have worried, for all gleaming and curried
She came down subdued, although late;
And the men swarmed like flies when she batted her eyes,
More than one of us that night lost her date.

It was, "I'll teach you to dance," "Baby, give me a chance,"
And "Where have you been all my life?"
Mel said, "What a gas! I dress up like an ass,
And they all want to make me their wife.
Furthermore, up til now, I was named a 'bow wow,'
But it's still little me in this mold.
I'm going to make hay 'cause someone should pay
For us 'dogs' who're left out in the cold."

Then cool and serene she made Homecoming Queen
And Sweetheart of old Sigma Chi;
Next she elbowed her way up to Miss U.S.A.,
Kissing many a sad jock goodbye.
Then our Melba was seen on the big silver screen
When Hollywood made her a star.
A suave billionaire from a manse in Bel Air
Sent her jewels and a sleek silver car.

A box-office queen (and on *Vogue* magazine)—
Now who could have bargained for more?

But Mel said, "Farewell." ("They can all go to hell—
This vacuous life is a bore.")
So she flung off her finery and fled to her swinery
To that place in Dark Holler, Missouri.
With the warts on her chin and the fur back again
Her identity's never a worry.

She's completely anonymous, writing novels pseudonymous;
Home folks never knew of her fame;
That creature they'd seen on the big silver screen
Was some glamorous big city dame.
Her fans think she died (it was never denied)
In a mishap of gristle and gore.
She's now a cult queen between Bogart and Dean,
But her pals from Blake Hall know the score.

We've all kept in touch. Her secret is such
That we've never revealed what we know;
She now makes top dollar writing books in Dark Holler
And she's married a farmer named Joe.
He'd been given the boot by a blonde with big fruit
And a brain like a pea sliced in half;
She drove him to drink, but Mel makes him think—
"Better yet," he says, "she makes me laugh!"

There are tales that are queer from L.A. to Tangier
From Shakespeare to "Days of Our Lives";
A history text leaves a student perplexed
From the Pyramids through Brigham Young's wives.
Whether history or fiction conveys more conviction,
That's a judgment I'll leave to a jury—
The tale queerest of all began in Blake Hall
When we beautified Melba Lou Burry.

Sylvia Swain Rummel　　　161

JO SCHAPER

DEAR UNCLE WALTER

Gazing out the mirrored window
from the toy train coach, how did you guess?
Rolling crossprairie through tall grass
hiding sons and daughters unborn and numerous
voices sprung from the laconic midwest
messages like locomotive sparks which catch
when drought dries up a once rich land
no flood huge enough to quench the fire—
did you dream me in that sleeping car?

Now that Gotham's gone down to Gomorrah
and California is a dollar sign dream
no one gives a damn, dear uncle,
for the farmer, the laborer, the mechanic you sang:
the only work worth doing, now done by machine
data preprocessed until even the truth
functions randomly. No analogy
holds up under this electronic assault
converting all essences to zeroes and ones.

Somehow we survive, hardscrabble and weary
along the Missouri, the Mississippi
noises caught in our raw, rasped throats
foreheads scarred from banging on bricks
interfaceless creatures in a plugged-in world
where it's not the thought, but the expression
not the heart, but the technology
nor an audience, but only the money
the glittering grease, green electric money.

And sometimes we see you, Uncle Walter
hitchhiking along the night interstate
gray grizzled, barely visible in your dirty coat
just the sort the authorities warned us about
and if we stop we find you've vanished—
it's not you. . .the song's the thing—
sometimes it hardly matters that no one listens
to that ballad drowned in the roar of exhaust
We have heard it. And we sing.

JO SCHAPER

MURDERING THE BLOOD NUNS

they're there whole convents of them
stomping down the waxed blood halls
shushing, shoving, covering my eyes
the mustn'ts shouldn'ts dasn'ts in black
all armed with rules and rules to rap
the knuckles of wandering hands
running faster, trying to rescue
me from their devils I've never forgotten
and what do you use to kill them
unholy hosts like they forced on us
sending a parade of first graders
to the water fountain wondering
why God stuck to the roofs of their mouths
like peanut butter, these solemn ladies?
strangle them with crystal rosaries
let them choke, hung by their scapulars
on the lies they told us of being human
theirs the original sin gnarling the twigs
of little children not content
until they shrunk like angels on pinheads
and jumped into our ears where they scream
if you stabbed them would they bleed
where's the vaccine against these mites
who congregate in the brain's choirs
flapping like bats in steel toed shoes
I've had it up to here with them
I'll point this silver crucifix
in their whirring pencil sharpener
fling it like a throwing star
into their ranks spilling
black and leprous white
and red all over.

KAREN WARREN SCHEIDER

THE YARD MAN

He seemed lost   half
Indian   no one knew
how many parts of everything else   nor age
long true nose   ancient eyes   red-clouded-white
ice blue   the Indian   pushed through
Sky Face   the name I gave   wrinkles.

He seemed lost   out of place
like he ought to have been   dragging a buffalo
instead of   a wheelbarrow.

Every year or so he'd appear with one less   finger
or toe   or tooth   didn't seem   to bother
chiseling granite   never took a big enough chunk.

                Sky Face, do you hurt?
                No it don't bother me.

I watched for his truck   window hunt
he was friends   with his truck
he called her Truck   and let me play in her
he said if I was quiet   she would talk to me
                it didn't work.

He lobbed apples   rotten   into his wheelbarrow
a slow lob   he did it slowly   took him awhile
to sieve the sky aside so his   two-fingered hand
could get the right crook   on the apple   on and
on he sieved the sky away through   four   or three
or two-fingered hands   with a labored gradualness
that comes   from hauling   buffalo.

One afternoon he huddled   over a strange pile
Grandma had put out by the trash   old underwear
newspapers magazines socks tuna fish oil she'd saved
in a can bruised bananas a coat with no buttons or-
            phaned shoe laces cheese.

He seemed lost   half
called me Miss   and left
I laid off my
                window hunt.

                Sky Face, do you hurt?
                No it don't botter me.

VICTORIA SPAIN

I MOVE WITH THE MOON
(for Russell)

Half-sleeping,
I offer you my shoulder
as your anchor.
We knot and tumble
as you move through the channel
of my arms.
All sounds muffled,
our love lowers us like a fisherman's net
from our home in the wave's curve.
We become the sea's sediment.
Here, the pictures from your mind
spill into mine.
Our pores flush a deeper coral
until spindles from elbows and knees
jerk us to sleep.
Wrapped in seaweed,
we shift.
There is nothing here
but the black sea's ceiling,
the weight of stars,
and a moon climbing
across a cold sky.

Victoria Spain

—a version of this poem published 1984, *Number One*

MARILYN TATLOW

JENNIE LOWE, AGE 77 — A VERY COLD WINTER

It was the kind of day to get your running done early, not so much because of the heat, but because of the humidity which bore down and robbed you of your breath and made you feel like you were moving under water. Suzanne Billings approached the Stanton Lake dam at a steady pace, ignoring her perspiration, concentrating, instead, on the water beside her. She looked past the slick green moss toward the lake's center, which was a deep, dark blue. As she moved, her vision shifted to the far shore where water lillies grew. In that instant, reflecting sun overwhelmed the colors of leaves and the water drew them into overall brightness. It was a perfect moment, an illusion from a childhood fairy tale where glimmering landscapes held mysterious secrets. Suzanne almost laughed aloud at the thought of an enchanted frog swimming in Stanton Lake, or a princess with a golden ball hiding in the woods beyond the water. I'm not apt to find any magic in this setting, she thought, as she left the park and headed up Rollins Hill.

The three mile course ended at her driveway and she walked through the grass toward the sound of the lawn mower. She saw Adam at the far end of the lawn under the big oak tree, looking more like one of his students than a thirty-five year old man. When he noticed her, he smiled and motioned to invite her to trade places. She shook her head, pulling her damp shirt to show how warm she was and then ran into the kitchen to answer the phone.

It was Captain Thompson, a pleasant man with silver hair who waved to her in a kind of salute when she saw him patrolling the park during her morning runs. As far as she knew, he had never used the black revolver strapped to his belt even though there had been one bank robbery attempt in Stanton. She wished she'd been there when the unlucky out-of-towner demanded they fill his grocery sack with money. Everybody stared at him like he was crazy until Leroy Brooks knocked him cold to the floor. They hadn't needed the police that day, although she supposed they did call Captain Thompson.

His voice sounded intense and Suzanne's inner alarm triggered, in spite of the fact that she could see Adam on his riding mower and she knew Tracy was upstairs sleeping. Maybe one of Adam's students was in trouble again; they sometimes called at odd times when their parents were nowhere to be found.

"We've got a woman who walked into the lake sometime early this morning, Suzanne. The biology teacher found her when he went out for algae samples. The thing is, we're not sure who she is, but she's got on jogging shoes. We thought maybe she was one of your morning regulars, someone *you* see every day."

Suzanne's mind was blank. "She walked into the lake? You mean she drowned?"

"We're not sure what time she went in. Dr. Long found the body sometime before his class, which starts at eight."

"Who—?"

"Right now we're trying for a positive identification."

"I'm sorry, Captain, I can't—"

"Excuse me for a second." He put her on hold and when he returned, his voice was coldly efficient. "Her car's been found so we're running a check on it. Thank you."

"But—"

He cut her off, and Suzanne stood motionless, trying to absorb what he had told her. What did he mean 'morning regulars'? Sometimes she saw Fred Selzer who'd taken to walking regularly since his heart attack, or Molly James who's trying to lose a few pounds; and if she went before six, she saw Shorty searching for beer cans to recycle. But she didn't think of them as regulars. She poured a cup of coffee and sat down, inhaling the hot steam without taking a drink.

She had never actually seen a drowned person, had only heard about bloating and discoloration. Why wouldn't someone take pills instead? Surely the woman hadn't intended to do it, you wouldn't get up in the morning and put on jogging shoes if you planned to die. Was she there, caught in the weeds, staring through the water, while I ran across the dam?

There had been other drownings in the lake over the years. The water curved, gently like a comma, so you couldn't see from one end to the other. Oak trees, trees that didn't seem to belong on the bank, grew up and shaded the silver row boats turned upside down. It was artificial, originally built for the Wabash steam engines. When Suzanne and Adam returned to Stanton, they'd taken Tracy to swim in the roped-off section near the swings. And soon as they could afford it, they'd joined the country club so she could dive for pennies in nine feet of bright turquoise.

The mower's engine stopped and Suzanne heard Adam enter the utility room and turn on the faucet. He came into the kitchen quietly, leaving a trail of grass clippings behind him.

"How was the run?" he asked.

"Fine."

"Is Tracy still asleep?"

Suzanne set the butter, eggs, and milk on the counter without reply and he asked her what was wrong. Before she finished telling him, he had picked up the phone. "Adam, please. Don't call."

"I won't have it. It was very unprofessional of him to ask you."

"Don't be silly," she said. "This is Stanton."

After Adam hung up the phone, he motioned her to sit and he began to cook the eggs. "It was a checker at Food Barn, no one we know. She lived in Manning and drove in to work. Her husband just died, no children, only relative a brother."

Suzanne picked up her coffee and then set it down. "That's terrible."

"What's terrible?" Tracy came into the kitchen yawning, her uncombed hair curled tightly around her face. At the temple, the curls were unbleached in the same spot as Adam's neatly clipped hair, and she looked more like a ten year old than a teenager.

Adam hugged her. "Nothing's terrible. How about scrambled eggs and a visit to the Henderson sale with me?"

Tracy nodded yes and Suzanne explained what happened while Adam spooned the eggs onto their plates. "Who wants ketsup?"

Tracy grinned at him and he set the bottle by her plate and passed a bundle of toast wrapped in a paper towel. Suzanne stirred her food without taking a bite.

"I don't mean to dwell on this, but do you think she went down those old steps where we used to swim?"

"I remember that place," Tracy said. "Every once in a while you'd bump into something swimming in the water." She shivered as she said it and Adam laughed.

"It was just frogs or fish trying to get out of your way." He looked over his daughter's head as though to say, 'Drop it.' Suzanne knew how his mind worked, the incident was over, there was nothing to be done about it and therefore nothing to discuss. But she knew Tracy was right about the things in the water, they went after her too, always in the same spot, the mole on her shoulder. She wondered if the woman had any marks which would have attracted fish.

She pushed her plate back. Adam and Tracy turned to her with puzzled expressions.

"I think I'll go out and open the shop," she said. "You two can handle the sale without me."

"There won't be any customers this early," Adam said.

"Good. I need to clean it up," trying to concentrate on what she'd just said. "If you see any decent glass, we could use it. The people from St. Louis bought almost everything."

"That's what we like to hear."

She frowned at him. "I hated to lose the bread dish."

He smiled blandly. "We're in business, remember? We buy things at one price, sell them at another, and use the profit to buy more. Eventually we'll come out ahead. In the meantime—"

"In the meantime, it gives me something to do besides moon around the house all day, right?"

Adam spoke deliberately. "I was only going to say, in the meantime, we're learning the trade and building our reputation. When I stop teaching, hopefully the antique shop will support us." He winked at Tracy, "Unless your mother treats it like a private collection and won't sell anything." He patted his daughter's arm. "But today, Tracy and I are going to get some guaranteed turnovers, right?"

Tracy smiled uncertainly. "I think it's funny that people want all that old stuff."

"It reminds them of the past, of happier times," Suzanne said.

Adam corrected her, "You mean, of times they imagine were happier."

"You can't deny that it was different then. People took time to talk to each other. Now we're all too busy."

168

He shrugged. "Give me the fast pace along with central air, indoor plumbing, and antibiotics."

"Me too," Tracy said. "Grandma told me it was miserable in the winter. Those heavy quilts weighed you down so you couldn't move, but you never got warm."

Adam nodded. "The best cure for nostalgia is to talk to *her*. On her last visit she saw your mother's kerosene lamp and said that nobody who had actually used one of those things would want it around now."

"I know," Suzanne defended. "I've heard all about how it was Grandma Billings' job to clean them."

Tracy said, "I bet she never thought it would be like it is now."

"Nobody ever does. When I was in school, they said in the eighties we'd have miniature helicopter blades with power packs strapped onto our bodies to fly us wherever we wanted to go."

Tracy laughed aloud, "You're kidding."

"And," Suzanne interjected, "houses would be plastic bubbles with everything inside washable or disposable. You flip a switch and jet sprays clean everything." Tracy looked skeptically at her mother. "I'm serious," she continued, "and there would be no meals to prepare because you'd take pills instead of eating."

Tracy grinned. "That means no dishes to wash."

And none to save, Suzanne thought. Grandmother Nancy's amber glass pitcher is the only thing left from that side of our family. "It makes you wonder what'll survive from our generation."

Adam ceremoniously picked up the yellow plastic juice pitcher. "Someday this fine relic will rest in a lighted case and be known fondly as Granny Suzzie's juicer!"

Tracy giggled. "I wish I could peek into our future."

Suzanne stood up. "I'm sure your father can tell you whatever you want to know. Just ask him." The two stared at her, startled by her tone. But she couldn't apologize without explaining that she was sick to death of having him joke her out of her opinions. "I'll see you after the sale," she said, taking the quickest way out.

The shortest route to Adam's grandparents' old place was through the park, down double K to the gravel road turn-off. The log cabin was the original homestead, and when Adam inherited it, he remodeled it himself. She'd been happiest then, that first summer. Sometimes they'd camped out in the cabin to get an early start on the work: he added a long porch across the front, she filled the black hominy kettle with geraniums, and they sanded and varnished the interior together, trading Tracy back and forth like a papoose.

Today Suzanne avoided the shortcut through the park. She drove down the highway until she saw their spinning wheel sign. Seldom did she take this route. She drove up the rode with care, studying the shaded woods as though she'd never seen them before. The clearing was bright and sunny and her geraniums, loaded with blossoms, pleased her. She stuck her finger in the dirt and reminded herself to water them as she walked onto the porch.

Inside, the air felt cool, and she silently thanked old Adam for creating such a sturdy place for them. Looking at the thick walls and smooth floors covered with braided rugs made her feel like she had stepped into another era. The sense of timelessness usually isolated her from worry, but today she couldn't shake the uneasy feeling that settled onto her with Captain Thompson's call. She decided the best thing to do would be to follow her ordinary routine. She picked up the Windex bottle and sprayed the glass doors of the china cabinet. Instead of admiring the familiar silver service on the bottom shelf, she imagined the yellow plastic pitcher sitting in its place. Slick, hard unchanged despite washing, dropping, slamming against a faucet, it irritated her from the minute Adam brought it home, and she now saw that he was absolutely right. It would survive.

It was so unlike the plastic one, the piece of amber glass safe in her cabinet at home, damaged by circumstance, too fragile to use. A legacy from her Grandmother Nancy, the white-haired woman had told Suzanne the story of the carnival, how she had sneaked out to go, how her boyfriend Ben pitched pennies to win it for her. Suzanne had half-listened until the woman took her hand and traced her finger over the raised grape design and up the handle of similated vines. Even though she couldn't see it, her finger felt the thin crack running along its side. Her grandmother laughed softly and squeezed her hand. 'We had fun that night, we forgot the time,' she'd said. 'Ben had to push the horses to get them home, and I made him stop down by the gate to let me out. Mama knew where I was but if my dad had heard us, no telling what would have happened. I picked up my skirts and ran so fast, and then do you know what happened, Suzzie? I dropped my pitcher, and it cracked here, where you felt it.'

Suzanne remembered her grandmother's blue eyes then, and tried to picture her white hair as dark as her own, pulled up with a red ribbon, or maybe a blue one to match her eyes. She was so enthralled with the image of Grandma Nan as a girl, that she'd paid no attention to the woman's reasons for keeping the cracked pitcher, but right then she remembered her words clearly: 'It wasn't perfect after that, but even so, it was worth hanging on to.' And when she'd given it to Suzanne she'd said, 'We invested too much time and effort in this to throw it away.'

Suzanne rubbed the glass with her cloth and as she stepped back to look for streaks, there, in the shining light was her own reflection. She watched her arm drop to her side and the dark mass that was her body begin to undulate and move, almost as though it were caught under the surface of water. Her face contorted and she realized she was holding her breath. She filled her lungs with air and breathed rapidly. This was ridiculous, there's no water here, only a trick of the light, the imperfections in old glass making things shimmer and move. Besides, she thought, I'm an excellent swimmer. Hadn't she eared her WSI and taught Red Cross lessons? It was insane to imagine herself below the water, no matter what the circumstances. . .unless she were held there by something. Suddenly more than anything else, she wanted to see the face of the woman in the lake. She felt compelled to know if it

170

were someone she had seen before.

A car turning in from the highway brought Suzanne from her reverie. It was too soon to be Adam and Tracy unless they had left the sale early out of concern for her. That must be it, she thought. Even though the drowning meant nothing to him, he was worried about me. Oddly, she took little comfort in his early return, for she couldn't shake her disorientation, the feeling that she had floated for so long she couldn't tell up from down. She reached into the trunk where the quilts were stored and selected one to display so she'd be busy rather than daydreaming when he came in. There were no problems between them, she told herself firmly, only differences. He prefers to ignore unpleasantness, and I examine it endlessly, but he's a good counselor, everyone says so. She reminded herself to be grateful that his calm attitude carried over so that he never raised his voice at her. From the beginning he had avoided confrontations by joking or studying the newspaper or leaving the room. He finally explained that arguing would ruin Tracy and make her as insecure as the children he counseled. 'Kids always know when their parents don't get along; you can't hide it.' he said, and even though it sounded logical and right, something about it felt wrong to her. She responded quickly, without thinking, saying she wasn't one of his kids, for God's sake, she was his wife, but she was crying by then, and her words seemed only to prove his point.

On the porch, Suzanne shook the quilt and breathed deeply, trying to forget her old complaints. With brisk efficient movements she draped the quilt across the church pew bench, working faster, pulling at the folds of the fabric as though by directing her body she could quiet the undercurrents splashing into her consciousness. She told herself Adam was right, that it's impossible to know why the woman walked into the lake, so she must forget it. But she'd no sooner told herself that than a new idea popped into her head. What if Adam's indifference to the drowned woman carried over? What if the truth is that pain simply did not interest him? Even when it was hers? Her stomach lurched at the possibility, but once the idea was there it would not be dislodged. It flooded her with the certainty of truth.

She looked out to the parking lot to see why they were taking so long. The sun glared on the windshield of a silver van. To avoid staring at the out-of-state license plate, she turned back to rearrange the folds of the quilt and then realized that she'd selected the wrong one. This was her friendship quilt, discovered in the bottom of a trunk she'd bought at a sale. The pieces of fabric had been carefully cut and fit into an overall pattern which focused on a half dozen squares of white. Those blocks carried the names of their creators, embroidered in black and embellished with a cluster of flowers or a message. The center one belonged to the Martins: Tad, Gladys, and Jimmy. Suzanne believed the quilt had been assembled in Gladys' kitchen and probably kept by her to use on a spare bed. In the corner of the quilt was Suzanne's favorite square: *Jennie Lowe, Age 77, A Very Cold Winter.* Even though Suzanne knew nothing of Jenny Lowe's history, she never imagined her with the other women— starting with their random scraps of material from a dress or a curtain that was too worn to use—creating something whole and new between them. As she studied the quilt, she wondered if the woman. . .the drowned woman whose name she didn't know. . .had ever helped to create a friendship quilt.

The door to the van slammed. A man in silver rimmed sun glasses and a woman in high heels carrying a shoulder bag walked across the gravel.

Suzanne called to them, "Hello. Beautiful morning isn't it?"

They nodded, looking at the friendship quilt.

"There are other quilts inside, if you'd care to look."

They glanced at each other and the woman appeared to come to a decision. "Are you the owner here?"

"My husband and I."

"Fine. We'll take this quilt, and I want to look at others you have like it."

Suzanne hesitated. "Actually this particular one isn't for sale."

"We'll give you three hundred dollars for it." The woman motioned to her companion and he reached into his jacket pocket.

Suzanne took a deep breath. "As I said. . ."

The woman didn't waver. "Cash." She held out the money.

"It's already sold," Suzanne said, not looking at her.

"Four hundred."

Suzanne turned away and opened the door to the cabin. They followed her inside and the woman leaned against the rolltop desk. "I'm Erin Finley, and this is my associate. We're assembling an exhibit of folk art for a gallery, and these signature quilts—"

"Friendship quilts. The women worked on the individual blocks at home and then assembled them in each other's houses at social gatherings. Sometimes they kept them, and sometimes they gave them for wedding gifts and such."

"Well, whatever—"

Suzanne opened the trunk and pulled out a quilt of pink and lavender print with a scalloped edge. "These really are very fine quality, more elaborate than ones found further west where each woman had to make her own and didn't have time for detail work. They're pieced together, not appliqued like ones from the deep South. .made of imported chintz which the planters' wives ordered and had slaves put together." Suzanne smiled, imagining how pleased Adam would be that she was telling the history of a sales item. He thought it professional to give the background of a piece, and she knew most people appreciate the time it allows them to imagine the piece—a quilt, a cherry dresser, oak commode —in their bedrooms at home.

Before she could finish the history, Adam walked in. "Don't let me interrupt," he said, smiling at all of them.

"We're just leaving," the woman said. "We enjoyed the lecture, but we came here to buy, not to listen."

"Oh?"

She was all business. "Let me give you my card. We're staying at the Ramada, in case you change your mind."

As their van pulled away, Adam asked, "What was that all about?"

"I'm taking my quilt home. I don't want to sell it."

"Why not? She seemed ready to pay a bundle."

"There are others, if she wants them."

"But it's not a family heirloom. You didn't know you had it until you opened the trunk. You almost missed it completely."

"You're right. I almost missed it completely."

Adam stared at her. "I keep telling you, this is a business. You put a price on things and when people want to buy them, you accept their money."

"Adam, all day I've been immersed in this, but just now, when I told them about the quilts—"

"What are you talking about?"

"I mean, I felt caught by it all, but now—"

He shook his head slowly. "Sometimes I think you don't live in the real world, Suzanne."

Suzanne closed her eyes briefly, and opened them to meet his gaze steadily. She leaned forward. "This *is* real to me. When I'm here in this cabin, I think about how your grandfather built it, and how it will be here after we're gone."

He stared at her without changing expression. "Grandpa built this place so they wouldn't have to sleep in the woods, Suze. As soon as he could afford it, he put up a new farm house near the road, and after that, they never came back here." At first his reasonable tone of voice made her think he understood what she had said. It took her a minute to realize that he hadn't even glimpsed what she felt.

Tracy entered and Adam smiled at her as though to say, your mother is at it again. He looked back at Suzanne, and his face broadened into a grin. "If you want to spend all day dreaming about this junk, dear, maybe we should run a museum not a shop."

If only he wouldn't smile like that, she thought, I might be able to swallow it again, but he won't stop smiling. She blinked rapidly several times before she spoke. "You never lose your good humor, do you? No matter how bad it is, you smile tolerantly and wait for it to pass."

"Suzanne—", his voice was low.

She stood motionless, unresponsive, until he opened the door and left. She turned to Tracy. "You wait here, I'll be right back."

Adam was leaning against the porch rail. "You upset her."

"What about me? I'm upset too, or don't you care?" He refused to look at her, so she stepped closer to him. "Is it too much trouble to deal with me? Is the real secret that you're not laid-back at all, just plain lazy?"

Adam continued to look straight ahead. "You have quite an imagination, Suze. I'm not sure it's good for you to spend so much time out here alone."

Suzanne pushed the quilt aside and sat on the bench. A corner of the fabric brushed her knee and she began to trace an embroidered name with her finger. "Do you think anyone ever made a quilt with that woman's name on it?"

"What woman?"

"You know, in the lake."

"The *lake*." He looked at her squarely. "Is that what set you off? Have you been out here brooding about that all day?"

"Not brooding, just thinking."

He shook his head slightly. "Think rationally for a minute, Suze. That woman's problems had nothing to do with you."

"I knew you'd say that," she said under her breath. For a minute the old tension grabbed her. It was a mystery to her how he could always make indifference sound so sensible. She folded her arms in front of her and looked into the woods beyond the clearing. Under her gaze, the shadows beneath the trees became pools of water, and gradually, almost without her realizing it, her anxiety began to pass. Slowly she saw that they were each immersed in their own worlds, that there was little she could do to change this. She felt strangely calm and heard herself saying words she had not intended.

"I'm keeping the quilt, Adam. I bought it, so it's my prerogative. The same goes for your purchases or for Tracy's. From now on, I'll run three balance columns and handle our transactions separately."

"That's crazy. You know it's not what you want."

"It's a good plan."

"How can you say that?"

"Let's try it, Adam. If it doesn't work, we can always go back to the way we were before." The words played over in her head with a crazy senseless rhythm, 'we can always go back, we can always go back,' and she clung to those words, telling herself they were true, wanting to believe they were true. She looked toward the woods again. They seemed ordinary now, there was no water, only grass, trees, shaded light, and ground. And from somewhere, deep in the woods, the sound of a bird calling.

Marilyn Tatlow

174

JUDITH TOWSE THIES

FIRST DAY OF SCHOOL

When I was five, you made me
a new checkered dress.
I had shiney patton shoes
and new braids pulled my eyes
slanted like a chinaman.
The bus was a yellow monster
who ate little girls, rattled
them around like ice cubes
in a blender
and spit them out.
You blew me a kiss as I sat
uncomforted and watched you grow
tiny on the window.
Some boy named Billy Claxton
threw himself next to me and
untied my ribbons and said,
"Your mother is a whore and
everybody knows it."
So, I spit on him and told him,
"Liar, liar, you take that back."
I hate Billy Claxton and that's why
"I'm never going back."

MARLENE TRICE

THE UNYIELDING MOMENT

Rhea peeked out from behind her mother's skirts. The knock on the door was expected, as it was every Sabbath morning, but the five-year-old shyly awaited her grandfather's request for her to accompany him to shul. The old man stood on the stoop dressed in his Sabbath finery and carrying his prayer shawl and tfilah. Rhea watched the sun flicker off his tie pin and highlight the brocade threads in his cream and rust colored tie. Even the satin ribbon on his hat seemed to shine in the early morning light. The sun danced in the small girl's vision and blessed the Sabbath morn.

He was her first teacher, the Zeda, so warm and giving during the week, beckoning her onto his lap, and calling her his "boopschelah." But laughing and whispering together in Yiddish were for weekdays. On the Sabbath, the walk to shul was accomplished in silence, the moments laden with expectation. Inside the shul door, Rhea was usually ushered upstairs to the woman's balcony where the women dovinned out of sync from the men. Rhea hung over the balustrade watching for the moment the old man would rise to take his turn removing the Torah from the ark. When he read from the Torah, she hung on his every syllable though she herself knew not a word of Hebrew. His prayers rose to her ears like a song and filled her with a quiet ecstacy. When the cantor sung, the walls fell away and time was without limit. Perhaps it was that the child was born with an old soul. Perhaps it was the quality of the ancient sung words themselves, mystic and forceful, that inevitably struck the sensitive chords. Whatever the reason, promise and pain rushed upon one so small and carved out recesses yet to be filled. The resonance of the cantor's voice struck chords the precocious child could feel yet not name— serenity, now turmoil—hope, now despair— benevolence, and, one day, pity. The shul too was a teacher, not of Torah for the small girl, but of life.

Friday evening. The sun not quite set; the Sabbath not quite begun. The Zeda begins to assemble his Sabbath garb, while Rhea's mother and grandmother, the Baba, prepare the Sabbath meal together. Rhea awaits her father at the door. She does not understand the fluttering heart, the long minutes, the heightened senses. A little girl's heart teaches the grown woman passion. The door opens and the young man swoops his daughter into his arms. He holds the evening paper in the crook of his arm. Has she been good today? Shall they read the funnies together? Of course, Rhea knows already it is an idle question. They read together by long established custom. Tonight his breath smells of beer of which Mama and the Baba disapprove—vocally. But Rhea is in on the men's secret. The Zeda throws Papa a wink. It has been a long week, Samuel, and the Sabbath has not yet begun—time enough for the beer, the paper, the sunset lush of gathering and family, ritual and tradition.

176

This Sabbath morning is particularly special. It is Simchas Torah, the celebration of the Torah. Today Papa will accompany Rhea and Zeda to shul. The yarmulka balances unsteadily on the young man's thick black hair. Rhea is near bursting as she walks between the two men, both so dear to her, one who teaches her the past, one who nurtures her present. And today she is not ushered upstairs. She is not set apart with the women. Somehow, she dare not question how, she shares a downstairs bench with her father and grandfather. The rabbi leads the congregation in prayer. Without understanding the words, Rhea recognizes every cue. The Zeda is the first of the congregation to rise and remove the Torah from the ark. He walks to a raised step and begins to read the week's Torah portion. The shul rocks back and forth as men and women, their voices now in unison, now a jumble, dovin, their words lilting, remembering and hoping, praying and cajoling, comforting and threatening. The cantor sings and all voices give way to his plaintiff cries.

Two other men have removed Torahs from the ark and carry them high above their shoulder throughout the congregation. Men rise and lift their prayer shawls to their lips before touching it to the Torah. The Zeda nods to Rhea's father and he begins to walk to the alter. Rhea beams as her father approaches the ark. But he is so new to faith and family that he stumbles on the alter steps. Once at the ark Samuel makes no motion to remove the Torah; he neither turns nor walks away. He stands, not knowing his next move, unmoving for longer than Rhea can hold her breath. Let the earth open and swallow them all. The child does not understand her father's hesitancy. It cannot be forgiven with a wink. Even her love offers no redemption. It was her love for her father that transformed such significance to this hour. That same love can not yet forgive the moment; it is not of the moment, but a recess yet to be filled.

The Zeda goes to Samuel's aid and pulls the Torah forth. He places it upon his shoulder and whispers the ritual Rhea knows by heart into the young man's ear. Once around the shul and Samuel returns the Torah to its place. He steps down from the alter and returns to the bench where his young daughter sits alone.

She does not look at him, her Papa, in his shame. As he takes his seat, Rhea slides toward the wall and peers out the window. She sees neither swatches of green nor blue, hears no raised mystic voices; the walls hold tight and time focuses only on this one unyielding moment.

MARLENE TRICE

THIS TIME I CLOSE THE DOOR

This time I close the door
briefly
—on the dishes askew in the kitchen sink,
—on the menacing portends
of congealed drippings on the stove
from other people's meals,
—on the hamper overhung
with other people's clothes
strewn in provocative postures,
providing each other intimate solace
as if conspiring to escape their doomed shelving
to linear folds and segregated stacks.

I close the door
—on the accruing circles of speckled grey,
dabbed as if by an artist's brush
in the shadow of the long suffering Frigidaire;
—on the corrogated cleric's box
(no briefcase with dignity)
of bundled overtime from a job
I do detest,
(let me this time discount it directly,
not elevate it with imagery)
a job to which I daily drive,
the road occasionally blurred,
but disjointed by brimming eyes.
Between car and cubicle
I manacle my inner scream
and resist the urgings of public radio
and Susan Stamberg's interviews with
the writers, artists, playwrights, and political activists
I once-upon-a-time intended to be.

This time I choose not to snivel
in the back seat of anyone's car
about the contender I might have been.
This time I point to center field,
swing the bat in wide loops above my head,
and promise myself the long ball.

DONNA L. TRUSSELL

BIRDS

I ask my boss for a raise.
She looks embarrassed.
How much you want?
How much you wanna give me?

After work Jim and I
eat Mexican food, have a Bud.
It's not much of a celebration.
A raise just makes it harder to quit.

At home I get another beer,
put it back.
Maybe what I really want is a cup of coffee
maybe ice cream
maybe sex
maybe a movie
maybe a bath.

I splash hot water on my face,
remember last night's dream:
I'm afraid—
my cat is loose in the basement
with the Brown Recluse spiders.
She's going after birds.
A big black panther is going after her.

DONNA L. TRUSSELL

LOST

I take a little walk,
end up in Nebraska wheat.
Turn around to go back home,
find myself in Omaha.

Yellow Pages no help.
Braniff, American—
all the numbers are in code.
I dial and cry, dial and cry.

I shrug and say okay fine,
I'll go on to the next dream.
Plot thickens: he's kissing my thigh,
plunging in.
I shudder.

Suddenly the phone, the Yellow Pages
intrude.
I'm alone, slumped in a chair,
still in Omaha.

EARRINGS

Your niece says, you go first.
Okay sweetie.
First or last, you know it will hurt the same.

It's over.
You grip the vinyl upholstery,
stare at the worn brown carpet.
"Oh!" she cries. You look up.
Blood streams down your niece's pale slender neck.
Trembling, you pay the woman.
You whisper, did I bleed too?

The first week
you arrange your hair different ways,
buy punkish earrings intended for teenagers.
Soon your jewelry box is full
and you're back to watching Cable News Network,
drinking tumblers of Gallo wine,
striking matches and blowing them out.

CORINNE UNDERWOOD

EXPLAINING DREAMS AND EVOLUTION TO THE BIOLOGIST

I'm not superstitious—
never fool with tea leaves or Tarot.
I believe in your double helix, DNA,
Glycolysis and Golgi bodies—
that you produced two haploid daughter cells,
your electrons got excited,
and your chromosomes crossed over.
Now, believe in my dreams:

Slithering in hot soup warmed by the Jet Stream,
evolving through thousands of opening doors,
riding cycles of waves,
smothered by seaweed
pulling against the undertow,
we slid onto obsidian
and lay gasping.

We changed into cypress trees
swaying with Spanish moss—
then into lotus blossoms,
iridescent raindrops and blue glaciers.

Lions chased us through Valencian streets,
up cathedral steps,
through velvet mazes.
We quaked with the earth,
swam in the floods,
clawed through the clay.

You say my dreams have no meaning—
only neurons firing like ladyfingers,
ions deserting and invading cells.

But these dreams, these electrical currents,
like the sparks of St. Elmo's Fire
flickering in my sleeping brain
galvanized me,
made me believe
in everything—
even in you.

CORINNE UNDERWOOD

NO ONE WILL SING

She kept the Star in the same window with the milk card,
checked every morning that it hadn't fallen.
With the window open, she could hear singing
from the high school: "The Caissons Keep Rolling Along." .
She remembered "Over There, Over There,"
and her middy blouse with gold stars.

And when it was time to say goodbye in California,
she dressed up special—wore her plum velvet hat
with pheasant feathers.
She rode the glass-domed train,
saw the mountains for the first time.

Red-stained meadows splashed by Indian Paintbrush
cradled Columbine—fragile purple hearts.
As she railed across Colorado, bits of ash filtered down,
showering dandelions—millions of gold stars.

No one had ever heard of Iwo Jima or Treblinka;
never dreamed there'd be a grandson at Da Nang.
She leaned back on the plush seat,
admired the landscape,
watched the night coming on.

Corrine Underwood

182

CONSTANCE URDANG

APPROACHES

Sensing the approach of the poem, I resist its power
    over me, like a woman who resents her body's involuntary
    response to the insistent caresses of a lover;

Or, I see the poem coming toward me through the crowded
    street, advancing with welcoming smiles and arms
    outstretched, and for no reason at all I quickly turn
    down the next corner, or dart into the anonymous maw
    of a Walgreen's Drugstore to avoid its eager embrace.

Maybe the poem is already growing inside me, even though
    my womanly rhythms have not as yet been interrupted
    and life goes on day by day in the same old way; it's
    possible that in spite of the fact that as yet I am
    not conscious of any change, inside me the poem lives,
    has developed a tiny skeleton, a thready network of
    nerves, and nourishes itself, feeding on what I take in.

It's nighttime, and the poem is knocking at the gate.
    What a loud, insistent sound! I don't want to open
    to it, to have to entertain its company just now
    when I'm ready to go to sleep. Maybe I can pretend
    nobody's home, turn out all the lights, and tiptoe up
    the stairs to bed. . .

In the gathering dusk, like the early twilight of winter,
    I see that already on the page, one after another the
    little doors are opening, some of their own accord,
    others waiting for me, clumsy-fingered, to pry them
    apart. Now all at once I am brimming with impatience,
    eager to see what lies behind that last unopened door.

CONSTANCE URDANG

AT FRANK 'N' HELEN'S

It's Nostalgia Week at Frank 'n' Helen's;
The two cops at the table near the door,
Ordering pepperoni pizza, have hung up
Their two blue coats, and on their brawny thighs
Their blunt black holsters dream. Under tinsel stars
Left over from Christmas, a party of seven,
Every one a senior citizen,
Is making itself at home. Over baskets
Of steaming fried chicken or shrimp
Carried by waitresses gently perspiring,
Sweethearts and strangers catch one another's eyes.

Here, in the odor of down-home hospitality
Dispensed for a price (but reasonable),
America rediscovers herself, all the homely virtues
Displayed in the mirrors behind the booths
Where time has been arrested, and everything
Remains what we recall, as Frank—or Helen—
Dreamed it. Here we are all fed, we can all
Love one another. Let the scarlet hearts
Festoon the ceiling, let the walls leaf out
With mammoth cardboard shamrocks, greener far
Than anything in nature, under the dreaming stars.

DEBORAH UTHE

A THING ABOUT TO HAPPEN

Something is going to happen.
I can feel it
like a six-year-old wiggling
her front tooth
with her tongue
feels a cold wind
on the exposed nerve,
tastes the first drops
of her own blood.

No, it is more than that.
I pace these rooms like a pregnant cat
looking for a warm place,
a safe place for it to happen.
This box. . .no, this closet,
if only they'd open the door. . .
or here, under the bed:
we'll be safe.

But that is not it either.
This is the feeling:
clouds burst free
waking me
to the wet song of the sky,
and feeling very alive,
very thirsty,
I run through the rain
with my mouth open,
my arms raised,
inviting lightning.

DEBORAH UTHE

ABSENCE

There are no people
in my dreams
anymore.
I suppose
they have run away
or perhaps they died.
Where is the dark-haired man
who used to shout at me
in a language I didn't understand,
the woman in gauze and lace
who danced midnight pirouettes
and cried silver tears,
the peasant couple
he with the hoe, she with the burlap sack,
who tended purple orchards,
and the fair child who needed
to hold my hand as we jumped
from cloud to cloud?
They are gone,
and I am left with
white curtains blowing in empty rooms,
desolate squares full of hungry pigeons,
fields of silent stars.

GLORIA VANDO

OUT OF BOUNDS IN KANSAS CITY
(for Pearse A. Mitchell)

These days I live in a treehouse
Above the green,
Where golfers swing their arms and bodies
In time to the wind, in keeping
With the driven branches of the basswoods.

It is Labor Day. Hot September gusts
Split the air like golf balls whizzing
Down the treelined alley to the 16th hole.
I watch the hackers,
Their white caps and gloves reflecting
The early morning light, file by
In a rhythmless conga line,
Lifting first one leg, then the other—
But no kick to it, no passion,
Only the ritual motion of body like ball
Dribbling from fairway to fairway.

Not my stepfather. He had a knack
For it. His feet in their metal-laden,
Multicolored oxfords trotted like a lithe fox
Across the grass. "My heart quickens
When I see a green," he told us
That one time he came to visit.
And he might have stayed—his heart intact—
Viewing the course each day
From our high perch, had not the ocean
Beckoned to him—as it does me—to come home.

GLORIA VANDO

IN THE CREVICES OF NIGHT

There's a man in my dream,
A man with a hatchet,
Ransacking my bureau,
Hacking at the doll asleep
In the bottom drawer.

A bloodless ritual.
He calls himself a surgeon, says
He's up on the latest laser beam
Techniques. I know better.
I know the jig's up.
Youth is waning and the end
Is closing in on the beginning—
A telescopic fantasy focused
On dismembered limbs, a glass eye
Rolling across the parquet floor,
Tiny fingernails scattered
In my underwear scratching
At the obscenity of early death.
But not a drop of blood. Not a cry.

I turn from the dream, reaching
For you across the thin ice of night
And pressing my body to yours
Long, foolishly, to bear your child.

Gloria Vando

Jim Goss photo

MONA VAN DUYN

THE INSIGHT LADY OF ST. LOUIS ON ZOOS
(a found oral poem)

The other day I had an insight.
I suddenly realized why I hate zoos.
You know how they build those enclosures
for an animal or two, and if the animal
is the kind that lives in a rocky country
they put one rock with it and then they say,
see, there it is in its natural habitat?
And if the animal is a forest animal
they plant one tree with it and then they say,
see, there it is in its natural habitat?
Well, the handyman had put up the new bookshelf
on the only wall in the house
that isn't already covered with bookshelves,
and I organized all the books I had used
to write my book on Svevo, and then
all the books I had used for my book on Kierkegaard,
and then I saw myself as a zoo animal.
They would build a bare room with three bare walls
and put me and one book in it and then they would say,
see, there she is in her natural habitat?

And that evening I went to a party
and when we left I went upstairs to get my own coat,
and you should have seen that upstairs—
how can people live in a mess like that?—
it looked as if the drugbusters had made a raid
and left every drawer half open
with the clothes and stuff dumped out on the floor,
and there was one book lying on the floor
and I picked it up to see what it was,
and then I had another terrible insight.
I knew what book they would put in my zoo pen.
It would be that book, *Building Bicycles*.

189

MONA VAN DUYN

THE LEARNERS

We slapped the smirking mother
and the swollen father
and went to live in museums
and anthologies. Around us
were images of such fairness
that the world outside
was smoothed into smog.
We knew it was hard.
We were bony and strong
but our knuckles broke
as we cleaned and copied.

When rocks split the cellophane windows
we stumbled outside
leading the eldest.
Sun seared our eyeballs
and the cramp of the journey
crazed some of the seemliest.
Some of us dried to jerky.
When the light lowered a bit
some of us said they found
beauty beyond belief
in the ashes and oilspills.

When darkness came down
some mated, some murdered each other.
Some of us shook our fists
at the moon and the stars
for disdainful distance.
All over creation
there were sounds and shadows.
Digging into a cockpit of earth
with our broken knuckles
some of us sat and waited
with whatever was in the world.

from *Letters From a Father and Other Poems*, copyright Mona Van Duyn, permission Atheneum

MONA VAN DUYN

EARTH TREMORS FELT IN MISSOURI

The quake last night was nothing personal,
you told me this morning. I think one always wonders,
unless, of course, something is visible: tremors
that take us, private and willy-nilly, are usual.

But the earth said last night that what I feel,
you feel; what secretly moves you, moves me.
One small, senuous catastrophe
makes inklings letters, spelled in a worldly tremble.

The earth, with others on it, turns in its course
as we turn toward each other, less than ourselves, gross,
mindless, more than we were. Pebbles, we swell
to planets, nearing the universal roll,
in our conceit even comprehending the sun,
whose bright ordeal leaves cool men woebegone.

Thomas Victor photo

Mona Van Duyn

from *Merciful Disguises, Published and Unpublished Poems*, copyright Mona Van Duyn, permission Atheneum

MARGIT VINCENZ

WORDPOWER

Since her confinement to a home
her outer world became quite small,
yet even if no friends came by
she has the company of guests
who come and go according to her mood.

WORDS are her unseen visitors,
the whispering voice of memories,
soothing sayings, prayers learned by heart,
the joyous text of childhood's songs,
some breathless phrases of astonishment,
of courtesy and gallantry
woven with unwrapped naughty words,
words of delight and of distress
and of such daring attitude,
words of advice kept heavy on the tongue
that rattle later out of tune,
words of praise that stroke with gentle hands,
words of precious books and letters,
a play or just a proverb which proved true,
mixed with expressions of mere sound,
cascading laughter, missed so much,
the sounds of crying, kept awake,
yet mainly words describing her,
tossed words of various sentiment,
all strewn along her path
emerging as a vocal sculpture.

So many words indeed were said,
yet she remembers mostly the harsh
that poison with sharp needle pricks
and stop the spirit's happy rise.
She thinks about the power of such words:
One can forgive them, but they still exist,
often not meant, yet they live on.

Amd when sweet words come back to her
she smiles, considers them a special treat,
but they are few and far between
and some of them have paled with age.
She found that they exist combined
with hugs and kisses intertwined;
if either fades, both lose their power.

And yielding to a longing mood
she keeps searching for those words,
and tiring soon, the loss makes her too sad.
And when she sits there forlorn and still
she tries to gaze beyond her room,
it happens that the silent sun
rests on her outstreached hands and fills her palms.

DEANE WAGNER

RINGS AND NAILS

Write me a dirty poem, he says; but she doesn't want to. She
might want sometime to perform a dirty poem, and with him, but she
won't write one.

Poetry is her love and she writes it clean. She writes of lovers,
lechers, perverts, and wistful underachievers, all couched in sensuous,
no Saxon, words. She's fond of puns, too. She did, though, write one
dirty poem, just to prove to herself that she could. While waiting for a
left-turn arrow, she decided to write one in what she thought of as the
genital genre, and in the six minutes it took her to drive to Pratzel's
to pick up fifteen little chocolate cakes, she made up six lines of free
verse about semen:

> Sweet moonlit silver
> is international currency
> illegal(ly) tender
> This is a night depository
> You cannot withdraw
> your savings

She scribbled them, small, on the bakery's cash register tape. Her
cliterary jewel, she thought it—but not dirty, after all.

> The gem cakes were well received at the meeting.
> She won't show him that poem.

He reads widely, but little poetry. He likes words. He'll call her
up to introduce one to her and, like her southern aunt, he'll discuss his
new acquaintance's background. "Comes from the Middle English, you
know; descended from Old French, and can you imagine? on the Italian
side there's. . ." She has likely already met the word's cousins, at least.

One day he called to say he'd seen an axolotl. A wnat? she said.
"An axolotl," he said, "it's an animal at the zoo." No it isn't she said.
"What the hell do you mean, it isn't? I SAW it." Nevertheless, she said,
it's the answer to a riddle: Axolotl? That's what you do to learn a lotl.

They both think the pun and word itself are funny. But she won't
say his favorite words because she doesn't want to, and although she
shucks off inhibitions with her clothing, she won't do two things he
wants. She says one of them sounds distasteful. The other, she said when
cajoled, is *in*sanitary. He rolled right off her. "My god, woman, what a
word to use at a time like this!" Nevertheless, she said composedly, I
prefer what you were just doing. So he did it some more.

He does find her exasperating, which she enjoys. She considers
him domineering, which he admits. You want to be in control of me,

she states. "Yes." But I want to be in control of myself. So he tries a new tactic. If he succeeds a little, she'll remember it.

She knows how he watches her hands, in public. She sketches vivid little pictures in air: the futility of a project, the expansion of a problem, the meshing of functions. He watches, not her face, but her flashing nails and distinctive rings. When she's remembering, she wears the ring that's his favorite. She bought it for herself, and he likes her taste. Although he shares her ex-husband's taste, he likes this ring even better than her wedding ring, which he admires very much. He may like either or both even better than his present wife's wedding ring, although he doesn't mention that. She, of course, wouldn't ask, but when they talk of rings she's afraid he'll tell her. So when they are both in public and he watches her hands as she speaks, she looks at him as often as she dares, enjoying his temporary ensnarement in the net she weaves of air.

Last week at a meeting she had a lot to say. She had chosen not to see him alone for a while, and as she talked he stared. His face, usually so noncommittal, showed interest, then absorption, then something very like greed. She finished her talk with her hands clasped lightly on the table. After the meeting, she remarked blandly that he looked hungry. He invited her to lunch.

She went. She accepted coffee, a salad and eventually half of his grilled cheese sandwich. She rejects everything else on his menu.

He says, "You did this to me once before, when you were screwing that guy." Yes. "Now you tell me you want to make changes in your life. Are you exchanging me for him again?" No. That's finished. "Isn't he the one you introduced at that dinner this spring?" No. That was a friend. "A friend? You mean he takes you out and doesn't screw you?" Right. I consider him a friend.

"Well, you're seeing *someone* who's not just a friend." In the lightest musterable tone (but he's gripping his coffee cup) he adds: "You are, aren't you? Joe saw you with someone at Balaban's last week." That was *another* friend. "Two of em?" Three. "God. Three! and not one of them gets to—?" The newest one may be different. He's, well, he appeals to me.

"I'm enjoying this, you know." She looks at him. His forehead is pink. He laughs. "I'm enjoying putting this to you." She thinks his choice of phrase amusing, and because his forehead is pink, she knows he's angry. Ha ha.

She doesn't notice that he doesn't call the next day. He always calls sometime, and when she's choosing not to see him alone he delights in encountering her in corridors or committees. "Want you to see this," he'll say, and while she looks at his report or grocery list, he'll murmur the sexiest specificities he can think of, and she'll note the inordinate number of ears their colleagues are wearing. So for now she's avoiding all likely encounters.

But a few days later, when she has an appointment in his building, she wonders if she'll see him, but doesn't. Then while she's buckling her seat belt, he walks into the parking lot just behind one of the secretaries in his department. She waves to both as she passes them. The randy bastard, now he's firing on *her*! And before she thinks further, she whips her car into the next driveway, U-turns and is re-entering his parking lot when the secretary drives out, alone.

He's nowhere to be seen, but come to think of it that was Joe's car that left as she returned, and he often lunches with Joe, his colleague and informer. She skulks her VW in behind a van and pretends to look in her briefcase for something she pretends to find.

She doesn't want the non-existent object any more than she wants him. Or rather, she thinks, vice-versa. So why is she hiding here behind a van, pantomiming Eureka!? She wouldn't marry him if he were free and asking; she doesn't want to marry anyone and would never trust *him* anyway; she's tired of smiling at an interesting new face and seeing, instead, him and his damned axolotl. She really *wants* to make changes, to get him out of her life.

But does she? She wants to ignore his body and engage his mind. She already misses him: his polished public and bawdy private discourse, the contrast; their talk of words, of wars and myths, of when and how and why. She misses his hands on her nape, soothing, although they never soothe for long; misses his hands, his lips, and she's working right down the list when she stops herself. O yes.

But she's glad she told him, with a sweep of her hand, Th-that's all, f-f-folks.

Now she's sitting at her desk, at a stack of the yellow second-sheets she writes on. She looks at her hands. They pick up the stack, tap it straight—bottom edge, top edge, left side, right; then place the now-neat stack precisely before her. She's glad she didn't write him that poem.

She looks at her left hand. The smooth cool richness of the carnelian ring is somehow gratifying to her. The diamonds of her wedding ring glint as her right hand picks up a pen.

> I remember Cyclops
> forger of thunderbolts
> one-eyed giant.

MARYFRANCES WAGNER

GIANT CLOWN

"There's no clown at your window,"
Mother insisted when called
to my bed late at night.
His painted frown,
his tapping, gloved hands,
his polka dot tie
haunted the window of childhood nights
where I tried, under a flood of sweat,
eyes squeezed tight, to lie still
until he went away.

At six, my nephew
called me to his bed,
sheet tugged to his eyes.
"A giant clown at my window."
"There's no clown,"
I started automatic as closing doors
then bit those words, then began again.
"Where?"
"Right there. He's got a rifle
and a polka dot bow tie."
"Wanna sleep in my room?" I asked.

When Mother started killing cancer pain
with methodone, she was certain
elves built puppets at night across the street,
cows stomped through the house.

"Those things aren't really there,"
I insisted. "It's just the medicine."
One afternoon she added,
"I saw a giant clown
outside the window last night."

"A clown?" I asked.
"What did he look like?"

JANE O. WAYNE

THE TRESPASSER

One slat half-twisted in these blinds
and I can see him out there in the alley
reading through all my trash:
my old shoes, my empty envelopes,
a bare-boned fish.

My thick hedge can't keep him out.
He reads right through it to my dandelions,
my uncut grass. If I'm not careful,
he'll get in the house, brazen past me
like a spider on a houseplant.

In my sitting room
he'll find the white scars
glasses leave on all the tables
and that pale square hanging on the wall.
He won't stop there.

He'll read my favorite chair
like the lines in my palm,
and on my face dark thoughts surfacing
as clothes do in a tub of water.
But I won't talk.

So what if he ransacks every closet
and empties drawers onto the floor.
Shake me, turn me inside-out
like some old sock—
I won't yield.

JANE O. WAYNE

IN YOUR HOUSE ON ELIA STREET

If it was summer
when she happened on their empty cottage
in the middle of the woods
and tried their table and their chairs,
their porridge in their bowls,
She might have taken off her shoes afterwards
as I do in your house.
She might have listened for them
when she climbed the stairs that night
or opened drawers—
might have heard what I do,
turning doorknobs, turning pages
that you've turned.

And if she stayed until the cut flowers
wilted on the mantle,
she might have thrown them out,
holding stems that they had held.
She might have changed the water in the vase
on a murky afternoon, and cut more flowers
for the house, the color of the ones they'd left.
At someone else's sink,
someone else's towel against her face,
she might have hesitated at the mirror
as I do early in the morning
rubbing off the cold, damp glass,
half-expecting you.

JANE O. WAYNE

OUT OF THE ORDINARY

First, the milk must boil:
three times the wave of white
rising in the pan,
three times descending;
then before you add
a spoonful of yogurt,
the milk must be no cooler
than your blood,
no hotter. For years,
I've followed the same rules
from some forgotten book,
followed rites
that I don't understand—
the wooden spoon,
the thick ceramic bowl—
followed a recipe
as others do religion.
I always stir the warm mix
clockwise, always leave it
covered with a plate
on the same window sill
in the kitchen, and by morning
I can always thicken milk
and feed my family
from a bowl of partial knowledge.

Jane O. Wayne

HUBA WELLS

GRACEFULLY

Using planets
as stepping stones.
April arrived.

MARILYN WILLIAMS

HIGH WIND IN GEORGIA

Marilyn Williams

Shades flap their wings.
Blinds rattle their bones.
Everything windblown. Even my thoughts
strain like dogs on their leashes.
No hurricane warnings, no warnings at all,
but red dust is rising all over the South.
The South could be rising without me
while I stand here watching,
gathering dust like my crystal goblets,
those one-legged dancers,
standing for years on their stems,
just waiting to break. I know how they feel.
I've lived here too long, waging my wars
against ants and tarantulas,
routing out spiders.
I understand spiders,
their lives hanging on by a thread,
and I know how a fly feels,
caught in some fiendish contraption,
so soft to his feet, he was
thinking of clouds, not webs.

SUZANNE WILSON

THE SUNDAY BEFORE ST. PATRICK'S

Yesterday was a poem I could not write
a country afternoon that would not word itself.
In at the eyes, straight to the heart.

Now I know it was
wash on the line
matching the blue rooftops,
couples tilling their gardens,
a man standing in the loam
with a coffee mug to his lips,
a family playing ball—
and you and I, driving by,
stopping, wandering.
We lay claim to all,
we hungry lovers savoring the meal
without writing down the recipe.

For us the small creeks floating green cress,
for us, bits of blue glass
against the moss in the country park,
for us, the emerald winter wheat
among the pale of last year's fields,
the budding broomlike trees
on the far hillside,
the light-rimmed cattle
in the evening pasture.

SUZANNE WILSON

TWICE DREAMED

Two people dreamed my death.
One dreamed I died
before this coming Christmas,
the other dreamed the same night
and agreed
I'd go.

God knows, I've dreamed.
Tornadoes,
fires in the sky,
lunatic marshmallow people,
getting-there dreams,
never really getting there.
Now, they say, I will.

And well I know the dream of falling
outward slowly
to the bottom of the stairs,
ended by my waking
with a thud.
Now, they say,
I'll land.

But I've been through tornadoes—
Smack! (Neighbor's roof against my window)
—and survived.
I have fled the fires,
slid on ice.

Oh, they could be right—
there's a certain malaise here,
and hair comes out in the comb.
I've noticed my handwriting
shrinking away.

I won't subscribe.
I plan to sleep,
to dream my death to death
in mild December,
to wake and dream my life.
But pray for me, friend,
now and at the hour
of my waking.

MAXINE

My mother, a pudgy woman with straight brown hair combed to one side and steel-framed glasses, kneads a lump of bread dough with plump brown hands, smooth from years of hard work. I perch on a step-stool she has drawn up to the counter for me, eating a piece of the lemon meringue pie she has made in honor of my visit and calculating the number of days I'll have to skip breakfast to make up for this indulgence. No one else in the family even likes lemon meringue pie, but it's my favorite, and she makes it every time I come, along with macaroni and cheese and stuffed cabbage. I'm aware of how she fills out her flowered housedress and have said, my whole life, this will not happen to me.

It's the first day of my visit. My luggage is still sitting inside the door off the side porch, not yet carried up to the room that used to be mine.

"This doesn't have anything to do with you, Mama," I say, awkwardly trying to rekindle a conversation she seems determined not to have. "You know I'd never be disloyal to you. If I thought you were going to be hurt, I'd never do it."

She turns over the mound of dough and pounds it flat with the heel of her hand before setting the rolling pin to it. I have to raise my voice to get over the noise.

"She wrote me a Christmas card. I never would have thought of it otherwise. It was her idea, really. She wrote that she saw my car over here last summer when I visited, and if I came again this year, she'd like to see me. Just two sentences on the bottom of an ordinary Christmas card. After I got it, I told myself it's time we laid that all to rest. It's been fifteen years. Long enough." I'm talking too fast out of nervousness.

She greases a bread pan vigorously with lard. While she's doing this she squints out at my dad who's pushing a rototiller in the garden, something he's too old to do. She wants to make sure he doesn't hear what she has to say to me. When she looks back at me, her eyes are narrow and her jaw is set, like we're conspirators in an unpleasant deal. She puts one hand on her hip and with the other shakes a greased and floured finger at me. "That woman caused me a lot of pain, missy. Maybe you don't remember the summer I lost twenty pounds and cried myself to sleep many a night. There were times I cried all night long, and your daddy would go out onto the porch swing, just so he could get up and go to work the next morning."

"Yes, Mama. How could I forget!" I move a piece of fluted crust around on the saucer with my fork, avoiding her eyes. "But you're all out here in the country. She's alone, and you and Daddy aren't kids anymore. What if you need each other? It just seems crazy, carrying a grudge like that."

She covers the dough with a wet towel and sets it on the stove so the warm oven will cause it to raise. Her back's to me. "You do what you have to do. You're a grown woman. I can't stop you."

In the living room, where my purse sits on top of my overnight bag, I brush my hair and put on lipstick. I slip out the side door without telling her I'm leaving. Outside the sun bakes down. My dad stops to take a handkerchief out of his overalls pocket and mop his forehead. He sees me and waves. I've always loved summer in the midwest. It's hot and moist in the day, but at night everything cools down. There are bees swarming around my mother's petunia bed, and the tabby cat, a fat old lady now, lies up against the step in the only pool of shade she can find.

I walk across the gravel road determinedly and push Maxine's doorbell before I can think about it. I'm not crazy about this errand, either, but it has to be done. Maxine wants to see me, and if I don't, I'll never be able to come home again without her watching my car, wondering if I'm going to come over, and thinking I buy into this feud my mother has had with her since I was in high school.

I haven't seen her up close in all these years and am surprised to see she looks better than I remembered. Her hair used to be long and stringy and tied back with a rubber band so tight her eyes seemed to pop out of her head. I never could see what she had my mother didn't, except she was thinner and had a job. Her house is the same but much different on the inside. She was divorced back then with three small children to raise. Then she married a man my mother said gave her everything she wanted, but he died, and now she's a widow. And someone who's spent a good deal of her life being alone.

Her eyes crinkle up at the corners when she sees me. "I'm so glad you came," she says and hugs me, although we are both embarrassed. "Iced tea?" she asks.

"Please," I say. I will need something to occupy my hands here, as I did in mother's kitchen.

Her kitchen has been remodeled so she doesn't have to carry water in a bucket from the pump outside, and there's a bathroom where the hall closet used to be. "Your house is beautiful. You've done a lot with it," I say to fill the awkward silence after we sit down and have our first sips of tea.

"My second husband, Jason, was very good around the house. He put in my kitchen and bathroom by himself. He liked to work inside during the winter, but he was always outside in the yard and garden in the summer. I can't get things to grow the way he used to. Sure do miss him." She stares at her tea. I sense she's about to talk about what she wanted me here for. "I never wanted your father, Pat," she blurts out finally, and now she looks straight at me, without smiling.

"We don't have to talk about this at all, if you don't want to," I say quickly, holding up my hands as if to ward off her words. "That was all so long ago."

She shakes her head no. "It has to be said, and you're the only one I can get to listen to me." She pauses and lets out a deep breath. "He was so kind to me the year Claude left. I don't know how much you remember, but I'll never forget it. I'd never worked a day in my life away from home, but he gave me a job at the hardware store, and he put up with a lot while I was learning." She laughs shortly at the memory. "He let me off when the kids were sick, without any questions, and he never docked my pay because he knew how much I needed the money. He even let me ride with him so I didn't have to buy gas." I nod. From my vantage point in the adult divorced world, I understand better than I'd like to.

"It only happened once." I steel myself for what's next. "It was spring, May, I think, a Friday, and we were riding home with the windows down and the radio on. I had on a cotton dress with lavendar flowers around the hem. Isn't it funny I'd remember that? They say a woman does. Anyway, all of a sudden he pulled the car over to the side of the road by the rest stop, where the picnic table used to be. I thought he was having car trouble. He turned and put his arm up on the back of the seat. 'Maxine,' he said, 'I'd give everything I own to kiss you one time.' Well, I knew it was wrong, but it was so unexpected, and he had been so good to me. Maybe I was afraid I'd lose my job if I didn't. Anyway, I let him kiss me. It wasn't passionate or long. It reminded me of the first time a boy ever kissed me in fifth grade. Just sort of. . .tender."

"I felt guilty right away and told him we should drive on, and he did, he started the car up again, but he seemed to think that since I kissed him, I was agreeing to something more. He told me, 'Dorothy's going to visit her mother next weekend.' He said, 'and she's taking Pat with her. Maybe I could come over Saturday evening after the little ones are asleep.' "

She pauses, sets her glass on the coffee table. "Your mother was my best friend, Pat." I nod again. There is no other way to respond to what she's telling me. "Before all that happened, we were in and out each other's houses a dozen times a week, drinking coffee, borrowing things. Before she got her driver's license, I'd drive her to the store every week. Well, there was no way I was going to betray the best friend I had. I told Willard no. I said I couldn't do it to Dorothy. He didn't even answer me, just started driving and nodded his head one time. I would've missed it if I hadn't been watching him."

"I thought that was the end of it. That we'd go on like always. But I guess I wounded his male pride. I don't know what he told your mother. But, the next Monday morning he called and said he couldn't give me a ride anymore because he was going to have to work late on inventory or payroll or something. The whole weekend had gone by and I hadn't heard from Dorothy. So I called her. 'Is anything wrong?' I asked her, 'I haven't heard from you in three days.' 'I think you know what's wrong,' she said and slammed down the phone.

"That's how it's been all this time. When she drives by, she turns her head if I'm out in the yard. Sometimes when we're both working in our gardens, we'd be within yelling distance, but she acts like I'm "not there. Maxine looks out the window, off into the distance, where my father has cut off the tiller and is walking toward the garage.

"What do you want me to do?" I ask. Her story is obviously finished, and she sits still, like a mechanical fortune teller whose prophecies have run down.

She shrugs. "I don't know if there's anything you *can* do. It couldn't ever be the same between us again, of course. I just wanted somebody to know it wasn't my fault."

I swirl the melting ice in the glass I still hold. It's sweaty and I wipe the bottom on the knee of my jeans. I don't like thinking of my dad this way. I liked it better when she was to blame.

"I don't mean to discredit your dad," she adds quickly, as if she's read my mind. "I think they must have been having problems of some kind then, and I was just the closet woman to turn to. I'd be willing to bet he's never been unfaithful to her. Before he retired, he came home at five-thirty every night of the world, regular as clockwork. Now he's home all the time. I see them outside doing things together and they look real happy."

I change the subject, and we talk for another hour about her children, who are now grown. The sun is no longer high up, and I know my mother will be waiting dinner for me. When I leave we hug again. "I'm going to tell her this," I say. "I don't know how much good it will do. . ." I leave the sentence trailing behind me as I go through her picket gate and back across the road toward my parents' house, thinking of how I can phrase what I have to say to my mother.

Inside the table is set, and I hear the valve jiggling on the pressure cooker. The loaf of fresh bread sits brown and shiny on a board next to a slab of home-churned butter. She sits in the living room by the window facing Maxine's, casually turning magazine pages. She looks up and smiles, determined not to ask. I sit on the hassock in front of her and put my hands on the magazine so she has to stop flipping the pages. "Mama," I say, "I want to tell you what Maxine said. I think it might change everything." She turns her head away from me. "Maxine said nothing ever happened between her and Daddy. She said he kissed her one time in the car and asked her if he could come over sometime, but she said no, Mama. She said you were the best friend she had. You've been mad at her all these years for nothing. She didn't start it, he did. But even so, it was nothing." I'm excited about my role as peacemaker. I want her and Maxine to get together right now. Maybe we could ask Maxine over to dinner.

"I know that, Pat," my mother says and looks defiantly right into my eyes, something she seldom does. Her thick glasses make her eyes look bigger than they are, and she knows it. "He came home that very day and told me he had made a fool of himself. He said they pulled over at the rest stop and he kissed her, asked if he could see her when I took you to visit your grandmother. Is that what she told you?"

I nod my head, frowning. "And she told him no because she didn't want to betray me?" I keep nodding. Abruptly she stands up and drops the magazine on the hassock beside me. Then she turns around and rearranges the curtains behind the chair. "I think supper's almost ready," she says.

"What are you going to do?" I ask, still thinking something is going to change.

When she turns around again, an artificial smile is glazed across her face. "Why don't you go out and see if Dad is ready?"

I push through the screen door and clatter down the back steps and across the patio to the garage, glad to get away for a minute. Through the glass in the side door I see him take a last swig from a pink bottle, screw on the cap, and replace it on a shelf behind the waders he says every spring he's going to use. When I open the door he's squatting down, wiping oil off the tiller. In the last fifteen years he's put on a lot of weight, and his hair has thinned.

"Supper ready, sweet pea?" he asks.

"Yes, Daddy," I say. "Mama's putting it on the table right this minute."

CAROLYNE WRIGHT

HEAT WAVE: LIBERTY, MISSOURI
(August 27, 1983)

I can't wait to see
that evening sun go down.
In this first-floor hotbox,
no Billie or Bessie or Big
Mama Thorton to remind me
where we've been:
                    New Orleans,
easy city where a white woman's
dark-skinned lover could steal
away through the grillwork
and disappear into the Creole wards
while the nay-sayers shrugged
and went on pruning the brown leaves
from their family trees. City
where we walked home from the Quarters
past the multi-colored stalls
of the fruit and flower market,
cries of the Cajun vendors;
where we made love under the ceiling fan
as mid-summer rainstorms swept the yards
and lightning touched down around us
like incoming fire.
                    Here, derailed
from my big-city expectations,
I'm on my own. Whatever I choose
to make of it. Every suitcase I unpack
a concession. A border state's chance
to ask the hard questions.

Dogs in the front yards
bark at my accent and my bedroom-
colored skin, the red dress
I wear Thursdays that says
I don't give a damn. Through jalousies
the neighborhood watches—I'm part
of all that's wrong with America.

Only the radio gives the facts.
Twenty years to the day
from Selma. Twenty years from the hoses,
dogs, demonstrators lying in rows

in the squad cars' shadows.
Two blocks from the Kappa Alpha house
with the Confederate flag
still hanging between white columns.

Every night, someone stands under my window
smoking Camels. I lower the bedframe
from its closet, sleep in a room
with screens unlocked
and a fan that drowns out
the footfalls of intruders.
Every morning, I get right up
against day's burning wall,
the I Have a Dream speech
fading from air above the marchers.

What else could we have said
even if I believed my life here?
If I dreamed the crossed sticks
on the lawn, waiting for evening
to burst into spontaneous flame?
One signature in the wrong place
and this old world of have-to's
got me good, twenty years
from the Freedom Riders
and Rosa Parks' *I'm tired.*

We know which side this town took.
My parents are proud
of how far from you I've come,
justifying my silence in the looped
shadow that falls down between us.
They don't see how I stand
before the bedroom mirror,
touching my nipples to the glass.

published 1986, *Missouri Review*

CAROLYNE WRIGHT

NOTE FROM THE STOP-GAP MOTOR INN

*"The man who crosses the street
may be already out of reach."*
  —Bertolt Brecht

Blues librettist, piano vamper,
transposer of the heart's iambics
to the ideographs of anything goes,
I'm a fool to leave you.

I've traded you for this
dead-end town, this South
by Midwest zipcode. What the hell
for? friends ask. Don't I know

a good thing? I tell them
I've led a charmed life.
Whatever I wanted
I got. Whatever I didn't

drove off alone. In a country
where it's dangerous to say No
to strangers, I've walked the streets
wearing my silent majority look,

my Welcome to America complexion.
I've got no talent for concealment,
and no profile but yours
is missing from the picture.

What would the true believers
say if they knew? The preacher
who crosses the street to avoid me?
Who, if I asked the time of day,

would turn his digital watch dial
off? Too late to change us, lady.
Too late to take the next train
or erase the lovers pressed back

to back in the ink blots,
in a town where everyone thinks
memory is enough. Who's laying bets
we get out of this alive?
I'm drawing my own geography
of cowardice, and you're home, not even
whistling Dixie to remind yourself.
You know the old score—

those who live in the dreamstates
of the saved, calling themselves
the Beautiful People: your name cut off,
a broadcast across enemy lines.

R. Miller photo

Carolyne Wright

published 1984, *New Letters*

JOAN YEAGLEY

THE KEEPER OF THE FIRE

My lover waits.
I catch his fleeting shadow
Behind and always on my left side
As one notices
The soft, throated dart of the quail.
He is beautiful
But I disdain his grace.
I was a proud woman
And not easily taken, nor suprised.
Once in a glade I met a doe
But the castle in its eye was strange.
I turned in time
As it reared to trample me.
His respect is great.
All these years I have kept the fire
And must be accorded the last privilege.
The women will tear away my rags,
Dress me in new clothes.
They will comb down this old white head.
My hair will fall to my waist,
Black, glossy as the upstart crow's.
I will dance.
All the others will fall away.
I alone will step to the right, making small feet,
Beat sticks, sing a tremulo,
Homage the four directions,
Only then, only then,
Shall I cover my head,
Taste the bright flame of his mouth.

JOAN YEAGLEY

THE SHRINK SAYS

I learned good scotch
Like I learned good men;
Belly laughs when the punch line
Drops decorum
With a ribald poke;
Straight from the shoulder stuff
Like a fast horse under my heels
Or the sure sense in my right shoulder
When bullets spin a Schlitz can
Floating by, spink, spink, again, spink.

Trying he says,
To be a father's need,
Son,
Wish of himself.

The shrink says—

But no tad this—
Out at the elbows with herself—

Her mother's child
Learned one good man,
Loves a good drink,
A good shot,
A good ride.

WILMA YEO

MIRACLE AT CROOKED CREEK

Our town sits right back of Crooked Creek in the Ozarks hills. It's not much of a town, hobbling along side of a hill the way it does like a hound dog with a broken leg. It's sure not the kind of a town you'd expect a miracle to happen in. But then as far as that goes, Barney Calloway was not the kind of man you'd expect to see a miracle happen *to* either.

There wasn't a soul in town could beat Barney at playing gin-rummy. And I guess that except for Miss Lucy who ran the boarding house, and the church women, most everyone in town had tried—tried right here in my filling station.

It could have been that Barney was just plain lucky at cards. On the other hand, it could have been that Barney had a system. Barney was a talker. Seemed like he could keep one eye on the discards and his big mouth shootin' off—all at the same time.

Like as not when the stakes were high and the game really tight, old Barney would be telling one of his wild stories like: "Hey, did you hear about Mrs. Littlefield trying to hang herself over at the boarding house last night?" And without missin' a draw he'd go into an impersonation of poor old Mrs. Littlefield, who weighed three hundred if she weighed a pound, trying to get herself into a dress that was three sizes too small. About the time Barney had all the players a laughin' good, he'd say, "Gin," and put his cards down easy like.

Except for the tourist season, when he might make a few dollars by signin' up to go along as guide on a couple of float trips down the White River yonder, I reckon Barney made most of his livin' right here in my station at that corner table.

Day and night Barney had a can of beer in his big hairy fist. All in all you can imagine he was not too popular with the women folk—especially Miss Lucy, although it had been talked around that Barney hankered after her affections somewhat more than a little.

Miss Lucy was kind of pretty and although she's gettin' on toward forty, people still mentioned that she would make some man a mighty fine wife, and they wern't speakin' of her cookin' either—leastwise the men wern't.

All I had to go on, about how Barney felt toward Miss Lucy, was that I never saw him do no imitations of her nor tell any funny stories on her. In fact, come to think of it, he never mentioned her at all, which should 'fatten the hog' as the sayin' goes, seeings he made jokes about everybody else in town, includin' hisself.

Well the start of the miracle was one Sunday morning. It was too dry and too hot for fish to be bitin' so the game was pretty big and it was serious.

Barney was in his usual spot, one big shoulder sloped back against

215

his chair like winning was easy, when the new preacher went into the church right across the road there.

Barney was facin' the window and when he got the first glimpse of the skinny, blonde reverend, he said, "One thing sure, *he'll* never work no miracles." Shows you how wrong a man can be, especially if he talks all the time and increases his chances the way old Barn did.

There's never much excitement around here so it was not unexpected when everybody in town turned out for the first preachin'.

I was wipin' off the counters for Irma when I heard Barney say, "Reckon there ain't no reason for us to miss his first show. Heard over at the boardin' house he's gonna preach on hard liquor. Knew a fellow like that once myself," he went on, spreadin' a winnin' hand, "he did his best preachin' on 'rot gut'."

I didn't see any reason I should miss out on the fun so I asked Irma to mind the pumps and went along with the boys. After some shovin' we all got ourselves across the road and into the last row seats in the church. Up front the new little preacher was lookin' like a loud Amen would scare him clean out of town.

When that poor feller got around to the sermon, he talked about the evils of drink all right, but with him the fire of hell wasn't burnin' no hotter than a pilot light. Even Miss Lucy, up front, got fidgity. This new parson didn't exactly *fill* the pulpit, as they say, he just kind of *leaned* against it.

After the preachin' was over and the game was started anew, I was surprised that Barney never mentioned the funny new parson. He didn't have much to say at all—appeared to be brooding over something which was not like old Barney. He even came out loser for the afternoon session.

But then on Monday he seemed his usual self, and I didn't think no more about it till I checked up on my beer sales on Saturday night and didn't show the usual profit. Then I realized Irma hadn't popped one single can for that fool Barney all week long!

Sunday morning he didn't show up at all. I figured he'd gone over to Whillers Dock to sign up for the day, when all of a sudden I saw Barney, big as life, followin' a little knot of folks into the church across the way.

I nudged Irma to take over and went across the road and peeked into the back window to make sure I hadn't been seein' things.

Sure enough! There sat old Barney all by hisself on the back row. He sat there in the exact same spot he'd been sittin' in the Sunday before when we all went—meek as a trussed up bull. The sun was pouring through the skylight above him like a big spotlight on his face and well—old Barn looked as out of place as Billy-The-Kid at a Ladies Aid meeting.

The window was open and I heard the little parson's words meander across the congregation like a gentle breeze that stirred folks just enough to make them restless—all except for Barney. He was starin' at that parson like the parson had him hypnotized.

The followin' Monday Barney showed up, but he didn't drink a single beer and his heart didn't seem to be in the game at all.

Then he quit comin' in the station altogether and someone said he'd signed up permanent over at Whillers—which none of us could figure at all since it wasn't even good fishin', what with the drought and the heat. Every Sunday I sneaked over to the church and took a peek. There'd sit old Barn in that same seat, still big as life but different from the old Barney as a wild cat from a kitten. It seemed to me like his big face looked sad with all the joking gone out of it, but his eyes never strayed from the pulpit. It was sure hard to figure since the parson wasn't improvin' any with practice. That preacher was so meek you expected to see him inherit the earth any minute.

It was plain to see we had lost the old Barney to religion, and the mystery was, knowin' that preacher feller—where the religion was coming from.

Over at the station we all tried to figure it out. We talked about the old days when Barney entertained us with his rip-roarin' stories and his goofy imitations. Someone dug up the one about Barney's pa who'd married twice. By each of his wives, his pa'd had eight kids. Barney was never funnier than when he told about his pa thinkin' Barney was a neighbor kid and tellin' him to go home.

"But, Pa, I *am* home. I'm Barney," he'd said.

Or the time his ma, who was the second wife, said to Barney, "I don't like to speak disrespectful of the dead, but you get your big mouth from your ma and I'm gettin' mighty sick of listenin' to it."

"But, Ma, *you* are my ma!" Barney said, imitating hisself as a kid—pullin' his wide clown's mouth down at the corners. Watchin' him—you would almost swear those were real tears, tears like a ten-year-old would cry, you know, bitter about never gettin' no attention unless in trouble.

Barney had a real talent for entertainin' all right, and I suppose it was remembrin' all those belly laughs we had here in my station that kept me goin' over to the church Sundays to check and see if he really had left us for good and gone over to the other side, so to speak.

The summer was a scorcher with the hills turned a dusty grey. Then one Sunday when I was over there lookin' in at the open window, I heard the parson apologize, sayin' he had to be out of town for the next Sunday's preachin'.

"Could someone—er—do something—er—like speak in my place or something?" he asked.

My feet almost went out from under me when Barney raised hisself half way up from his back pew and said, "I'll be glad to."

Every mouth in that church fell open, but I will say that nobody snickered, which will show you the state of affairs things had gotten into with Barney.

This news was too big to keep to myself. As soon as I got back across to the station I told the boys about it. We all agreed that at this point the least we could do for our old buddy was to pay him the respect of attendin' what would surely amount to him preachin' his own funeral.

When the next Sunday came we all marched halfway down to the front of the church. I guess we was secretly hopin' old Barn would let lose with one of his roof-raisers and give those long sufferin' folks some real entertainment.

Well, he didn't. But at least he filled the pulpit when he stood up there. He had some words on paper and he said them off good and loud. Even though it was another hot, sunny day, folks sat still and listened.

But Barney was no more than good and started when a strange thing happened. While we watched, this bewildered look began to come over Barney's face and he quit talkin'—right in the middle of a sentence. You could of heard a pin drop. Barney just stood there starin' over our heads.

Suddenly, like he was coming out from a daze, he shook his shaggy head and then that old trouble-startin' grin come over his face.

"Now it's a-comin'!" I nudged Ben next to me.

But all Barney said was, "Amen." Then he stepped out of the pulpit and marched down the aisle and disappeared through the church door.

Folks began whisperin' like a deck of cards being shuffled, so we got out of there.

When I got back to the station I saw poor old Barney sittin' out back on the bench all by hisself. Had his head in his hands and his shoulders were shakin' so hard I thought he must be terrible sick, or maybe even cryin'. I put my hand on his shoulder and when he looked up I saw he was laughin' fit to kill.

"What in tarnation's so funny?" I asked sittin' down beside him.

"Promise you won't go tell it?"

I nodded and Barney said, "Remember the day the parson gave his first sermon and all of us went over there to listen? The day he talked about drinkin'? Well, he preached every last word straight to me—never once took his eyes off my face. I never enjoyed another beer after that. I had to go back the next Sunday to make sure he had really singled me out from his whole congregation."

"It was the same thing that next Sunday." Barney shook his head. "I tell you it does somethin' to a man when someone looks him straight in the eye and names off his sins."

"But—" I began.

"I know what you're thinkin'," Barney said. "I'll admit the parson isn't one to look you in the eye, but can't you see— that's what made it all the more important—knowin' how much courage it took for him to find me and speak directly to me. One Sunday he spoke on bearin' false witness against your neighbor and it came to mind that all those stories I told was mostly false witnessin'." Barney looked out across the hills and said, "You see, I ain't never been singled out in my whole life before! The only time I can remember anyone payin' attention to me was when I yelled so gol-durned loud they had to."

"It was me—and nobody else—that parson had his eye on the day he asked for someone to preach in his place," Barney went on. "He's chosen me out of his flock, I thought, he's offerin' me my reward for

218

givin' up my sins one after another like he's a-been askin' me to do every Sunday mornin'.'"

And then Barney smiled, half embarrased. "But this mornin'," he said, "when I stood up in that pulpit for the first time, I found out I'd made a terrible mistake. I didn't discover it right off. Not until I happened to look back at that pew where I'd sat."

"I couldn't see it at all! You just simply can't see nothin' back there from the pulpit, and it's on account of the skylight. There's nothin' to see back there but glare!"

"That's when I knew the little parson hadn't singled me out at all. He didn't even know I was back there. He was so scared he couldn't talk if someone's eye caught his, so he stared at blind spot every single dang Sunday."

Barney grinned, so I said, "Then you'll be comin' back to the games?"

"No, I reckon not," Barney said. "You see, I've changed my ways some. There's someone else has singled me out—Miss Lucy— and there ain't no mistake about this one, that's for sure."

I looked at Barney and it was written plain there on his face—he was a man who'd had a miracle happen to 'em.

BIOGRAPHIES

MAYA ANGELOU, born in St. Louis, was nominated for the National Book Award in 1970 for *I Know Why the Caged Bird Sings*, & a 1972 Pulitzer Prize for *Just Give Me a Cool Drink of Water 'Fore I Diiie*, a 1973 Tony Award for her performance in "Look Away" Her books include *Gather Together in My Name, Oh Pray My Wings Are Gonna Fit Me Well, Singin' and Swingin' and Gettin' Merry Like Christmas*, & *All God's Children Need Traveling Shoes*.

JEAN BAKER, born in a tiny Colorado mining town on New Year's eve, was 8 when her family moved to a farm in Missouri. After a stint with the Peace Corp in Ghana, West Africa in 1973–74, Jean traveled the world on the S.S. Universe, taking a Semester-at-Sea course that eventually lead to a B.A. Her work appears in *Poetry Scope, Western Poetry Quarterly, Cape Rock*.

ALICE G. BRAND, a migrant to St. Louis from New Jersey, is an assistant professor of English & director of UMSL Communications Programs. Her poetry appears in *Helicon Nine, Descant, Literary Review, Confrontation, Berkley Poets Cooperative, Croton Review, Kansas Quarterly,*; essays in *New England Quarterly, The New York Times*. D.C. Heath published Dr. Brand's *Therapy in Writing*, 1980; with a New Jersey Council on the Arts fellowship, *as it happens* (Wampeter Press) appeared in 1983. While at Yaddo Artists Colony, Alice began her third book.

MARILYN CANNADAY, born in rural Missouri, spent most of her life in the La Plata-Kirksville area. After her youngest chiid began school, she earned a BA & a MA degree at Northeast Missouri State University. Her career spans secretarial work, teaching, editing,writing. She's an executive staff assistant at UMKC.

LENORE CARROLL, a Kansas Citian, teaches freshman composition & creative writing at UMKC. Lenore & friend Pat Huyett (also in this anthology) admit to having a great deal of chutzpah.

JAN CASTRO, editor of *River Styx*, authored *The Art and Life of Georgia O'Keeffe*. Her poems appear in numerous anthologies & periodicals. Jan is the driving force behind Big River Association, a St. Louis artists/writers collective.

T. D. CIACCHI, a resident of Columbia, became a self-employed artist after graduating with a degree in Interdisciplinary Ecology from Stephens College.

S. R. CLEMENT is a pen name for a 31-year veteran of Missouri. She has a MS in Counseling & Guidance from Northeast Missouri State University, & freelances for the greeting card industry. Her haikus published in *Nit & Wit Literary Magazine*.

NADINE MILLS COLEMAN, Columbia, Missouri resident, grew up in Moberly, Missouri. She began to do "serious writing" at the age of 40. In 1986 she was given honorary life-time membership to the Missouri Writers' Guild, & elected to Theta Sigma Phi honor society, now called Women in Journalism. Her work is in *The Reader's Digest* & in various Missouri newspapers & magazines.

ELLEN COONEY, born in St. Louis, now lives in San Francisco. Her most recent book is *House Holding* (Duir Press, 1984). Ellen is interested in mythology & music prior to 1750.

MARY K. DAINS, associate editor of *The Missouri Historical Review*, was born in Glasgow, Ill. She has BS & MA degrees from UMC.

CAROLYN DELOZIER came to Deepwater, Missouri in 1970. She self-published *Home*, a book of poems about people, places, & things found in her town. Her Pageant Play for Deepwater's Centennial Celebration was presented to an audience of 1700. In 1985 she won the Missouri Arts Council Fiction Contest.

ANGELA DOUGHERTY, resident of Columbia, Missouri, is active with women's programs at KOPN community radio. She studied English at UMC as an undergraduate.

DOROTHY DUNARD, of Columbia, Missouri, won the Gamma Alpha Chi Award upon graduating from UMC with a BJ degree. A past president of the Missouri Writers' Guild, Dorothy's freelance work appears in: *Parade*, *Let's Live*, *Women's Circle*, *Lady's Circle*, *Grit*, *Capper's Weekly*, etc.

MARY EATON resides in Kansas City, where she writes poetry as well as short stories.

CRYSTAL FIELD, born Crystal Joy Groulx at the base of the "thumb" in Bay City, Michigan, attended Park College, Parkville, Missouri. She received an MA from Indiana University. Her poems are in *Missouri Poets: An Anthology*, *Voices from the Interior* (BkMk Press), *Bloodroot*, *Helicon Nine*, *Chouteau Review*. Her first book: *The Good Woman*, 1977; her second *My Sister's Leather Bag*, 1982. Crystal writes reviews for *Literary Magazine Review*, teaches English, & conducts poetry writing seminars.

MARIAN FLEISCHMANN, native Missourian, is a stringer for the Associated Press & Field Coordinator for the March of Dimes. She spent 5 years as a newspaper reporter in Jefferson City, & con- tinues to freelance her "Ozark Series Collection" of short stories compulsively, whileattending Lincoln University.

KAREN FOX, member of the Fulton Writers Group, co-authored "Patterns of Life," a video production funded by the Missouri Arts Council.

VICTORIA GARTON, a Poet-in-the-Schools participant in Nevada, Missouri, has published in many little magazines, *Focus/Midwest*, *The Little Balkans Review*, *Kansas Quarterly*, *The Spoon River Anthology*, *The Chariton Review*, *Webster Review*, to name a few.

JOAN GILBERT, a native of Pulaski County, attended Southwest Missouri State College, Springfield. Joan has freelanced about 400 works of short fiction & sold 2 novels. She's been contributing editor for *Saddle and Bridle*, *Today's Farmer*, *Missouri Life*. Joan is a former women's editor for the *Columbia Daily Tribune*.

JOAN GILSON, a native of KC, says her claim to fame is that she was given birth by the same doctor who delivered Hemingway's kids. She teaches composition at UMKC; her poems are in *Number One Magazine*, *The Country Poet*, *Newsletter for Teachers of ESL in High School*.

DIANE GLANCY, born in KC, high schooled in St. Louis, BA-ed at U. of MO., is Artist-in-Residence for art councils of Oklahoma & Arkansas. She's Poet-in-the-Schools for Arts/Humanities Council of Tulsa, & Writer-in-Residence at Heller Theater. Of Cherokee heritage, Diane won an American Indian Theatre Company Prize, & a Pegasus Award given by Oklahoma Federation of Writers, & others. Her poems & short stories are widely published. *Offering* (Holy Cow! Press); her *Two Dresses* will appear in a volume of 12 Indian writers called *I Tell You Now* (U. of Nebraska/CooperUnion).

VALERIE GORDON, born in KC, is Research Analyst for the Missouri House of Representatives. She has a BJ from UMC & wrote a weekly column for *The Northwest Dispatch* when in Tacoma. She was named 1984 Woman of the Year by the Pierce County YWCA in recognition of her community activity in minority affairs.

PAMELA HADAS, an associate staff member at Bread Loaf Writers' Conference 1980-86, has a BA, MA, PhD from Washington University where she has lecturered since 1976. She is a recipient of the Wittner Bynner Award of the American Academy & Institute of Arts & Letters, 1980. Her poetry, articles, reviews appear in major literary publications & popular magazines. Of note for this anthology is Pam's "Marianne Moore: Poet of Affection".

SHARON KINNEY-HANSON, born in E. St. Louis, Ill., earned a BA from SIUE & an MEd from UMC. She's author of *Art Museums & Galleries in Missouri* & 1986-87 president of Missouri Writers' Guild. Her non-fiction & poetry appear in various newspapers & magazines. Sharon is Publications Coordinator for O'Missouri: Irish Missourians Research Group, & 1987 Project Director of the Let The Women Speak Authors Tour.

LINDA HATCH, from Tela, Honduras, currently lives in St. Louis, Her "Lysis" won the 1985 St. Louis Branch of National League of American Pen Women; "Company" won Honorable Mention in the St. Louis Writer's Annual Fiction Contest.

LUCY REED HAZELTON, native of Webster Groves, is former editor of *Poetry Speaking* & member of the T.S. Eliot Society, The St. Louis Poetry Center, & others. Her paintings & poetry appear in small press efforts; her chapbook: *Eros/Agape.*

LUCILLE M. HEFT, who moved to KC close to 40 years ago, is past Missouri state president of the National League of American Pen Women. She teaches fiction at UMKC's Communiversity; her work is in the *Kansas City Star Magazine* & elsewhere. Lucille is a former contributing editor of *Discover North.*

JULIE HEIFETZ, Clayton, Missouri resident, is co-founder of Child Development Project of the St. Louis Psychoanalytic Institute. With a BA & MA from St. Louis University, Julie did post-grad work at Washington University with Mona Van Duyn. As Writer-in-Residence for St. Louis Center for Holocaust Studies, she gives dramatic readings from her *Oral History and the Holocaust.*

KRISTEN HEITKAMP, writer, poet, graphic artist living in beautiful uptown Rocheport, Missouri, started writing in the 70s. Her work appears in *Midlands, Webster Review, Missouri Short Fiction.* A journal-keeper, Kristen is an author in search of a publisher for her "three books in the closet—in Kinkkos boxes."

SHARON HIBDON lives on a farm in Centertown, Missouri. She is a grad of Lincoln University & prior to having children, taught in Missouri's schools. This is Sharon's publishing debut appearance, although she's been writing for some time.

BEV HOPKINS, born in Springfield, Missouri, a grad of Southwest Baptist University & has taught English for Ferguson-Florissant School District for 17 years. Bev serves as Academic Coordinator at McCluer High School & is president of St. Louis Poetry Center.

EDITH HOWINK, a St. Louis native, is a MSW graduate of Washington University with Ph.D. studies at U. of Chicago. Since 1977, Edith has had 7 books of poetry & prose published.

PAT HUYETT, a native of KC who has taught English at the KC Art Institute & UMKC, has work in *Poet & Critic*, *Midway Review*, *New Laurel Review*, & *Uncle*. As Associate Editor at BkMk Press, she helped produce *In the Middle: Midwestern Women Poets*.

JANE ELLEN IBUR, born in St. Louis during the 50s, writes fiction, non-fiction, poetry that appears in *Eads Bridge*, *River Styx*, *Slipstream*, *Pastiche*, *Webster Review*, & others.

LYNNE JENSEN was born on an airforce base in Newfoundland, Canada, grew up in the south, & came to Columbia, Missouri, in 1977. She teaches emotionally-disturbed children & adolescents in a hospital setting.

BEE NEELEY KUCKELMAN lives in Columbia & is a member of the Missouri Writer's Guild. Her poems have been published in *Grit*, *Harbinger*, & elsewhere.

MARILYN LAKE, resident of Columbia, is information officer for the Coordinating Board for Higher Education. Marilyn writes plays for children, poetry, short fiction, & novels.

DORIS LANDRUM grew up in Missouri's Ozarks but now lives in KC.

SHIRLEY BRADLEY LEFLORE is a poet, performing artist, counseling psychologist living in St. Louis. Shirley is director of the performing arts group "Free n' Concert" & editor of *And We Rise*, an Afro-American poetry anthology of St. Louis writers & poets.

ELIZABETH LEXLEIGH, St. Louis-born, has written poetry, essays, fiction "since early childhood," although she's only begun to publish within the last 5 years. Before establishing her own business, she produced advertising/marketing materials, manuals & brochures for KETC-TV, St. Louis Symphony Orchestra, etc.

SHARON LIBERA, born in St. Louis, won a Fulbright Fellowship & pursued a master degree at U. of Manchester, England; she PhD-ed at Harvard & studied poetry with Robert Lowell. She's widely published: *Parnassus*, *Ploughshares*, *Italian Quarterly*. Sharon's co-authored with John Peck: *Mr. Jefferson's Horses*, 1985.

LYNNE LOSCHKY, raised in New England, is a Brown University grad. As Professor of English at Lincoln University, Dr. Loschky's main focus is the honors program where she works with young writers & poets.

JANET LOWE, a native of Hutchinson, Kansas, became a KC resident in 1977. While pursuing a master degree at UMKC, Janet is a teaching assistant. She participated in the 1986 poetry workshop of Maple Woods Community Collge; her work appears in *Number One*, *Modern Maturity*,

EDITH MCCALL moved to Hollister, Missouri, in 1955, after living in Illinois, Iowa, Wisconsin. She earned an MA from University of Chicago & taught elementaryschool while a resident there. Her first book,a pre-primer used in schools, was published in 1953. Edith now has 47 published books as sole author, plus almost as many co-authored books. Her most recent titles: *Conquering the Rivers: Henry Miller Shreve and the Navigation of America's Inland Waterways*, 1984; *Message from the Mountains*, 1985; *Mississippi Steamboatman: The Story of Henry Miller Shreve*, 1986.

PATRICIA MCCARTY moved to KC 20 years ago. A newspaper reporter & editor who holds a BJ degree from Marquette University, Milwaukee, Pat attended the Mark Twain Writers Workshop in 1985.

ELLEN GRAY MASSEY, born in Nevada Missouri, was "the" teacher & editor for 10 years of *Bittersweet*, a cultural journalism magazine about the Ozarks. She edited 2 books about her students' works: *Bittersweet Country* (Doubleday), *Bittersweet Earth* (U. of Oklahoma Press). Ellen retired from teaching English at Lebanon High School in 1986 to write & to do educational consultant work.

LESLIE ADRIENNE MILLER has lived in Missouri 9 years, & is Poet-in-Resident at Stephens College & managing editor of *Open Places*. Leslie has published in over 40 magazines/anthologies, including *Northwest Review, Poet Lore, Georgia Review*.

MARLENE MILLER, of St. Louis, studied writing at Washington U. with David Clewell & Pamela Hadas & privately with Sue Adylette. Marlene is a Board of Directors member of St. Louis Poetry Center & organized the first Poetry in the Neighborhood Series. She has had 2 residencies at Ragdale Foundation.

CHARLOTTE NEKOLA, born in St. Louis, received the Avery Hopwood Award for poetry given by the University of Michigan & a Fellowship in Poetry from the New Jersey Council on the Arts. Charlotte has a PhD from U. of Michigan, teaches women's studies & literature. Currently, as Schweitzer Fellow in Humanties, she's working with Toni Morrison on a first collection of poems.

HELEN PATMON was born the 7th daughter & 12th child of Bose & Bessie Patmon of Crescent, Oklahoma. She holds degrees in acting & directing & teaches at Lincoln University. Helen's aspiration is "to retire from academia in the near future so to dedicate all my energies toward a professional theatre & writing career."

JUDY RAY, born in England, studied English Literature at the University of Southhampton, has lived in KC for many years, but takes visits to other parts of the world. Judy was associate editor of *New Letters* until 1985 & is a producer of "New Letters on the Air," a weekly half-hour, NPR program. *Pebble Rings* (Greenfield Review Press) is her first poetry book; a second unpublished manuscript is *Pigeons in the Chandeliers*.

MARIA A. REED, born in Nurnberg, Germany, in 1946, is a librarian residing in Jefferson City with her husband & two sons. Maria has written poetry for years—without much concern for publishing it. Her work is in *The Soon-to-be-Popular, Unpublished Works of Previously Unknown Persons* (River City Press, 1984).

C. A. RHOADS says of herself: "Female. Born 1944. Married 25 years (to Bob). Four sons & only slightly insane (this information always filed together). Former editor of the short-lived *Thornleigh Review*, a past love. Currently Branch Supervisor, Sedalia-Boonslick Regional Library. Good job, nice people."

PHYLLIS J. ROSSITER, born in Carthage, Missouri, has recently completed a juvenile historical novel & is working on another. *Stoney Lonesome* won 2nd place in the 1986 Short Story Contest of the Ozarks Writers League. Her work is in *The Mother Earth News*, *The Ozarks Mountaineer*, *Farm Woman News*, *Ford Times*, *Missouri Ruralist*, *Missouri Conservationist*.

BETTY COOK ROTTMANN, Columbia resident with a BJ from UMC, created a children's program for KSGM while writing a column for the *Ste. Genevieve Herald*. Her work is in *Missouri Ruralist*, *Kansas Farmer*, *St. Louis Post-Dispatch*, *Women's Wear Daily*, *Saturday Evening Post*, *New York Herald Tribune*, etc.

SYLVIA SWAIN RUMMEL, born in Salem, Missouri, but grew up in Lee's Summit, says she "defected from Missouri long enough to attend the University of Kansas" for a degree in music therapy/ education. Sylvia is a "piano technician in Callaway, Audrain, Montgomery counties & I compose light verse either while traveling between clients or while doing the dishes."

JO SCHAPER, a lifelong Missourian, is "a printer by trade, & poet by inclination" Jo's a member of the St. Louis Poetry Center Board of Directors; she teaches creative writing for St. Louis public schools. Samisdat Press published: *WAM&T*, 1978, & *Riding the Twister*, 1985. Jo won the 1986 Poetry Center's Halley's Comet contest, & a book award of the St. Louis Wednesday Club.

KAREN WARREN SCHNEIDER, born in New York, lives in Chesterfield, Missouri. She studies poetry at UMSL with Dr. Alice G. Brand. She has a BA in General Literature from the College of Wooster, Ohio. Karen's work is in *Lindenwood Griffin*, a publication of Lindenwood College.

VICTORIA SPAIN was born in New Jersey, but has lived in KC since 1972. Her poems appear in *Missouri Poets*, *Kansas Quarterly*, *Poetry Australia*, & elsewhere; she's co-authored with Valerie Hubbard Damon *A Creative Teacher's Guide to Willo Nancifoot* (Star Publications, 1986). Victoria is Education Librarian at UMKC.

MARILYN TATLOW, from Columbia, now Moberly, Missouri, writes essays & articles for *Boston Herald American*, *The Chicago Tribune*, *Modern Bride*, *The Midwest Motorist*. She won Honorable Mention in a 1982 *Writer's Digest* contest. Marilyn has an MFA in creative writing from Warren Wilson College, North Carolina.

JUDITH TOWSE THIES is a native Kansas Citian who chairs the English Department at Notre Dame de Sion French Institute in KC. She's conducted workshops throughout the state & taught "Communal Poetry" at UMKC, & was chosen for the 1985 Excellence in Teaching Award. Judith edited several poetry books of student work; her own poetry is in Missouri & Minnesota publications.

MARLENE TRICE—about herself & her work she says: "obviously of & for women & were written on my recent release from pumpkin shell &

kitchen. These days you will find me a gloomy, stoop-shouldered cleric, a beggar of measured time & fresh air from 9 to 5. Evenings I'm a Bombeck-esque parent & overzealous student. (The closer I get, the more I slip/slide away.) A believer in process over product. . ."

DONNA L. TRUSSELL, born in Texas, has lived in KC since 1977 & is the editor of *KC Pitch*, a music newspaper. Her work appears in *West Branch, Puerto del Sol*; her story "Someone Could Do That" is written from a male point of view.

CORINNE UNDERWOOD was given birth in Sioux City, Iowa, is a grad of Stephens College, Columbia, Missouri. She has a master degree from UMKC, has taught at UMKC & Johnson County Community College, participated in art/poetry exhibitions & was a finalist in the Lichtor Poetry Contest & winner of the StorckFiction Prize.

CONSTANCE URDANG, from New York city, is a Smith College grad (AB, Cum Laude). She has a MFA from University of Iowa. Her work is in many publications; she won the Carleton Centennial Award for Poetry for *Natural History* (Harper & Row) & a NEA Creative Writing Fellowship in 1976; the Delmore Schwartz Memorial Poetry Award in 1981. Her poems have been twice chosen for Borestone Mountain Poetry Awards. Her books: *Luncha, New & Selected Poems, American Earthquakes, The Woman Who Read Novels*.

DEBORAH UTHE is a political science-with-writing-certificate grad of UMSL. Deborah's work is published in local & national small press mags: *Impetus, Up Against the Wall, Mother, Litmag*. In 1986 she won Missouri's Robert A. Smith Memorial Award.

GLORIA VANDO, born in New York city of Puerto Rican parents, studied at New York University, University of Amsterdam with a Tolstoy Foundation Scholarship, & graduated from Corpus Christi State University, Texas. Gloria is founding editor of *Helicon Nine*; her poems appear in *New Letters, Rampike, Espuela Lirica, Organo Literario*.

MONA VAN DUYN's many literary awards include a National Book Award in 1977 for *To See, To Take*, Yale University Library's Bollinger Award, 1970, the Borestone Mountain Award, 1968. Books: *Valentines to the Wide World, A Time for Bees, Bedtime Stories, Merciful Disguises, Letters From a Father, and Other Poems*. Mona & husband/poet Jarvis Thurston founded *Perspective*.

MARGIT VINCENZ, born of Austrian parents in Czechoslovakia, has lived in Missouri since 1961.She successfully published poems & articles in Europe & in the Caribbean before coming to the states. Margit & geophysic professor/husband see traveling as a way of life. After visiting China in 1986, Margit quickly sold a travel piece to a St. Louis paper.

DEANE WAGNER was "an infant in Columbia, a child in Jefferson City, an adolescent in St. Louis" An adult in Ferguson, where she's director of the city's community development, she writes for the local paper. Her award winning fiction & poetry appears in *River Styx, Image. Rings and Nails* won a Missouri Writing! award & a St. Louis Writers Guild award.

MARYFRANCES WAGNER is an English teacher at Raytown High & has given workshops & seminars as well as poetry readings statewide.

Her poetry books: *Bandaged Watermelons and Other Rusty Ducks*, & *Tonight Cicadas Sing*. She's served on the Committee for the American Poets' Series, & chaired the Lenore Anthony Poetry Work- shop & the Randall Jesse Poetry Fair for 7 years.

JANE O. WAYNE resides in St. Louis. Her *Looking Both Ways* is in its second printing. Her poetry appears in major small press publications: *Poetry, Ploughshares, Michigan Quarterly, Southern Poetry Review*, etc.

HUBA A. WELLS, born at Ongo, Missouri, lived in Douglas County most of her childhood & "grew up thinking there would be trees any direction I looked" Huba is a member of two writers' groups in Jefferson City & is known for writing "long, epic poems."

MARILYN WILLIAMS was born in D.C., but as an army brat lived in many states. Marilyn, who graduated from Washington University & "studied with the Finkels," says St. Louis felt like home. An active member of the St.Louis Poetry Center. She's won the 1984 Wednesday Club of St. Louis award & others. Her work appears in *Cedar Rock, Child Life*, etc.

SUZANNE WILSON has lived in Joplin, Missouri since 1967 & teaches writing workshops in Missouri schools in the Artists in Education program of the Missouri Arts Council. She is the author of *The Midnight Flight of the Moose, Mops and Marvin*.

GLENDA WINDERS is a BJ grad of the University of Missouri who, while in Warrensburg, taught writing at Central Missouri State University. She's a contributing book editor for *Kansas City Star* & also is a winner of the 1985 Missouri Writing! competition sponsored by MAC, & a PEN Syndicated Fiction Award recipient.

CAROLYNE WRIGHT received a doctorate in English & Creative Writing at Syracuse University. As a Fulbright scholar in 1971-72 in Chili, she transcribed Spanish. She's held fellowships from NEH, Bread Loaf, New York State CAPS, Fine Arts Work Center & is a winner of many prizes, including the Pablo Neruda Poetry Prize, Celia B. Wagner Award of Poetry Society of America. In Missouri, she taught at William Jewell College. Her books: *Stealing the Children, Premonitions of an Uneasy Guest, Returning What We Owed, From a White Woman's Journal*.

JOAN YEAGLEY, Denver, Colorado born, is Coordinator of the Great Books Program for KC & the Great Books Foundation, Chicago. As Consultant for Program Activity for Northeast Kansas Library System, Joan teaches Creative Writing at Missouri Southern State College & Crowder College. Her book: *Four Bookmark Poets*; her work is in *Voices From the Interior: Poets of Missouri, Above the Thunder,Poetry of Love, Past & Present, How to Eat a Poem*.

WILMA YEO, a resident of KC, authored: *Girl in the Window* & *Gypsy Summer* (Scholastic), *Maverick with a Paintbrush: Biography of Thomas Hart Benton* (Doubleday), *Oliver Twister & His Big Little Sister* (Simon & Schuster), *Mrs. Neverbody's Recipes*, & *Mystery of the Third Twin*. Wilma has over 50 works in magazines,including *Writer's Digest* & *Reader's Digest*. She's a member of the Society of Children's Book Writers.